# THE FOURTH BATTALION
*Duke of Connaught's Own*
## TENTH BALUCH REGIMENT
### IN THE GREAT WAR

# BRITISH AND INDIAN OFFICERS, 129TH D.C.O. BALUCHIS

## Indian Expeditionary Force 'A'

### KARACHI, AUGUST 1914

Jem. Masaod Khan  Sub. Azad Gul  Major G. G. P. Humphreys  
(127th Q.M.O. Baluch L.I.)  
Jem. Lal Sher  Lieut. and Adjt. F. M. G.-Griffin  Jem. Abdullah Khan  Capt. P. C. Hampe-Vincent  Jem. Mir Bad Shah  Jem. Jafar Ali  
(127th Q.M.O. Baluch L.I.)  
Sub. Ghulam Mohd,  Capt. W. F. Adair  Sub. Zaman Khan  
Major J. A. Hannyngton  Lieut.-Col. W. M. Southey  Sub.-Maj. Mala Khan  Sub. Adam Khan  Jem. Nawab Khan  
(127th Q.M.O. Baluch L.I.)  
Major P. P. L. Atal, I.M.S.  Sub. Mukhmad Azam  Sub. Amir Khan  
Sub. Ahmed Din  Major H. W. R. Potter  Jem. Mir Bad Shah  
Jem. Imandar  Lieut. H. V. Lewis  Jem. Karim Khan  
127th Q.M.O. Baluch L.I.)

For complete list of British and Indian officers see Appendix

# THE FOURTH BATTALION
## *Duke of Connaught's Own*
# TENTH BALUCH REGIMENT
### IN THE GREAT WAR
#### 129<sup>TH</sup> D.C.O. BALUCHIS

by
## W. S. THATCHER

The Naval & Military Press Ltd

Reproduced by kind permission of the Central Library,
Royal Military Academy, Sandhurst

Published by
**The Naval & Military Press Ltd**
Unit 10, Ridgewood Industrial Park,
Uckfield, East Sussex,
TN22 5QE England
Tel: +44 (0) 1825 749494
Fax: +44 (0) 1825 765701
**www.naval-military-press.com**
**www.military-genealogy.com**
© The Naval & Military Press Ltd 2007

## The Naval & Military Press ...

...offer specialist books for the serious student of conflict. The range of titles stocked covers the whole spectrum of military history with titles on uniforms, battles, official histories, specialist works containing Medal Rolls and Casualties Lists, and numismatic titles for medal collectors and researchers.

The innovative approach they have to military bookselling and their commitment to publishing have made them Britain's leading independent military bookseller.

*In reprinting in facsimile from the original, any imperfections are inevitably reproduced and the quality may fall short of modern type and cartographic standards.*

Printed and bound by Antony Rowe Ltd, Eastbourne

*To*

ALL WHO SERVED AND ENDURED FAITHFULLY

كَمْ مِنْ فِئَةٍ قَلِيلَةٍ غَلَبَتْ فِئَةً كَثِيرَةً بِإِذْنِ ٱللَّهِ

Koran ii. 250

*How often has a little army defeated a great army
by permission of Allah!*

# CONTENTS

PREFACE                                                    *page* xi

CHAPTER I                                                  *page* 1
4 Aug.–18 Oct. 1914: Mobilisation; Voyage to France; Egypt; Landing at Marseilles; Journey to Orleans; Departure for Front

CHAPTER II                                                 *page* 8
18 Oct.–31 Oct. 1914: Arrival in fighting line; Attached to 3rd Cavalry Brigade, 2nd Cavalry Division; In the trenches at Hollebeke; Attack of 26 Oct.; German attack of the 30th; Khudadad Khan's V.C.; Loss and regaining of Farm; Regiment leaves Ypres sector

CHAPTER III                                                *page* 20
1 Nov.–20 Dec. 1914: Regiment rejoins own Division on Indian Corps Front; In the trenches; Reinforcements; Inspection by the Prince of Wales; Enemy attack on 23 Nov.; Trenches and billets; Attack on two enemy saps; Further attacks on 19 Dec.; Excessively bad weather conditions; German attack; Remnant of regiment with Lahore Division withdrawn for rest

CHAPTER IV                                                 *page* 37
Jan.–24 April, 1915: Lahore Division in line again; Regiment in billets until battle of Neuve Chapelle; In trenches once more; Reinforcements

CHAPTER V                                                  *page* 44
24 April–2 May, 1915: March to Ypres; Position at Ypres on arrival of Lahore Division; Attacks north of Ypres

CHAPTER VI                                                 *page* 55
2 May–25 Sept. 1915: In billets; Reinforcements; In line again; Ayub Khan's exploits; Trenches and billets; Reinforcements; Preparations for the offensive 25 Sept.; Withdrawn from trenches

CHAPTER VII                                                *page* 71
25 Sept. 1915–1 Jan. 1916: Behind the line; Decision to withdraw Indian troops from France; Departure from France and arrival in Egypt

CHAPTER VIII  *page* 74

JAN.–4 MARCH, 1916: Regiment leaves Mombasa for Voi; Training for new type of fighting; Arrival at Kajiado; Part of 2nd East African Brigade, 1st East African Division; Headquarters move to Longido West; Changes in composition of regiment; All ready

CHAPTER IX  *page* 82

5 MARCH–25 MARCH, 1916: Review of general situation; Offensive begins; March from Longido round south of Kilimanjaro; Arrival at Moschi; Advance from Moschi; Attack on Store; Enemy night attack; Van Deventer's flanking movement; Smuts's general plan; Attack by 2nd East African Brigade on Ruwu; Enemy withdrawn during the night; Kahe occupied

CHAPTER X  *page* 101

25 MARCH–21 AUGUST, 1916: On outpost duty along Ruwu; Rainy season begins; Havildar Zerdad's exploit; Relieved and withdrawn to Moschi; Malaria; New drafts; New general advance begins; March down Tanga railway; Arrival at Kwa Mdoe (Handeni); No longer fit for service owing to sickness; Recuperating in camp till 21 August

CHAPTER XI  *page* 117

21 AUG.–28 SEPT. 1916: Occupation of Tanga; March via Korogwe to Tanga; Embark for Bagamoyo; March from Bagamoyo to Dar-es-Salaam; Rest in Dar-es-Salaam; Re-embark; Detachments occupy Mikindani and Sudi; Headquarters return to Dar-es-Salaam

CHAPTER XII  *page* 121

28 SEPT.–3 DEC. 1916: Transfer of regiment to Kilwa area; Occupation of Kibata; Patrolling

CHAPTER XIII  *page* 140

6 DEC. 1916–13 JAN. 1917: The fighting in and around Kibata; The enemy retire north; Action at Mbindia

CHAPTER XIV  *page* 165

13 JAN.–18 JULY, 1917: Rainy season begins; Effect on general plan of campaign; Condition of troops; Regiment back in Kibata; At Ngarambi Chini; Floods; Very short rations; Back in Kibata; Concentration at Chemera; End of rains; Offensive reopens; Arrival of fresh drafts

CONTENTS ix

CHAPTER XV *page* 183
18 July–18 Sept. 1917: General situation; Nanyati affair; At Mssindy; Preparations for marching out

CHAPTER XVI *page* 196
18 Sept.–29 Nov. 1917: Attack on Ndessa-Mihambia line; Offensive continues along valley of Mbemkuru; Action at Namehi; Advance on Ruponda; Fighting at Lukuledi; Back to Ruponda resting; The final drive; Von Lettow crosses into Portuguese territory; Operations against Tafel; Final fight of regiment at Mwiti Water

CHAPTER XVII *page* 215
1 Dec. 1917–11 Nov. 1918: March to Lindi; Arrival at Dar-es-Salaam; Sail for Karachi; Arrival in India; Reorganisation; Armistice

APPENDICES

I. Indian Army List, July 1914, Officers of the 129th D.C.O. Baluchis *page* 221

II. British Officers with the regiment in France and East Africa 223

III. Indian Officers who served with the regiment during the War 226

IV. Composition of the Indian Army Corps in Flanders 229

V. Organisation of the British Forces in East Africa 231

VI. Note on the composition of the regiment 234
(By Lieut.-Colonel H. V. Lewis, D.S.O., M.C.)

VII. Casualties 242

VIII. Recommendations in France and East Africa 248

IX. Decorations 277

INDEX 281

# ILLUSTRATIONS

### PLATES

Regimental group taken in 1914 *frontispiece*
Major-General W. M. Southey, C.M.G. *facing page* 32
The Flag at Kibata 154
Brigadier-General J. A. Hannyngton, C.B., C.M.G., D.S.O. 192

### MAPS

#### In the Text

Trenches October 1914 at Hollebeke *page* 15
Sketch of attack at Ruwu River 95
Sketch Map of Kibata 143

#### Outside the Text

Lahore Division at 2nd Ypres *facing page* 54
Indian Corps Front in Flanders 72
Sketch Map: January–August 1916 120
Sketch Map: September 1916–May 1917 182
Sketch Map: May–December 1917 214
Key Map of East Africa 220

# PREFACE

THIS history of the 129th (Duke of Connaught's Own) Baluchis, now the 4/10th Baluch Regiment, is in reality almost, or at least in part, a history of the Baluch Regiment itself. For throughout the War the regiment was continually reinforced from the other Baluch regiments except the 130th, which was itself on service in East Africa. The regiment naturally claimed as its own all reinforcements sent to it and, in so doing, claimed their honours, though at the same time all the survivors of the original 129th would freely acknowledge the debt owed to these regiments. Fortunately the present grouping, effected since the War, has made one regiment of all, so that now there is no need to vindicate one's rights even in a friendly way. The regiment was also reinforced both in officers and men from many other regiments outside the Baluch group. These, too, contributed their share to the reputation and honours of the 129th.

The offer to write the history was made at the Baluch Dinner in London in 1928, some time before dessert had been reached. I did not realise then how difficult a task I was undertaking, but nevertheless the offer was not made light-heartedly.

There had been published, even at that date, a very large number of histories and books dealing with the Great War, but little had been done to make known the valour and devotion of the Indian troops. This was and is due largely to the fact that there are so few British officers with each Indian regiment, and Regular officers have been too well trained to write books. Further, there had been a marked tendency in certain quarters to minimise the services of the Indian troops and to forget their achievements and sacrifices.

As one who joined up for the War only, my service in the

PREFACE

Indian Army, first with the 54th Sikhs for training and then with the 129th on service, was and still is the great adventure of my life. We Indian Army Reserve officers, certainly the first batches, were very 'jungli' creatures who could never claim the finish of the Regular officers under whom we served. Nevertheless we did our best, though more often by the dim light of nature than by the stronger light of training and regulations. But whatever we did not do, we did learn to love the Indian soldier, no matter what his rank, just as we learned to admire the high efficiency and devotion of the Regular British officer.

It was in the hope of repaying, in some small measure, the great debt which I owed to all with whom I served in the 129th and with whom I trained in the 54th Sikhs that I offered to write the war history of the regiment. Perhaps, not being a Regular officer, I was in a better position to write. The whole training and environment of the Regular Army officer tends to make him a poor speaker and a diffident writer. There are notable exceptions, but in general the well-trained Regular officer is mute. An amateur may get enough knowledge to understand and interpret what he sees and hears, and not having been trained in such a Spartan school may also express in words or writing what the Regular officer would be too modest to say or even allow himself to think.

I am only too conscious, now that the history has been written, that I have not succeeded in my hopes. I had hoped that I might be able to do the impossible—write a regimental history which would appeal to more than the very narrow circle of the regiment itself. I had hoped that perhaps a few might be attracted to read the story of an Indian regiment for its own sake. I can see now that such a hope was an impossible one. A history such as this must eliminate the personal too much, must record much that is dull, must be too disciplined to appeal to a wide public. Only those who served with the regiment during the War will be able to clothe the dry bones of record with flesh and breathe into them the life which they must lack to all others.

In other respects also I feel the record is inadequate. It has been compiled from the Regimental Diary, Brigade Diaries, letters, notes and memoranda contributed by many officers: but these records are all inadequate. The Regimental Diary was kept as an official duty by overworked and often exhausted Adjutants wherever they might find themselves and their so-called Office—on the march, in a dug-out, in the bush, anywhere. They certainly had no idea that they were collecting material for a regimental history. On the whole the record is good. One of the worst patches is that period written up by myself, but here my memory came to my aid. The latter months also are very bad. This is easily accounted for by the great paucity of British officers, the endless demands made upon them, and the exhausting conditions under which they lived. No wonder then that from time to time even the arrival of drafts is omitted.

Two defects, however, cannot be remedied, and account for what would otherwise appear to be serious omissions in the history. The list of officers who came and went was not always properly kept. This is particularly unfortunate in the case of the Indian officers. The British officers were fewer in number and it has been possible to discover the names of all who served, but the Indian officers being more numerous the task has been more difficult, so that the list is, I fear, not complete. Secondly, the casualties were very inadequately kept. In the later stages of the War even the killed are not always entered. How many men died in hospital of wounds or disease is entirely unknown. The figures on the Karachi Memorial are undoubtedly incorrect and underestimate the death roll, while they refer only to 'pucka' 129th casualties and not to the total casualties. For instance, sick casualties in East Africa are not recorded at all. How great they were can be seen from the fact that the regiment had gathered in almost 700 men from hospital before it embarked for India on its return home. This great toll of sickness cannot be given in figures but must be borne in mind when estimating the total losses. It is again well illustrated, in Chapter XIV, when Major Gover could only muster 50 fit men for his fighting patrol out of all the regiment, and even then most of these went sick before the patrol returned to camp.

It may appear to the reader that the officers are too prominently portrayed while the men are rather dimly sketched. This is inevitable in such a history. It should be remembered that the officers are mentioned rather as symbolising the action of the men. The devotion of the men was beyond praise and but for this the officers could have done nothing. Leadership they provided, as was due to their training and position, but unless this leadership had been backed by the unflinching courage and patient endurance of the men, little could have been achieved. Further, many of the officers who could have supplied me with invaluable material about the men are dead. Thus Major Money told me, after he had returned from a long and arduous patrol with his Double Company, that one of his havildars had died of dysentery on the march back to camp. The havildar had been sick before marching but had refused to go to hospital and had insisted upon marching with the patrol. He had marched in the heat and the dust, unable to eat, constantly lacking water, but had struggled on until just before camp was reached he collapsed and died on the road. Such a man is worthy of a mention by name, but alas! he must be nameless for ever. Nevertheless the officer does count enormously. On the morale of the officers depends the morale of the men—and rightly so.

The history may appear to many to be disproportioned. Too much space is devoted to East Africa and too little to

Flanders. The losses from battle were much greater in Flanders than in East Africa and the actual fighting much more severe. But being concentrated in a small area there is less detail to narrate. After all if one leaves out the itineraries in Africa there is little to record. Actual battle casualties were small, and judged by the standards in France appear so trivial as to incline some to think that a history is rather superfluous. If one does not detail the fighting unless it is somewhat on the scale of, say, Loos, there would be nothing to relate. The biggest battle in East Africa, Mahiwa, could only produce some 5000 casualties if one took those of both combatants. The total casualties for 1917, of both British and German, were under 15,000—a bagatelle. We lost 80,000 at Loos in less than a week, and Loos was not a big affair compared with what followed.

In East Africa the combatants were fewer and reinforcements less frequent, the artillery almost negligible, while both sides had enough machine guns to put the defence always in a very strong position. Frontal attacks with such small numbers and no covering fire from artillery would have meant annihilation to no purpose. Hence the apparent slowness with which attacks were delivered and the seeming reluctance to assault what, from a Western standpoint, were comparatively weak positions. The attackers were driven to manœuvre to turn their opponents out of their positions. This in such a country as East Africa was always arduous and very frequently exhausting.

There is no doubt that the quality of the Indian troops was not nearly as good towards the end of the War as at the beginning, but this applied equally to the white troops as time went on. The Indian sepoy requires more training than a British soldier, and after 1916 he did not get sufficient: partly because the demand for men was so insistent, but chiefly because there was no really good organisation for training men. Training counts. A grave mistake was made in sending out weak and inadequately trained men to East Africa. They simply filled the hospitals in the former case, while their lack of training made them of little use in action. Bush fighting requires nerve and nerve depends partly upon ability to use one's weapons well and a knowledge of what to do. It is astonishing how well these inadequately trained men behaved. If the regiment in August 1914 had been asked what sort of an action would be fought by 250 inadequately trained sepoys, who had been half-starved for several weeks and who had been on their feet for the greater part of 40 hours, when suddenly attacked by five times their number, at a time when they were parched with thirst, there would have been no hesitation in saying that such an action could only end in complete disaster. Yet the action at Mwiti Water was such a case. The men fell back, but as one of their officers said they 'simply walked back': there was no rout and finally they beat off the enemy.

The Indian troops in Flanders were criticised by many, but such criticism must be tempered by the knowledge that they were fighting under very severe handicaps. Psychologically the Indian soldier had greater demands made upon him in Flanders than had the British and still more the French soldier. We were fighting for our skins and we knew it. Men may fight for their pay, for their honour, but for sheer stark butchery they require more than that to drive them on again and again. They need hate and the knowledge that defeat means annihilation. The French were better supplied in this respect than the British. Every Frenchman fought with hate in his heart as well as the fear of annihilation. The British lacked this hate, or at least the intensity of it, but they did know that they must win the War or be destroyed. The Indian troops lacked both motives, that is, they lacked the two most powerful driving forces which are necessary for such great massacres as took place in France. They were fighting for their officers, their honour and fifteen rupees a month.

Further, they were fighting under conditions entirely new and foreign to them. Not only were they plunged into Flanders in the late autumn to face the endless rain and mud, but they were asked to fight in a way entirely new to them. It may be replied that the method of fighting was new to all. So it was, but not to such an extent in the case of the European units. The Indian soldier is not so quick to adapt himself and does not display the same initiative. In addition to this he depended too much on his British officer, and in this he was not entirely to blame. Certainly it was his nature to do so, but his training encouraged him in this. It added enormously to his fighting power, provided his officer was not shot; and, of course, the Indian Army, being organised for frontier fighting in India, presumed that the British officers would not all be shot in one day or, say, a week. But having lost his British officer the sepoy lost fighting efficiency. He often failed to go on with the same determination, not because he was afraid but because he did not know what to do.

Another grave disadvantage which is generally overlooked lay in the lack of reinforcements. It is not good for the survivors of a regiment which has lost heavily in battle to be left, a mere handful somewhere in a back area, to contemplate their annihilation. The ranks should be filled with new men as quickly as possible so that fresh spirit can be infused through the sight of full numbers. The Indian regiments were rarely up to half-strength and were often mere shadows.

Yet in spite of cold and exposure to constant rain, and in spite of all these disabilities, the conduct of the men was heroic. If they did not come up to standard on all occasions it was because too much was asked of them by those who were ignorant of their psychology and needs, but it was not often that they failed.

In East Africa the position was often the reverse, and considerable numbers of the white troops showed up to disadvantage. East Africa was largely conquered by Indian and African troops. An analysis of casualties, especially battle casualties, will prove this. Even in sickness more was demanded of them. The white troops were withdrawn from time to time and sent to recuperate in the hills, or in the case of the South Africans even went home. Not so the Indian regiments. They might be riddled with malaria, worn out with sickness, but they had to remain. Only those who saw what they had to bear can appreciate their fortitude. No writing can bring this out clearly. One must have served with them day after day, month after month, to appreciate how much was demanded of them, to know how magnificently they responded. The East African campaign would have meant very great hardship and privation even if it had been well organised and run, which it was not. Rather it was a lesser Mesopotamia. Columns were only too often sent out with inadequate medical equipment, porters even without water bottles. Food was bad. Von Lettow would have managed it better.

It only remains to thank all who have helped me directly and indirectly in my work. I am grateful to all those officers who have supplied me with information, whether verbal or written, and for their kindly criticism. I am particularly grateful to Lieut.-Colonel H. V. Lewis, D.S.O., M.C., who has assisted me more than I can acknowledge, not least in his encouragement. I had the privilege of serving under Colonel Lewis in East Africa, and should like to record how much we junior officers and all the regiment owed to him for his magnificent example and leadership. I am also most grateful to Lieut.-Colonel W. N. Hay, D.S.O., C.I.E., and to Major A. C. Gover, M.C., for their invaluable assistance in writing the last chapters. Without their help I should often have been very much at a loss in obtaining information. Lieut.-Colonel G. V. Dreyer, R.A., also greatly assisted me in writing the account of the Nanyati fighting.

I must also thank Mr E. A. Dixon of the Historical Section (Military Branch), Committee of Imperial Defence, for his very willing help in assisting me to examine the various War Diaries at Audit House; Lady Willcocks for kindly allowing me to use two maps from her husband's book *With the Indians in Flanders*, and Mr W. H. Swift for reading through the proofs. Finally my thanks are due to Miss Boning who has typed and retyped the manuscript and who has done much to help me in this way.

W. S. THATCHER

FITZWILLIAM HOUSE
CAMBRIDGE
*June* 1932

'We are too much inclined to think of war as a matter of combats, demanding above all things physical courage. It is really a matter of fasting and thirsting; of toiling and waking; of lacking and enduring; which demands above all things moral courage.'
SIR JOHN FORTESCUE

'In this campaign the Hun has been the least of the malignant influences. More from fever and dysentery, from biting flies, from ticks and crawling beasts have we suffered than from the bullets of the enemy.'
'But if the soldier in the forward division knows nothing of the strategic events of his war, there are many things of which he does know. He does know the food he eats and the food he would like to eat; moreover, he knew, in German East Africa, what his rations ought to be, and how to do without them. He learnt how to fight and march and carry heavy equipment on a very empty stomach....He knew what it meant to have dysentery and malaria. He had marched under a broiling sun by day and shivered in the tropic dews at night....'
CAPTAIN R. V. DOLBEY, R.A.M.C.<br>Sketches of the East African Campaign

'...the 129th Baluchis...were without a doubt very good....'
VON LETTOW-VORBECK

# CHAPTER I

4 AUG.–18 OCT. 1914: Mobilisation; Voyage to France; Egypt; Landing at Marseilles; Journey to Orleans; Departure for Front

IN writing the history of a regiment it is inevitable that its movements and actions should tend to be thought of in isolation, as it is upon this particular unit that the writer is focusing his attention. This narrowness of vision has grave disadvantages both from the point of view of historical presentation and of the interest of the story. For, in the first case, one is concerned to present a true and accurate account of the particular unit, and this cannot be done unless the action is visualised in its proper setting as a small part of a combined movement, often of vast extent, stretching over considerable periods of time. Unless therefore this larger movement can be presented, regimental actions appear to be almost purposeless and chaotic, whereas, properly understood, they always form part of a definite plan, though whether this plan was rightly conceived is another matter.

Secondly, without the broader outlook, the story soon becomes a dull repetition of attacks and assaults, of endless turns in the trenches, dreary marches, and of fatigues suffered, until the reader is wearied and nauseated.

The task of writing is thus far from easy, and it is for this reason that regimental histories tend to be tedious and, to those unacquainted with the particular units, dull. The general public will always prefer to read the larger story unless it happens that the detailed scene is depicted with particular skill and insight.

Nevertheless, these lesser histories do serve a purpose in themselves—in so far as they are accurate and lifelike—as no true perspective of war can be attained even by those who study strategy unless it is vividly realised that the grand movements analyse down finally into brigade and regimental actions, and that, given equally good Staff work, battles are won or lost by the devotion and skill of individual officers and men. For the strategist, therefore, the study of these smaller and more intimate histories is far from being a waste of time. A careful study of regimental, brigade and divisional diaries will show how easy it is to forget the human factor and to think of the fighting men merely as robots. If such be so with these formations, how much more so must it be in the larger formations of the Corps and the Army.

But there is a further reason for writing. The regiment is a deathless organism which survives the individuals who for a time, longer or shorter, belong to it. It is just and proper that its members should be aware of its history, for only in this way can they really come to form an integral part of the greater spiritual whole: only in this way can they acquire that tradition and virtue which makes them something finer and better than their original selves. Finally, it is fitting and right that some record should be kept not only of those who fought and died, but also of all those who took a part in the great epic struggle of the World War.

War was declared against Germany on 4 August and the news reached India the next day. On the 8th orders were received to mobilise the regiment, which was then stationed at Ferozepore, forming part of the Ferozepore Brigade of the 3rd (Lahore) Division.

Ten days later, after a period of great activity—for the regiment had 30 per cent of its strength away on leave, while a detachment of 188 Indian ranks under Captain Adair was on duty in Simla—they entrained for Karachi, and finally, on the 24th, embarked with other units in the S.S. *Ellenga* bound for Marseilles. In the meantime the fighting strength had been brought up by recalling all men and officers away on leave or duty, and also by the addition of a Double Company from the 127th under the command of Major G. G. P. Humphreys.

Of the fatigues of the journey both by land and by sea little will be said save that travelling by troop train across the Sind desert is always exhausting, while life on an overcrowded transport through the heat of the East is under the best conditions an experience better appreciated after the event. To the older men it was not a new thing, as the regiment had been overseas before, but from all it demanded patience, endurance and discipline. Fortunately the weather was fair so that there was little sea-sickness, a devastating thing on a crowded troopship when men are herded together and the hatches and portholes are closed down.

The voyage was not a continuous one, but was broken by a short stay in Egypt from 11 to 17 September, when, with the exception of a small detachment under Captain Vincent, all the troops disembarked at Port Tewfik and entrained for Cairo, passing *en route* the battlefield of Tel-el-Kebir, where in 1882 the regiment had fought under Lord Wolseley. The camp was pitched on the Racecourse at Heliopolis, which in its flatness and general semi-desert-like surroundings recalls the parade grounds of Karachi. Here the time was filled with routine duties, training and route-marching. Here, too, they 'received news of the Battle of the Marne, and at the Hotel Heliopolis, which was used as a club by the Brigade, many were the complaints that the whole show would be over before we could reach France'. On the 16th with the whole Division they marched through the streets of Cairo, and two days later entrained for Alexandria, where once more they embarked on the same transport for Marseilles. During this time Captain F. A. Maclean, Captain S. Ussher and Lieut. C. S. Browning rejoined from home leave. Captain R. F. Dill also rejoined from embarkation duty.

From Alexandria they sailed in a convoy of 16 transports

under H.M.S. *Weymouth*. This was augmented by another five ships under the care of H.M.S. *Indomitable*. Eight days later, on the 26th, the convoy reached Marseilles. The voyage was uneventful and calm. It is recorded that, in preparation for the landing, the regimental musicians were taught to play the *Marseillaise* by the fourth officer of the *Ellenga*. It is also noted that they passed 'transports with Territorials bound for India'. So brief a note for so great an event! But less significant of the vastness of events than maybe a parallel entry in the Diary of some one of those Territorial regiments: 'passed transports with Indian troops for France'. It needed a world war in the twentieth century to bring Asia to Europe.

At 8 a.m. on 26 September the convoy steamed into the harbour at Marseilles, and disembarkation began at once. The 129th was the first Indian regiment to land in Europe and a very close second to come into action a little later.

Here, amidst scenes of frantic excitement and enthusiasm, they marched with others to the celebrated camp on the Borely Racecourse.

'No one who saw it will ever forget the landing from the great transports which began to swing into the harbour of Marseilles in the autumn of 1914, or the laughing, sunburnt, careless faces of the young British officers who leaned over the bulwarks and called aloud to learn whether they were coming too late. In six months nearly all were dead. The arrival of the Indian Corps was an event to him who could presage the future as fraught with tragedy and pathos and "the purple thread of doom" as the landing of that earlier force which marched to Mons with the same gaiety, the same valour and the same bloody predestination.'

Here they were joined by Captain S. Ussher, who had been acting as R.T.O. in Cairo. They had attached to them also two French interpreters—Corporal Le Comte Louis de Blegier Pierregrosse and the Adjudant de la

Charriers: also 2nd Lieut. Boulton as interpreter in French and German. What little time there was—they were less than four days in Marseilles—was spent in re-arming the troops with the new pattern rifle and long bayonet, with exchanging their ammunition for the new Mark VII, and with route-marching and routine exercises. On the morning of the 29th the Division marched past the French General Sevrieures, commanding the 15th Region. Afterwards surplus kit was stored and tents struck, and at 7 o'clock that evening they entrained at the Gare d'Arène in 'cold and very windy weather' for Orleans, with a fighting strength of 9 British officers, 19 Indian officers and 790 other ranks. Captain Ussher was left behind sick in hospital, and a few men were also left to form a base.

The train did not depart until 6 a.m. next day, but on this detail the Diary is silent, long and uncomfortable waits being too normal for comment. The journey took 52 hours and was broken at several points by halts. It was uneventful except for the novelty to the men of passing through new scenes and for the growing excitement that at last they were approaching the battle area. All along the route they were welcomed and cheered by the French, who were filled with enthusiasm and relief to see 'les Indiens' at last. Only one casualty is reported, that of a sepoy who tumbled out of the train and was picked up by the train following with the 57th Rifles. Fortunately it was only a troop train, so his injuries were slight and he recovered within a week, ready for more serious things.

On the morning of 2 October they detrained and marched to Cercotte Camp at Orleans, where they remained until the 17th awaiting orders. Already the more northerly climate made itself felt, 'cold at times', 'mild and cloudy at times; but always cold at night'. Here they were issued with woollen garments in preparation for worse times to come.

On the 5th the Division marched past the Corps Commander, and on the 7th H.R.H. Prince Arthur of Connaught visited the lines and inspected the regiment. After shaking hands with all the British and Indian officers he addressed them:

'I had the pleasure of seeing your regiment in Hong-Kong a few years ago, and I am doubly glad to have the opportunity of seeing you again on active service in Europe, about to fight side by side with the British Army. I wish you all the best of luck, and hope to meet you again in a few days at the front. I will write to my father the Colonel-in-Chief of the regiment and tell him what excellent condition you are in'.

The remainder of the time was uneventful, being passed in route-marching, rifle and machine-gun practice, transport loading and other exercises.

Very considerable difficulty was experienced in obtaining sufficient transport for the Division, as the supply of the orthodox military pattern was completely exhausted. The eventual collection savoured much of the civilian, both as regards vehicles and drivers, and was prophetic of the wide sweep of hostilities as well as symbolic of the unprepared state of the Empire for the war. The scene is graphically described by General Sir James Willcocks:

'A vast plain, now converted into a bog, was literally strewn with vehicles and horses; every species of conveyance found a place, and the fair at Nijni-Novgorod could not have shown a greater variety; the char-a-banc and the baker's cart; structures on prehistoric springs; pole and draught harness; horses in hundreds without collars, head or heel ropes—in fact just loose. It might have appeared grave if it had not been so amusing. But the cart-horses and harness were all as nothing to the drivers. Good fellows, who a month later had become useful soldiers, to-day they were indeed a sore trial. I went round to one diminutive man and said, "Do you know anything about horses?" "I do not", was his reply. "How many days have you been a soldier?" "Thirteen days...." The Indian soldiers could not understand all these things'.

There was much else they could not understand, as will be seen as the story unfolds itself. Meantime the regiment secured its share of vehicles and was now ready to move.

On the evening of the 17th the regiment, with the Division, entrained for the front, and after 39 hours' journey finally reached the war zone and detrained at Arques. Here for the first time the men saw aeroplanes flying overhead, symbol of the new type of warfare into which they were very soon to be plunged.

# CHAPTER II

18 Oct.–31 Oct. 1914: Arrival in fighting line; Attached to 3rd Cavalry Brigade, 2nd Cavalry Division; In the trenches at Hollebeke; Attack of 26 Oct.; German attack of the 30th; Khudadad Khan's V.C.; Loss and regaining of Farm; Regiment leaves Ypres sector

ON the morning of 19 October the Division, less the Sirhind Brigade, detrained at Arques. On the same day the German attack on Ypres began, and the series of battles which are grouped under the title 'First Battles of Ypres' continued until 22 November. The gravity of the position cannot be overstated. Lord French in his despatch of 14 November wrote:

'I fully realised the difficult task which lay before us and the onerous rôle which the British Army was called upon to fulfil. That success has been attained, and all the enemy's desperate attempts to break through our line frustrated, is due to the indomitable courage and tenacity of officers, non-commissioned officers and men. No more arduous task has ever been assigned to British soldiers; and in all their splendid history there is no instance of their having answered so magnificently to the desperate calls which of necessity were made upon them'.

The *Official History* also emphasises the intense gravity of the situation:

'The period was one of the most momentous and critical of the war, and only by the most desperate fighting did the Allies succeed in maintaining their front'.

The British Army was fighting for its very existence and breaking point had almost been reached, as the total losses up to the beginning of the new German offensive had been exceedingly heavy, while the remaining troops were exhausted by continuous fighting. Few reinforcements were available to make good the gaps and to oppose the new onslaught. The Territorials, except for a few select regiments, were still in training. The new Kitchener armies had only begun to exist and would not be available for another 12 months. The only considerable reinforcement available was the Indian Army.

After detraining at Arques the Division marched to Bailleul, which was reached shortly after noon on the 22nd. While resting here 'General French drove up in his car and ordered the Ferozepore Brigade to join the 2nd Cavalry Division'.[1] The rest of the Division, together with the Meerut Division, was sent as a reinforcement to the 2nd Corps, reaching Estaires on the 23rd, and went into the trenches immediately, where we may leave it to follow more particularly the fortunes of the 129th.

That same evening (the 22nd) the regiment was conveyed by motor bus to St Eloi, which was reached at 10.30 p.m. There it was placed at the disposal of Brigadier-General Vaughan, commanding the 3rd Cavalry Brigade, 2nd Cavalry Division. The next morning, at 5.30, it took over a portion of the firing line from the 16th and 5th Lancers and the 4th Hussars.

The Cavalry Corps was at that time holding the very important stretch of country between Wytschaete and Zandvoorde, with its right resting on the north-east corner of Ploegsteert Wood. This sector was part of the ridge which commences in the west with the Mont des Cats and runs eastwards for some 11 miles to Wytschaete between the Poperinghe-Ypres road on the north and the Lys on the south. Its occupation by the enemy would have necessitated the evacuation of Ypres.

Of this stretch of line the 2nd Cavalry Division was holding $3\frac{1}{2}$ miles between the canal bridge east of Hollebeke and Messines with the 3rd Brigade on its left.

So far the heavy fighting had been further north, but nevertheless the 2nd Cavalry Division, together with the other Divisions of the Cavalry Corps, had been pretty

[1] Note by Major F. M. Griffith-Griffin.

heavily engaged and its fighting strength was exceedingly small. The *Official History* records that 'attacks were made by the enemy, at intervals throughout the day and night. One and all of these attacks were repulsed, but the continuous strain on the defending troops was never relaxed and there were many casualties'.

General Vaughan himself accompanied the regiment to the trenches, which extended for about a mile and a half from Hollebeke in a southerly direction. These trenches were not continuous nor were they of the developed type which appeared later, being rather hasty improvisations, regarded as mere temporary shelters to be occupied until the next movement took place. As yet the front had not stabilised nor trench warfare really developed. Here they soon came under fire from the enemy's guns and suffered from snipers. The casualties for the first day were 5 killed and 3 wounded. Probably the first death casualty was that of Signalling Naik, Mazar Khan, one of the few Baluchis serving with the regiment, 'who had taken up an Observation Post in an attic on the top storey (of the house in which were the Regimental H.Q.) and who was blown to bits'. They continued to hold their trenches until the afternoon of the 26th without anything of importance happening, though there were frequent attacks on a small scale at night. These were beaten back without difficulty. Casualties were comparatively light, in spite of a steady bombardment and of a steadily maintained rifle and machine-gun fire. On the 25th all the cavalry supports were withdrawn except the machine-gun detachments, which remained in the trenches. So far the weather had been dry, which was fortunate, as they had 'no kit whatever save haversacks and no blankets',[1] but that night there was a heavy rain and much sniping, 'which made the night a most uncomfortable one in the trenches'—a phrase pregnant with meaning.

On the 26th orders were received shortly after noon that

[1] Both the 5th and 16th Lancers lent blankets to our men.

the Baluchis were to be ready to attack at 3 p.m. This attack was part of a much larger operation, involving the 1st, 2nd and 3rd Cavalry Divisions, ordered by General Allenby, who himself had been instructed to make a forward move in conjunction with the 7th Division on his left.

Owing to the scattered nature of the trenches, and the great extent of front covered by them, Lieut.-Colonel Southey was unable to collect his Company Commanders until 2 o'clock. By 2.30 p.m. the situation had been explained and orders issued. This, however, gave little or no time for the Company Commanders to return to their companies and make the necessary arrangements, so that much had to be left to chance.

The plan of attack was: No. 2 Double Company[1] under Major Humphreys, occupying trenches in the third section about Hollebeke, to advance with their left on Lock and occupy a front of 600 yards. No. 1 Company under Captain Adair to occupy the Roosebeek and, as soon as No. 2 Company came into line, to advance with them, their right directing on the farm on Contour 30. Two platoons, No. 3 Company under Captain Maclean with the Machine-Gun Section under Captain Dill, to co-operate with flanking fire from the trenches near Jardine's Farm. No. 3 Company, less two platoons, and No. 4 Company to be in reserve behind Jardine's Farm.

At 3 p.m. the preliminary 'bombardment' commenced. It was carried out by four horse artillery guns and lasted for 10 minutes. The advance then began, but was supported by the fire of one gun only. So scattered were the trenches that the men had to get out and advance in small groups. This they did, coming immediately under enemy rifle and machine-gun fire. The distance to be covered was something over 600 yards. In spite of the heavy fire and difficult country—for there was little or no cover in the flat

[1] In the rest of the history 'company' will be used for 'double company'.

country—they advanced to within 200–300 yards of the enemy, when they were stopped by the enemy's fire, losing in the advance some 19 men. Part of the company under Captain Vincent lost direction and came in on the right of No. 2 Company. Meantime Captain Adair, who had been waiting for Major Humphreys' advance before moving forward, having seen nothing and received no information from him, had asked Headquarters for instructions. He was ordered not to advance until Major Humphreys had come on. This message, however, never reached him and he began to advance. No. 3 Company and the Machine-Gun Section meantime were subjecting the enemy to a heavy and accurate fire and were themselves subjected to a heavy artillery fire, which fortunately could not quite find them. At 4.45 p.m. Captain Adair asked for reinforcements and two platoons of No. 4 Company were sent up to him.

By this time it was getting dark: firing was very heavy, and it was evident that the attack could not hope to succeed owing to the smallness of the attacking force and the lack of sufficient artillery support. The enemy machine guns, which were numerous and were too well hidden to be found, made further advance impossible. Captain Adair's company suffered somewhat severely, while Captain Vincent was shot in the head and died very shortly afterwards.

Meantime more important events on the right of the Corps made it imperative that the Division should break off the action, and at 5.15 p.m. orders were received to stop the attack and reoccupy the original trenches. Thus ended the first serious action of the regiment. The men are reported to have 'behaved very well under trying circumstances' and to be still 'very cheery and full of keenness'. Two mentions are made: No. 118 Lance-Naik Nek Amal, who went out alone to within 100 yards of the enemy trenches to aid Captain Vincent after he had been wounded. Unable to bring Captain Vincent back alone 'he returned to his company and with the aid of No. 250 Sepoy Saiday Khan, who was later killed, he succeeded in taking Captain Vincent back to hospital'. The casualties were Captain Vincent and 6 men killed and 40 wounded. Captain Vincent was the first British officer of the Indian Army to be killed in Flanders.

The next morning the regiment was relieved and went into billets at Hollebeke but found little rest, for it is recorded next day to be entrenching a position north of the Château, while in the evening two companies under Major Hannyngton were back again in A and B sections of the old trenches. On the 29th Headquarters and the remaining two companies which were still digging trenches were ordered at 11.15 a.m. to march to the bridge over the canal north-west of Hollebeke to support the cavalry in Hollebeke Château. At 1.10 p.m. they were ordered to Kleine Zillebeke to 'form part of reserve to the 1st Army Corps', marching back to billets about 7 p.m.[1] Such was the paucity of troops.

That night 'the position of the Cavalry Corps was the same as in the morning...the line was fairly dug in but there was very little wire up, and such as there was had been taken from the fencing of the farms near'. But the effective force was being very seriously reduced by the constant casualties, so that by the 30th the 'British line was already all too thin; it was indeed little stronger in places than an outpost system.... The total effective force of the Cavalry Corps, reckoning in the Indian troops, did not furnish 1000 rifles per mile, including supports and reserves.... They had no more artillery support than their horse artillery batteries and one section of old 6-inch howitzers could furnish'.

Upon this very weak and fatigued Corps the German attack was now to be made in weight. The 2nd Bavarian

[1] This small movement entitled the regiment to 'Ypres 1914' as a battle honour. They are the only Indian unit so entitled.

Corps, supported by very heavy artillery fire, concentrated on the sector held by the 3rd Cavalry Brigade on the left of the 2nd Cavalry Division.

The 129th had two companies in the line but were to be relieved at 7 a.m. by the 5th and 16th Lancers, while No. 1 Company had just taken over No. 3 Company's section of the trenches with No. 2 Company in reserve. The enemy attack, therefore, was by great mischance or otherwise just timed to catch these reliefs, and this added considerably to the confusion of the situation. No. 4 Company under Major Potter was withdrawn in spite of heavy artillery fire, but No. 3 Company was compelled to find cover behind a farm in a wood. Both companies were ordered to concentrate at Brigade H.Q. at the Château, but only Major Potter's company and one platoon of the 3rd Company arrived, the other three platoons being temporarily lost. They were eventually found by Major Stewart, the Guides, attached to the 16th Lancers.

Meantime the enemy pressure was increasing on the centre section, and about 12.30 p.m. all available men of the regiment at the Château were ordered to reinforce the firing line. Headquarters with No. 4 Company and the one platoon of No. 3 Company went forward, but when half-way up found the whole line in retreat, both British and Indian. These were rallied by Colonel Southey and made to take up positions behind hedges and farms, while No. 4 Company and the one platoon of No. 3 Company occupied a wood to hold and protect the right flank. 'The enemy were successfully held there until (4 p.m.) orders were received to fall back on the position entrenched during the last two days.'

All this time Nos. 1 and 2 Companies had been fighting and suffering even more severely, as upon them fell the brunt of the enemy's attack owing to the sectors which they held forming a salient. They had been subjected to a very heavy bombardment from close range and had lost many men, killed and wounded. Major Humphreys was hit by shrapnel and died early the following morning. His place was taken by Lieut. Lewis, who commanded the company till it came out of action at the end of the day. No. 1 Company, occupying C section of the trenches, was also severely handled. Shortly after noon it was ordered to

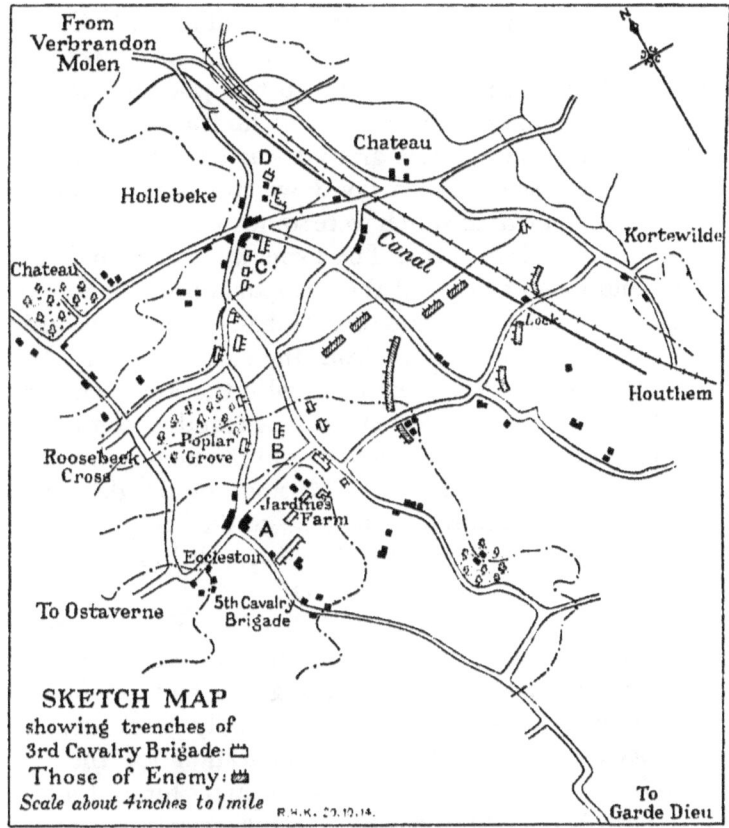

fall back via the bridge north of Hollebeke and to hold the crossing of the canal. The company was, however, more or less cut off by the enemy, and few men rejoined Headquarters that evening. Captain Adair was mortally wounded in the body, and knowing this refused to let his men be hampered in helping him. He was never heard of again. All his Indian officers were killed or wounded.

In B section No. 2 Company fought under exceedingly severe conditions, which are best described in Lieut. Lewis's own words:

'On my arrival the trenches in the salient were being very heavily bombarded: many were obliterated. Captain Dill with his machine guns and most of his men were, however, still in action. I brought up two platoons from the support to reinforce but could not find a yard of trench for them to occupy. The ground was levelled. For want of a better place the men lay down in the open near the farm in the salient in which were some men of the machine-gun sections filling belts. The farm was cut in half by a shell and caught fire and the occupants burnt before our eyes. Wounded were numerous, and as, owing to casualties, stretchers had not arrived from the supports, I ran back to fetch some. Coming up again with the stretchers I saw English, Indian and German troops together coming out from the salient. These wounded and the men burnt in the farm account for most of our "Missing" on this day. Each man extricated himself as best he could from this mêlée and fell back on a position 600 yards behind, which is mentioned by Major Hannyngton'.

It was in this great onslaught that Captain Dill and his two machine-gun crews so distinguished themselves. They had been in action all the morning and had fought their guns with great determination. Gradually the enemy shell fire became more intense in preparation for the final assault. One gun was wrecked by a direct hit and several of its crew killed and wounded. The survivors then attached themselves to the remaining gun. A little later Captain Dill was severely wounded, but refused to leave his men and continued to carry on until he was completely exhausted, when he was taken to the rear. His men, however, continued in action, firing and inflicting severe losses until the enemy assault swept over them. Every man was either shot or bayoneted at his post. Of these devoted men only one survived—Sepoy Khudadad Khan, who had continued firing until severely wounded, when he was left by the enemy for dead. Eventually in the dark he managed to crawl back and join the regiment. For his heroic conduct he was awarded the V.C., being the first Indian to be so honoured. The others of the team, all dead, who equally shared this great distinction though it fell to Khudadad Khan to wear the V.C. for them, were not forgotten. They were: Sepoys Ghulam Muhamad, Lal Sher, Said Ahmed, Kassib and Afsar Khan. All received decorations: Ghulam Muhamad being awarded the I.O.M., while the others received the I.D.S.M. The behaviour of all ranks had been splendid. Lieut.-Colonel Southey, who was then commanding the regiment, writes in a later note: 'Owing to the enormous extent of front occupied by the battalion, it was impossible to get any accurate information regarding the behaviour of the men on the left, i.e. No. 1 Company. All the officers, both British and Indian, were *hors de combat*, and undoubtedly many gallant deeds were left unmentioned in despatches. Five sepoys lost their way in the retirement and found themselves on the wrong side of the canal. They joined up with a British infantry battalion and some weeks later rejoined their own battalion, with a certificate from the Officer Commanding the British battalion to say the men had fought with them and done very well, and he was now sending them back as he heard the battalion was close by'.

At 4 p.m. the regiment received orders to retire to a position north of the Château. No. 4 Company went into trenches for the night, while the remainder went into billets about half a mile in the rear close to the canal bank. There they had the unpleasant experience of being shelled by a French battery which 'had been sent to the assistance of the brigade, and started off by shelling our line thoroughly, firing line, supports and reserves. Luckily no casualties, but many escapes'.

Next day these three companies and Headquarters moved up to support the 18th Hussars. They were shelled, but had no casualties. At dusk No. 2 Company relieved the Hussars in the line with No. 3 Company in support and No. 1 Company in reserve. No. 4 Company remained in its own section of the line. Towards 9 p.m. there was an attack by the enemy on the regiment's right but it was repulsed.

About midnight occurred one of those curious incidents always possible where troops of different nations are fighting together. During the day French reinforcements had been coming up and had taken over both on the right and left of the positions held by the Brigade. About half an hour after midnight a message came through from the French that the Germans had occupied the farm held by Major Potter. This proved to be true. The explanation was that the Germans had been mistaken in the dark for French troops and had been able to obtain possession without opposition, as fire was not opened upon them until they were almost in the farm. There they captured Major Atal, I.M.S., and also Captain Maclean, with a few other wounded to whom Major Atal was attending. Major Potter withdrew some 50 yards and entrenched. Orders were immediately issued for the recapture of the farm, and at 4 a.m. the assault was made, Major Potter attacking on the left flank while the remainder of the troops brought up attacked the right. The movement was very quickly and successfully carried out, all the German garrison being either killed, wounded or taken prisoner. Much of the fight was a room to room hunt, which was greatly to the liking of the men. Major Atal and Captain Maclean were released. The bag was a good one: 10 killed, 13 wounded and 14 others captured.

At 5 a.m. orders were received to hand over to the

French and to march to Vootmezeele. Then to Kemmel, which was reached in the evening. The next afternoon they marched to Westoutre via La Clytte, where they arrived at 4.30 p.m. and billeted for the night. Thence they marched to Strazeele and were inspected by the G.O.C. 2nd Cavalry Division, who thanked them for their work and services. On the 4th they marched to Estaires to rejoin the Ferozepore Brigade once more.

Thus they spent their first ten days of war. The total casualties were: 3 British officers killed—Major Humphreys, Captain Vincent and Captain Adair; 3 British officers wounded—Captain Dill, Captain Maclean and Lieut. Lewis; 3 Indian officers killed—Subedar Azad Gul, Subedar Ghulam Mohamed and Jemadar Jafar Ali; 2 Indian officers wounded—Subedar Zaman Khan and Jemadar Mir Bad Shah (127th). Of the men 26 were dead, 138 wounded, 67 missing (these were mostly dead; many were burned) and 11 sick.

Of the two machine guns, one had been destroyed by shell fire while the other had been captured after the whole of the crew had been killed or wounded.

They had thus lost 50 per cent of their British officers, 30 per cent of their Indian officers, and 33 per cent of their men—no mean record. There is little doubt that they had inflicted at least equal losses on the enemy, while they had played an important, though small part, in holding the enemy at bay during a very critical time.

Compared with some of the later and larger slaughters at Loos, on the Somme and at Passchendaele, it is not a formidable casualty list but it is sufficiently heavy. Nor were they being withdrawn for a rest, but only to pass on to another scene equally terrible and even more trying physically, for now they were destined to occupy an area which is always waterlogged, and which in the winter months is little better than a quagmire once one leaves the hard roads.

# CHAPTER III

1 Nov.–20 Dec. 1914: Regiment rejoins own Division on Indian Corps Front; In the trenches; Reinforcements; Inspection by the Prince of Wales; Enemy attack on 23 Nov.; Trenches and billets; Attack on two enemy saps; Further attacks on 19 Dec.; Excessively bad weather conditions; German attack; Remnant of regiment with Lahore Division withdrawn for rest

THE regiment, having rejoined its own brigade on 4 November, was now in the sector held by the Indian Corps, where it remained, with the exception of the few days interlude in April when it was again at Ypres, until the whole Corps was withdrawn from the Western Front. This sector stretched for some 8 miles, 'from north of Givenchy on our right passing east of Festubert and Richebourg l'Avoué, west of Neuve Chapelle, past Mauquissart, and taking a bend to Rouges Bancs on our left', and had been the scene of some very heavy fighting. For its defence the Corps was deplorably weak both in personnel and in materials. The total strength was little more than that of a British Division, and at the time amounted to some 3500 British and 9500 Indian rifles. In addition to this, the Secunderabad Cavalry Brigade could supply about 1000 more rifles. Wastage was much more difficult to make good than in the case of the British Corps owing to the very great distance from the base depôts and also to the lack of organisation in India for making good such heavy losses.

From the moment of its arrival the Corps had been subjected to very considerable casualties, so that when the 129th with the Ferozepore Brigade returned to the Lahore Division it was sent the next day to the trenches. At 5 p.m. on 5 November, therefore, they marched to trenches near Rue de Bacquerot, where they took over from the 59th Rifles.

The country in which the regiment now found itself has been described many times. 'A dismal dead plain, dotted with farmhouses and here and there clumps of trees.' Certainly those who knew it in the winter would subscribe to this description, which, however, must fail to register the real feelings of those who went through the winter of 1914–15. The Official Observer's description is equally adverse: 'The line held by the Indian Corps from the time of its arrival...may be fairly described as one of the least attractive sections, either from the picturesque point of view or from that of comfort...The eye was met by a vast expanse of low-lying cultivable land, cut up by innumerable roads and lanes, and dotted with small villages and isolated farms. During a great part of the year, as far as the eye could reach there stretched a dismal sea of mud, almost the only break consisting of suspicious-looking pools of water, which proved on further investigation to be flooded shell holes. The only prominent objects...were a few copses or woods, amongst which was the Bois du Biez, so long a stronghold of the enemy, and in the distance the Aubers ridge so near and yet so far....The short distance below the surface at which water was found rendered the digging of deep trenches impossible in places, while even a moderate fall of rain reduced the inhabitants of the trenches to a state of discomfort quite indescribable'. Such a description, whilst being accurate, can convey no meaning to those who do not know and did not suffer the country. To speak of a state of 'discomfort' is utterly to mislead the reader. The condition of the trenches was too appalling for description. Into such conditions the Indian troops were hurled by an unkind fate, and there they remained making the most of their position. Few, except their own officers, will ever realise what a physical and spiritual strain these men underwent. The contrast with their own country was as hell to heaven, while the lack of equipment with which they had to face their enemy made it necessary to suffer an unceasing toll of casualties which could never be adequately replaced. It may take three years to make a good sepoy; it required less than three months of such conditions to destroy him.

The regiment did not complete the relief until nearly midnight, as they did not know the trenches which they were taking over from the 59th Rifles. Nos. 3 and 4 Companies were in the firing line and supports, while Nos. 1 and 2 were in reserve. On the right was the 57th and on the left the 9th Bhopals. The 57th and 129th formed the right section of the Brigade under Lieut.-Colonel Southey.

Here they remained until the evening of the 10th, during which time all was quiet and nothing happened. The weather was bad. The Diary very tersely reports that the night of the 10th was a 'wet and windy night'. The next day it 'rained hard'. Two days later it was 'cold and wet', while the relief and march back to billets was effected 'in pouring rain and under heavy rifle fire'. There is little doubt, however, that on this occasion the rain depressed them less than it did those who took their place. Nor was the weather the sole trouble. The enemy continued to vex and harass them to the utmost of his ability. Rifle fire, gun fire, grenades, bombs of all descriptions were directed upon them, though fortunately without causing too great a number of casualties. But if the damage to flesh and blood was little, that to the trenches was great, so that it was necessary to be constantly rebuilding the sections blown in or destroyed. The cry of the Israelites was exceeding bitter when they were ordered to make bricks without straw: it would have been more so had they been compelled to repair and rebuild those trenches without wood or sand-bags and even without proper tools. But here there was no complaint, only a great fortitude and a stern endurance. All did their duty and no special mention is made of any, save that on the 15th the enemy shelled the aid post which had to be vacated. 'Major Atal, I.M.S., stuck to it with the greatest gallantry as long as he could.'

The relief took some five hours and the regiment marched to billets in La Gorgue. Here they received news of Lord Roberts's death and here their first officer reinforcements arrived: Major Buist, The Guides, Captain C. A. G. Money, 130th Baluchis, Captain H. C. Rome, 20th Punjabis, Lieut. C. M. Thornhill, 24th Punjabis, while Captain Ussher rejoined from hospital.

The strength of the regiment was at this time 10 British officers, 14 Indian officers and 520 other ranks.

During the next week the weather became more severe and there was frost and snow. On the 19th 'snow fell during the greater part of the day', while it 'froze hard' the night before they returned to the trenches.

On the 21st H.R.H. the Prince of Wales visited the regiment and inspected No. 1 Company under Major Buist. The next afternoon they marched to trenches at La Quinque Rue where, together with the 57th, they formed the left section of the brigade. Here the enemy trenches 'were very close up to us: in two places their saps have reached within 50 yards of our trenches'. Their time was not to be so peaceful as on the former occasion, for on the 23rd the enemy attacked all along the front. The attack was well timed, for it caught the Meerut and Lahore Divisions in the midst of a relief which added greatly to the general confusion.

The main weight of the enemy attack fell upon the centre section of the line held by one company of the Connaught Rangers, the 34th Sikh Pioneers and the 9th Bhopals—that is, on the right of the 57th and the 129th. With the details of this action we are not here concerned, and it can be studied in Chapter IX of General Willcocks's book. The regiment suffered little compared with other units which bore the brunt of the fighting, but it was due to the very prompt action of Lieut.-Colonel Southey that the enemy break-through was held up: 'The position here was saved by the coolness and grasp of Lieut.-Colonel Southey of the 129th Baluchis, who sent one and a half companies to entrench themselves on the road from Festubert to Ligny-le-Petit and to hold the neighbouring houses. This refusal by Colonel Southey of his right flank and the determination with which the position was held by his detachment, prevented the enemy from extending his success to the left'.

The Diary helps one to realise how much in the dark everyone was. First it is the 34th falling back and the Connaught Rangers being driven into the trenches held by the 57th. At 1.25 p.m. a counter-attack is promised, but 'no signs of any counter-attack were apparent in the left section'; so at 2 p.m. the reserves of the left section are sent up to entrench the right flank as already mentioned. Again, a counter-attack is promised, but at 6 p.m. they are informed that it has failed, which 'left us very much in the air, with only Germans on our right for at least 800 yards'. So the darkness falls, till at midnight the enemy are bombed out of the captured trenches and the affair ends with the line restored, though the Corps has lost 1200 officers and men. The regiment has lost Major Atal, who, with Lieut. Indajit Singh of the 57th and some 4 or 5 wounded men, was buried in the debris of the house where they had their aid post. 'He was a gallant and conscientious man and had twice been recommended for his work.'

The rest of the sojourn till their relief on 2 December was again of the routine order. The weather was warmer, but there was much rain, while the enemy by no means desisted in making himself unpleasant in the usual routine ways. But there were slight signs of improvement in the material side of life. Not enough to make any great change in the continual wretchedness, but sufficient to keep hope alive and help them to hang on for better things. Thus on the 24th it is noted that 'braziers and coke' were issued for trench use and were greatly appreciated: though on the debit side the Diary for that same day also records: 'A good deal of bombing went on on the part of the enemy. We have none to retaliate with'. The next day, however, the gods are good and they 'received some bombs'. On the 29th a trench mortar is recorded. Not the magnificent species of later days but an improvised tube almost equally dangerous to its owners as to the enemy. It 'did a lot of good, silencing enemy's mortar for some time'. Even a few rifle grenades appear, and finally a very few Verey lights to lighten the darkness. Hitherto they had had to depend upon the kindness of the enemy for such favours.

All these were but signs of the intense activity going on behind the fighting lines. In the meantime, like the rest of the British troops, they had to continue to hold out against an enemy who was well supplied with all these things. They were, however, helping themselves, and the Corps engineers improvised a number of types of amateur bombs from jam tins, nails, slabs of gun-cotton and such like. Thus on the 27th they were instructed to 'have old empty jam tins saved and sent in to Brigade H.Q.', not, as the uninstructed might at first imagine, to be refilled with jam.

The bad weather and sodden condition of the trenches caused a certain amount of sickness, but the men were rapidly learning their trade. 'During this time in the trenches the men suffered a good deal from swollen feet, otherwise their health was good. They now realise the importance of good trenches and the necessity for protection against bombs'—a note well calculated to call forth ribald and profane comments. But however bad the weather and the conditions in the trenches the spirit of all was splendid. Lieut.-Colonel Southey wrote:

'During this period the spirit of the men in the trenches was wonderfully good. A gunner officer in charge of the first field mortars (local manufacture) which operated in our area commented on the cheeriness of the men: his remark to me was, "It is a pleasure to come into your section, after seeing so many gloomy faces on the right. Every one of your men in the front line seemed to be enjoying himself".

'The Mahsuds especially seemed to revel in the fighting. Some refugees from "The Glory Hole", a trench on our right which came in for an abnormal share of bombing, were lying in one of our trenches and one man would now and then point his rifle in the air and fire without taking any aim. A Mahsud noticed this and went up to him and said: "That is not the way to fire; look at me". He deliberately stood up and fired over the parapet, taking careful aim; then reloaded, aimed and had another shot. Then he turned round to the man and said, "That is the correct way"'.

They remained in billets until the evening of the 15th. The weather was uniformly wet and cold, but out of the trenches life was possible although not exactly joyous. On 4 December they were notified that Khudadad Khan had been awarded the V.C., which news greatly pleased everyone. On the 6th General Willcocks inspected the regiment and congratulated them on the great honour they had received. Also short leave was opened for officers. For the men no such joy was possible, a fact which should always be remembered, as leave when one does not go home is not the same thing. On the 8th they received a draft of two British officers: Captain Robinson, 46th Punjabis, and Captain R. D. Davies, 127th Baluch L.I.; 2 Indian officers: Jemadars Dadin and Kadir Khan; and 202 other ranks. The next day they received Christmas cards from H.M. the King.

On the 16th, at 2 a.m., the regiment marched to Givenchy where it was to deliver an attack, the first serious action since coming into the Indian sector.

This attack was only an incidental affair in an ambitious

scheme of operations which the French had been gradually maturing, and serves well to give a sense of proportion when reading such a history as this. But to the regiment it was a very serious action in which severe losses were sustained. It also explains the unhappy events of the 20th when the German attacks broke through the Corps front.

The Germans had been withdrawing troops for some time from the West and transferring them to the Eastern Front. This movement had been watched very closely by General Joffre, who believed that an opportunity now presented itself for an effective break through on a wide front.

Plans were made accordingly for an extended offensive in which the British Expeditionary Force was asked to co-operate. For such an offensive the British were quite unprepared, being still desperately short of men and munitions. It was, however, impossible to refuse. Consent was given reluctantly, but the lack of confidence felt is very clearly reflected in the plans and confused orders which followed. That the French command had grossly underestimated the enemy's defensive strength was only too apparent when the offensive began. A series of actions followed which were hopeless in their conception, and which, being carried out without confidence by the Higher Commands, only resulted in a useless slaughter at a time when economy in both men and materials was of paramount importance. It not only reduced fighting strengths, but, coming at the end of a long and exhausting struggle when the troops needed rest, caused for a time a serious loss of morale. It is necessary to bear this in mind when dealing with the events of the 20th. The temporary collapse of the Indian Corps in these critical days reflects not on the men but upon the Higher Commands.

But to return. 'The British attack was to be made by the 2nd and 3rd Corps..., whilst the 4th and Indian Corps were to "carry out active local operations with a view to containing the enemy on their front".' As part of this scheme it was decided to 'capture two German saps opposite to the trenches of the 15th Sikhs in the neighbourhood of Givenchy, and then to extend the operation by securing a portion of the German main trenches'. For this work the Ferozepore Brigade was chosen, while the 129th was to lead the assault. The Diaries make no allusion to artillery preparation, nor is this strange in view of the dearth of ammunition and the still prevalent belief that gallantry was more than a match for machine guns, no matter how numerous and well placed. It was hoped, however, to take the saps just before daylight by a sudden assault, as they were only 25 and 35 yards respectively beyond our front-line trenches. While the assaulting troops were driving the enemy back, digging parties were to connect our trenches with the saps so that reinforcements could be sent up. Beyond these immediate plans it is unnecessary to go. The attack was timed to take place at 6.30 a.m. on the 16th. Major Potter with his company was to rush the left sap while Major Buist took the right. What happened is best described in Major Hannyngton's report:

'The method of attack was similar against each saphead, viz. the four platoons of a company to issue from our trenches one after the other, to charge down on either side of the sap, and to seize the points in the enemy's trench where the saps joined it.

'The attack was timed to take place as soon as the light was enough for the men to distinguish their objective, of which they had otherwise no knowledge, nor had they seen the ground. Both companies were timed to start at the same moment. This time was altered by 10 minutes owing to one company going wrong in the darkness so that it was nearly light when the attack started....

'Only two platoons could be packed into the front trench; the other two platoons were placed in the support trench, from which each platoon in turn filed into the front trench, extended and went forward. The first two platoons went forward on the minute, and in each case made good the sap-head and the major portion of the sap. The third platoon also made good, and a few men succeeded in reaching the main trench. By the time the fourth platoon was in position to go forward it was daylight, and the enemy brought a heavy cross-fire with machine guns to bear on the spaces between the sap-heads and trench. Both platoons lost heavily; a few men did reach the sap-heads...'.

Having got in they found themselves trapped. The digging of the communication trenches under heavy fire was exceedingly slow as well as costly of lives; that to the right sap was never completed. The enemy was much better supplied with bombs, both as regards quantity and quality. As a result, in spite of the utmost gallantry and devotion, our men were gradually driven back towards the sap-head. All day they were bombed systematically as well as shelled and sniped. Cramped in the narrow sap, impeded with their dead and wounded, without bombs, without food and short of water—those in the right sap without a British officer—they withstood for 12 hours all attempts to dislodge them. Lieut. Lewis, who was an eye-witness, writes: 'Of the 80 men who gained a footing in the right sap, 18 only, of whom about half were wounded, regained our lines after dark under Jemadar Id Mohamed, who was captured two days later. This remnant passed an incredibly trying day and returned much shaken. For some three hours before darkness fell, we watched them from loop-holes, imprisoned in the German sap-head. A German arm appeared above a traverse, a bomb was thrown, a scuffle among our men, and perhaps the bomb was thrown out to explode immediately just outside. Lance-Naik Sahib Jan on several occasions relieved the situation by charging single-handed with fixed bayonet down the sap.... And all the time we, in our trench about 20 yards or so away, were digging like maniacs, but otherwise powerless to help, except by raising cheers to keep up their spirits and to make the Germans less cock-a-hoop'.

On the left the situation was almost equally desperate. The first two platoons had been swept by machine-gun fire as they crossed the open and had lost heavily, Subedar Adam Khan being among the killed. The survivors under Captain Davies reached the sap and captured it, bayoneting the enemy or driving them back to their main trench. Here they were held up by a machine gun, and being unable to make further progress blocked the sap. But they were gradually bombed back again. Meantime Major Potter with the survivors of the other two platoons managed to reach the sap and tumble in.

Under the leadership of these two officers the men sustained the fight until it was dark, being bombed without cessation. Captain Davies writes: 'During the day I went back to see Major Potter whose Company H.Q. were near the sap-head... It was a most unpleasant journey. The sap was packed with the living, the dead and badly wounded men. As I went along I remember the advice given me by the sepoys I met: "You can walk on him, sahib, he is dead. No, not on that one, he is terribly wounded but not dead yet". They were so packed one could not get along in any other way'.

Gradually the dismal December day drew to its close and darkness fell, allowing a handful of exhausted men to withdraw from the right sap while the completing of the left communication trench permitted the 15th Sikhs to relieve Major Potter and his almost equally spent men. About 8 p.m. the survivors were withdrawn and the regiment marched back to billets at Bethune. The losses had been heavy: Captain Ussher and Subedar Adam Khan killed; Captain Money, Lieut. Browning, Jemadars Nawab Khan and Imandar wounded; 53 other ranks killed and 65 wounded. The Brigade Diary tersely summarises the whole action: 'This regiment suffered heavy casualties.... Net result, gain of 40 yards of German sap. Other units did not take part in attack as they were not to go in until 129th were all used up, which did not occur'. This failure to get 'used up' was largely rectified a few days later.

A series of mentions and recommendations were made which, though eminently earned, should not be allowed to belittle the uniformly high conduct and courage displayed by all ranks. The report ends: 'Finally I wish to bring to notice the splendid leading of Major Potter. The leading platoon... hesitated at the lip of the sap. Major Potter seeing this dashed forward and carried them right on. During the whole day when heavily bombed and pushed he kept perfectly cool and never allowed himself to be flustered. He was in a very nasty position—cut off for 12 hours—knowing I could get no help to him, and by his bearing so kept up the spirits of his men that the sap was held and fortified and made good'.

On the early morning of the 18th they were back again in the trenches at Givenchy whence they had made the attack on the 16th. Once more the whole of the Indian front was being stirred up into activity and both the Meerut and Lahore Divisions were involved. The first day they lost Captain Rome killed, while the following day two platoons of No. 3 Company under Jemadar Mir Bad Shah co-operated with the 59th in a similar attack to that of the 16th. This attack was delivered at 5 a.m. Mir Bad Shah and his men rushed the enemy's trench and occupied it. They were cut off for 24 hours, but in spite of continual bombing kept off the enemy until they withdrew. For this Mir Bad Shah was mentioned in the report to the Brigade. 'Jemadar Mir Bad Shah commanded the party which seized the right sap. This party was attacked pretty well for the whole 24 hours they were in the sap. This officer behaved splendidly. Had he failed to do so, the whole party would have been lost.' For this he received the I.O.M. 2nd Class, as also did L.-Naik Sahib Jan for his distinguished conduct on the occasion of the first assault.

The fighting had been equally desperate and bloody as on the previous occasion, while again little had been gained. 'The net result was that one platoon succeeded in holding about 90 yards of the enemy's sap on the left, while another platoon on the right, with some of the 129th Baluchis, kept its grip on a sap in front of the regiment (i.e. the 57th). With these exceptions the night of 19 December fell with all the ground lost which at bloody price we had gained during the day.'

The troops were utterly exhausted with the continuous fighting; their losses, especially in British officers, had been exceedingly severe, while their misery was completed by the perpetual rain which flooded their trenches and which had hardly ceased for 48 hours.

General Willcocks had already warned G.H.Q. that the Corps was in urgent need of rest, but the reply had been to extend slightly his front and to force him into the costly and exhausting operations just mentioned.

On the 20th the Germans opened with a heavy bombardment all along the front held by the Indian Corps. This was followed by infantry attacks directed especially against Givenchy and the trenches between Givenchy and La Quinque Rue. All night long the weather had been atrocious. 'The elements were warring on the side of the enemy, for torrential rain during the night had made the trenches almost untenable. In many places the fire-step had been washed away and the men were consequently unable to stand high enough to fire over the parapet. The trenches were knee and in some cases even waist deep in mud and icy water, which clogged a large number of rifles and rendered them useless.'

On the 129th front the captured parallel was heavily shelled for over an hour. It was then assaulted and recaptured. Meantime along the front of the Sirhind Brigade,

MAJOR-GENERAL W. M. SOUTHEY
C.M.G.

which was on the immediate left of the 129th, a series of mines had been exploded about 9 a.m. The survivors after desperate fighting were driven back, leaving the 129th left flank completely in the air.

Having recaptured the parallel the enemy now lifted his barrage and directed all his fire on to the regiment's front and on to Givenchy village, which were heavily assaulted by dense masses of troops. The right flank was overwhelmed, while at the same time the left company 'found the enemy in the support trenches behind them which they had gained by coming up the passage from the Sirhind Brigade trenches. With both flanks gone the centre gave way, the left company remaining prisoners in the hands of the enemy'.

Lieut.-Colonel Southey relates how, as he was writing in the Regimental H.Q., 'the right and centre companies of the firing line suddenly appeared retiring in good order. Some of the men said the order had been given to retire by a British officer, but I could not discover whether such order had been given or not. Anyhow the Germans were on the top of them; their rifles missed fire owing to having no bolt covers, and the only thing to do was to continue the retirement holding on to every bit of cover until the canal was reached. Artillery support was almost nil owing to lack of ammunition and want of communication, due to the destruction of the telephone wires'. He further relates an incident which may be taken as typical of the still undaunted spirit of the men. 'Owing to the surprise of this retirement some documents were left behind in the drawer of a table in the Regimental H.Q., and the loss was not discovered till late in the evening. One of the regimental signallers who was employed in the office volunteered to go up to Givenchy that night, and although the place was in the hands of the Germans he succeeded in rescuing the papers and returned with them in the early morning.'

It is difficult to give any idea of the complete confusion

of this day's fighting. Communication was practically impossible as the telephones were all cut and the bombardment was so heavy as almost to prevent messages being sent by runners. Moreover the trench system had been practically destroyed. Before the bombardment began it had nearly slipped away in muddy liquefaction which utterly defied all attempts to make repairs. All the reports insist with a wearisome monotony on this. 'During the night it poured with rain, the parapet was constantly dropping away, and the men were trying to repair it all night. Their rifles were clogged with mud, and only one in three or four would fire.' 'I was given the warning by my sentries of the advance, but owing to the nature of the trench and the liquid mass of mud round the loopholes the rifles jammed in large numbers....' Only those who have wallowed in Flanders mud will fully realise what this means, and even they have largely forgotten with the passage of time. For this was one of the worst sections in the whole Western Front for mud and water. The German bombardment completed the ruin, while it destroyed large numbers of the defenders who were not as yet provided with shell-proof dug-outs.

But the enemy advance, while it swept away the defenders, was not unopposed. Small groups of men fought it out to the last. Thus died Major Potter, who with many of his men was never seen again. 'He tells me Major Potter and his men resisted for some time and killed many Germans.... From his account and from what I know of Major Potter I am sure that he and most of his men fought till it was useless, as did the Machine-Gun Section under Lieut. Lewis.' Nor was Major Potter the only one who so fought.

The stragglers were rallied by Lieut.-Colonel Southey and the Adjutant, Lieut. Griffin, some 800 yards in the rear of the front line. Finally, what was left of the regiment was mustered some 500 yards still further back. Fresh troops were being rushed up to take its place, and at last the wearied remnants of the regiment with the Division were withdrawn and marched back to Pont Fixe—such as were left. For when mustered there were but 5 British officers, 4 Indian officers and 210 men. How many were dead was not known. The immediate casualty list showed—killed: Subedar Ahmed Din, Jemadar Karim Khan and 14 other ranks; wounded: Jemadar Lal Sher, Jemadar Masaod Khan and 104 other ranks; missing: Major H. W. R. Potter, Captain R. D. Davies,[1] Subedar-Major Mala Khan,[1] Subedar Amir Khan,[1] Jemadar Id Mahd. and 84 other ranks. Most of the missing were dead, buried in the falling trenches or stamped in the mud during the fighting. In those days corpses took the place of duck-boards.

So ended the fighting for the year 1914. The remaining days were hardly days of rest. The next day, after all this slaughter and exhaustion, they were digging trenches west of Pont Fixe—and the next, after which they marched to billets at Pugnoy. Christmas Day was hardly a day of great rejoicing for the few British officers who survived: for the men of course it meant nothing. But 'in spite of this reverse the spirit of the men was unbroken. Three days after the regiment had been taken out of the line, when going round the remnants of the companies, I was asked by the men to let them go up into the trenches again as soon as possible'.

During the remaining days the remnants of the regiment were gradually pulling themselves together. A few stragglers came in, and some sick and wounded returned, amongst whom was Captain Dill. On the 31st they marched to billets at Marles, where Major W. J. Mitchell, 124th, arrived and Lieut. C. M. Thornhill rejoined from special duty.

Such is the record for the first two months at the front: one of which any regiment might well be proud. During that time they had known no rest, while they had been

[1] Rejoined at the end of the war from Germany.

fighting against a much better organised and better equipped enemy. And their losses—'We have lost 13 British officers, 16 Indian officers and about 800 men. We have now practically no regiment left'. So wrote one of the survivors. The losses were equivalent to the full strength of the regiment. Who could demand more!

# CHAPTER IV

JAN.–24 APRIL, 1915: Lahore Division in line again; Regiment in billets until battle of Neuve Chapelle; In trenches once more; Reinforcements

DURING the fighting of 20 December the G.O.C. Indian Corps had reported that his troops were quite tired out and unable to fight any more, and that they must be relieved at once. At 6.30 p.m. on that day, therefore, G.H.Q. directed the 1st Corps to replace the Indian Corps, which was to be gradually withdrawn into reserve. By the night of the 22nd the Lahore Division had been entirely withdrawn. The Meerut Division followed a few days later.

A month later, on 24 January, the Corps was once again holding a front which extended from a point west of Neuve Chapelle on the north to the vicinity of Givenchy on the south, but everything was exceedingly quiet until early in March when preparations were made for a renewed offensive.

Until the battle of Neuve Chapelle the 129th did not go into the front line but remained in various billets, resting. 'Resting' during the Great War was a euphemistic term for the often very strenuous life behind the front line. It implied a state of not being actively killed or maimed by the enemy through malice aforethought, though he might quite well inflict damage by accident. It meant that one might walk abroad on the surface of the earth instead of leading the life of a mole or a water-rat. It meant freedom from immediate alarm, but it never meant rest in the dictionary sense of that word. The Diary records an endless succession of route-marches and close-order parades, of instructional parades for trench-digging, machine-gun instruction, signalling, bombing and other delights. During one of the bombing parades Lieut. Lewis and three sepoys were wounded by a premature explosion. Bombs at that time were by no means the safe and efficient things which they became later on. When not occupied the men were being inoculated. Occasionally there were bathing parades and clothes-washing, though the organisation for such activities was not as yet very highly developed. Towards the end of January there was an outbreak of measles, otherwise the health was good.

Meantime the regimental strength was being augmented by a constant trickle of reinforcements, chiefly from other regiments in India, but also of wounded and sick rejoining from hospital. In January Captain A. D. Radcliffe, 105th Marathas, Captain G. D. R. MacMahon, 124th Baluch Light Infantry, and Lieut. H. J. D. O'Neill, with Subedar Zerghun Shah and 74 other ranks of the 127th Baluchis, joined at different dates, so that by the end of the month the strength was 9 British officers, 12 Indian officers and 401 other ranks. On 26 February Major B. F. R. Holbrooke, 124th, and Major A. G. Crawford, 84th Punjabis, together with 7 Indian officers and 302 other ranks reported, so that by 1 March there were 10 British officers, 21 Indian officers and 704 other ranks. But the regiment had lost Lieut.-Colonel Southey, who had taken over the command of the Bareilly Brigade. During most of this period of recuperation the weather had been bad even for a Flanders winter. It rained incessantly during January, was only slightly less wet and cold in February, while March lived up to its reputation for bleakness. But this did not prevent them getting on with their task nor destroy the joy of living. It needed no philosopher to make them count their blessings. The worst billet is always superior to the best of trenches. Of billets they experienced several. They remained at Marles until 31 January when they marched to La Flandrie, a mile to the north-west of Lillers, where they were inspected by General Willcocks. Thence they went to Cornet Bourdois, where they remained until 7 March, when they marched to Guarbecque, after which the period of 'rest' came to a close.

During the month of February the award of several decorations, earned in the earlier fighting, was notified. On the 12th Captain Dill was awarded the D.S.O. for his services on 30 October. The following day the I.O.M. 2nd Class was conferred upon No. 4280 Naik Sar Mir and No. 2524 Sepoy Ghulam Muhamad for their gallant conduct on the same day. Ghulam Muhamad was one of the machine-gun crew which was wiped out save for Khudadad Khan. On the 15th Subedar Zaman Khan received the M.C., also earned in the same action. On the 28th came the award of the I.O.M. 2nd Class to No. 453 Lance-Naik Sahib Jan and Jemadar Mir Bad Shah for their gallantry on 16 and 19 December respectively.

Meantime with the spring came preparations for fresh offensives. For some considerable time the Higher Commands had been devising and maturing plans for attacking the enemy. In spite of the utmost secrecy signs of the coming events could be discerned by the wise and experienced. Over all came a great feeling of expectancy and a growing confidence that the coming year would see the tables turned on the enemy. One of the many hints of things to come is recorded early in March when it is briefly noted that the regiment, with other units, had 'practised attacks on trenches at Ham'. These practices were followed by discussions as to the best method of doing it. The Diary records no decision on this interesting debate: nor did the disastrous history of the year 1915. The time when assaults would be led by tanks and backed by massed brigades of artillery had not yet been dreamed of. Meantime the Neuve Chapelle offensive was drawing near. There were also many other signs. On 7 March the regiment was ordered to be in a 'state of constant readiness'.

With the battle of Neuve Chapelle the Lahore Division

had little to do, as the assault was delivered by the Meerut Division, while the Lahore Division awaited events. On the 10th the attack began, and at first all was expectancy and high hopes. The next day the Ferozepore Brigade moved to Les Lobes about 5 p.m. Early next morning it marched to Lacouture. Here orders were received to proceed to Richebourg St Vaast, where it came under the orders of the Meerut Division. All that day the regiment with the Brigade were in a state of expectation and increasing doubt. What had happened and what was happening could only be vaguely guessed at and pieced together from the fragmentary messages and odd bits of news which filtered through. Evidently everything had not gone to plan.

Meantime their movements, which in themselves appeared to have little reason and which ended in nothing, were being dictated by the fortunes of the battle still being fought in front of them. All day they waited until, just after 4 p.m., they received orders, together with the rest of the Brigade, to march to Neuve Chapelle via the Rue des Berceaux. Having arrived they again waited but filled in the time digging. Finally at 2 a.m., nothing having happened, they marched back to Lacouture. The Brigade Diary throws light on the darkness of these marches and waits. It had been intended that the Ferozepore Brigade, together with the Sirhind and Jullundur Brigades, should attack the enemy through the Bois du Biez, when, having carried the wood, they would consolidate their gains beyond. After considerable hesitation the attack was cancelled, chiefly on the grounds that a night attack by these Brigades over unknown country would probably end in disaster. The discussions about the whole of this proposed attack are astonishingly interesting to read in the light of our present knowledge. There is a touching simplicity of design, in which artillery preparation figures ever so lightly, while enemy machine guns and wire are hardly noticed. Did not the young French officers fresh from St Cyr thus lead their regiments in the early days of August and September? With drawn swords and kid gloves—and complete annihilation. Only the swords and kid gloves were lacking to make this attack equally picturesque. Fortunately the Officer Commanding the Ferozepore Brigade prevailed and the attack was not made. Major Holbrooke, who was sent to find out what was happening and to learn what was intended, describes the scene at Headquarters just before the decision was taken to cancel the attack: 'The Brigade Commanders, Divisional Commander and G.O.C. Indian Corps met in a cellar in a smashed-up house. They were there for some considerable time and we had no orders. I was at last sent to find our Brigade C.O. and get from him what we were going to do. Going down the steps of the cellar I had to step across three dead British soldiers and one Indian. The superior ranks were all talking at the same time, several very excited.... I could get no information so came away'. Perhaps the more silent dead may have helped in arriving at this decision. They were thus spared a little longer, though eventually destined for battle elsewhere, when they were to attack under conditions equally futile and with the disastrous and bloody failure which needed little imagination to predict.

On the evening of the same day, the 13th, they once more went into trenches, taking over from the 58th Rifles in No. 3 sub-section of the Rue du Bois. Nos. 1 and 3 Companies were in the line, No. 2 in Orchard Redoubt, and No. 4 in reserve. Here they remained until the 23rd. There was rather more than the usual shelling, as the whole front was still in a state of tension. Casualties, however, were small. While in the trenches they were reinforced by Major H. Hulseberg, 127th Q.M.O. Baluchis, and 130 men from the 127th, 129th and 21st Punjabis. Captain A. Delmé Radcliffe, and Lieut. Browning, a victim of the measles epidemic, also had rejoined a little earlier. On the 26th

Major Mitchell left them and Lieut. Campbell was transferred to the 59th. On the 28th Major A. G. Kemball, 31st Punjabis, reported for duty. Casualties during March were 'gratifyingly' small, being only 1 killed and 38 wounded.

April 1 found them in Brigade Reserve at Rue du Puits with their full strength of British officers, 19 Indian officers and 634 other ranks. The Diary records that on the 2nd there were three cases of mumps, but also notes three I.O.M. 2nd Class, awarded to Subedar Makhmad Azam, No. 118 Naik Nek Amal, and No. 250 Sepoy Saiday Khan. These were rather belated rewards, as the original list of recommendations had been lost by the Brigade. Naik Nek Amal, it will be remembered, had gone out into the open under heavy fire to help Captain Vincent after he was shot. He was recommended for the V.C. Saiday Khan had helped him on the same occasion. He was killed just a little later. Subedar Makhmad Azam was recommended for his devotion to duty and conspicuous services during the last week, 23 October 1914.

Once more they took their turn in the trenches from the 5th to the 12th. The period calls for no comment but is marked by the loss of Captain Dill, D.S.O., who was killed only a few hours before the relief was effected. The regiment lost a very gallant officer, while the original cadre of officers who had come over after the outbreak of war was further reduced. Captain Delmé Radcliffe had been dangerously wounded early in the tour, on the 9th. After this they were in billets until the 24th at Paradis, a place which sadly belied its name. The Diary reports much work and many fatigues of the usual routine character, but also reports much work of a sanitary nature, such as the covering over of middens and general cleaning up of the locality. One feels that it must have been a very select locality to call forth such entries, as Flanders was not famous for its model farmhouses, and Adjutants were usually much too preoccupied to note the obvious. During this time Major Kemball left for duty in England, but was replaced by Major C. A. James, 126th Baluchis.

On the 24th the Brigade suddenly received orders to march to Godewaerswelde *en route* for Ypres.

# CHAPTER V

24 April–2 May, 1915: March to Ypres; Position at Ypres on arrival of Lahore Division; Attacks north of Ypres

THE second battle of Ypres began officially on 22 April and ended on 25 May, 1915. It was almost as critical as the first battle and strained the resources of the B.E.F. equally. The employment of the Lahore Division on the 26th and 27th is an indication of this strain and also serves to emphasise the paucity of troops at the disposal of G.H.Q. With the battle as a whole we have nothing to do, but again it is necessary to look a little further afield than the narrow front of the regiment.

During the first weeks of April the B.E.F. had taken over nearly five more miles of front from the French—from the Ypres-Menin road opposite Gheluvelt to the Ypres-Poelcappelle road beyond Zonnebeke. This extension had left only two French Divisions on the Ypres front. These were the 45th Algerian and the 87th Territorial Divisions with a detachment of cavalry, under General Putz, stretching from the Poelcappelle-Ypres road to the canal at Steenstraat included. On the evening of the 22nd the Germans made their first gas attack, directing it against the French who were taken wholly unawares. Their front completely collapsed, and the Germans pressed through the gap within 300 to 400 yards of the Poelcappelle-St Julien road and Mouse Trap Farm which were held by the Canadians. With the magnificent defence by the Canadians we have no concern here. The position was, however, desperate enough. 'By 8.45 p.m. reports had come in to the 5th Corps that the French had no flank at Pilckem, that both their first and second lines and the guns had been abandoned, and that there were no formed bodies of French troops east of the canal, except at Steenstraat. Thus it was clear to General Plumer that the gap was not 3000 yards but 8000, and the way to Ypres was open to the enemy.'

On this broken front there now began a series of desperate and costly counter-attacks, most of which broke down hopelessly before they reached the enemy, as the attacking troops had to assault positions only vaguely located and without adequate artillery support. The net result was nil: the lost ground was never regained. The German advance was arrested owing to more fundamental causes.[1] The attacks by the Lahore Division on the 26th and 27th were directed against part of this new German front and were only a few among many, all equally unsuccessful.

The march to Godewaerswelde had been a long and fatiguing one. There the regiment rested for the night. Next day they moved to Ouderdun which was reached about 10 a.m., where they remained until, at 5.30 a.m. of the 26th, they 'marched to Ypres, getting into position of assembly at La Brique about 9 a.m.' The available strength, all ranks, is given as 470. The Brigade front extended from La Brique to St Jean, at which latter place were Brigade H.Q. The troops were 'placed under cover of hedges and made cover for themselves'. All the time the enemy 'Taube' were actively observing, a task 'which they carried out with impunity'. So that if the attacking force did not know where the enemy was, the enemy had very precise ideas as to the whereabouts of the regiment and which way it was coming.

While the troops were so employed the Commanding Officers of the various regiments were conferring at Brigade H.Q. about the attack, though there seems to have been little to confer about, as up to 12.30 p.m. no orders had been received from the Division regarding the plans. Orders came at 12.40 p.m. and were delivered verbally by Lieut.-Colonel Du Pree. There being no time to issue

[1] See *Official History*, 1915, 'The Tactics of Second Ypres', p. 210.

formal orders, everything had to be done verbally. The attack was ordered at 1.20 p.m. according to the Brigade records. This was the official zero time, but the real assault was not delivered until 2.15 p.m. In the interval the troops were moving forward to the assaulting positions.

While they are doing this we can go back a little in order to take a larger view of the game, in which the 129th was but a single pawn on the Ypres chess-board. After arriving at Ouderdun the Division came under the orders of General Sir Horace Smith-Dorrien, commanding the 2nd Army. The 2nd Army was to co-operate with the French in an attack in a north and north-east direction from about St Jean. The main attack was to be carried out by the French. Originally the French had fixed 5 p.m. as zero time, but late in the night of the 25th they had advanced the time to 2 p.m. General Smith-Dorrien had protested to G.H.Q., 'as the change curtailed the already short and inadequate time available for the preparations of the Indian Division, and for the rest needed by the troops, who would have been on the march all night'. He was, however, ordered to proceed. It is this change in the French plans which explains the lateness of the orders finally issued.

The French, who were supposed to be strongly reinforced, were to attack the enemy in their front with their right resting on the Ypres-Langemarck road. The Lahore Division was 'to attack northwards against Langemarck, on a front of 1000 yards, through the sector of the 5th Corps line held by the 13th Brigade east of the Ypres-Langemarck road'. The 5th Corps was directed to co-operate in the attack on the right of the Indian Division.

There had not been time to find places for the Lahore Divisional Artillery, except such guns as were required in close support of the infantry. It was therefore disposed of on the west bank of the canal. In preparation for the attack 'General Plumer in 5th Corps orders gave instructions that the artillery bombardment to prepare the advance should begin at 1.20 p.m. and continue for 40 minutes, followed by five minutes' rapid fire, after which a barrage was to be formed 200 yards ahead, and the assault would take place'. The *Official History*, which is always written with a perfect academic reserve, goes on to remark: 'but on 26 April, as on other days of fighting near Ypres in April–May 1915, the number and calibre of the guns, the amount of ammunition, and the advantages of observation, both ground and air, were all in favour of the enemy. Apart from this, the length of time allowed for the British artillery preparation, fixed by the amount of ammunition available, was wholly insufficient; whilst wire-cutting and proper support of the infantry was practically impossible owing to the absence of good observation posts and the long distance from the front of so many of the batteries'. Finally, as if the dice were not already overloaded, 'the front line (of the assaulting troops) carried little yellow flags to show its progress to its own, and equally to the enemy's, artillery'.

The orders to the Division were 'to attack northwards and assault the enemy's trenches wherever met with, the first objective being a frontage from Oblong Farm to the Langemarck road'. No mention is made of the further objectives, nor is it of interest to anticipate the operation orders of 1918.

We can now return to the Ferozepore Brigade and the 129th who, with the other Brigades of the Division, were still under cover of hedges and whatever impromptu shelter they could provide for themselves. The attack was to be made by the Ferozepore and Jullundur Brigades, with the Sirhind Brigade in support. Each of the assaulting Brigades had a frontage of 500 yards. The order of attack was the Connaught Rangers on the left, with orders to keep their left flank on the Langemarck road echeloned slightly in rear of the French, who were to include the road in the right of their advance; the 57th Rifles in the centre, and the 129th on the right. On the right of the 129th were the

47th Sikhs, who formed the left flank of the Jullundur Brigade. In support were the 4th Londons, some 400 yards in the rear of the Connaught Rangers. The 9th Bhopals were in reserve with orders to move forward to the trenches previously occupied by the Rangers. The divisional front faced direct north, and the troops in their place of deployment were just north of La Brique, between Wieltje Farm (500 yards west of Wieltje) and the Ypres-Langemarck road.

Already both the assaulting Brigades had suffered casualties from the enemy artillery as they had marched up to their places of assembly. While waiting there they had been further subjected to shell fire, so that zero time did not find them exactly fresh.

At 1.20 p.m., when the artillery opened, the Brigades immediately advanced in order to reach the position from which to deliver the assault at 2.5 p.m. The distance to be covered was some 1700 yards, over ground which offered no protection from artillery fire and which was swept for the greater portion with machine-gun fire. The *Official History* describes it: 'The ground over which the advance was to be made was the scene of the fighting of Geddes' Detachment three days earlier, so that the Division had to ascend a gentle rise to Hill Top ridge, then cross a shallow valley, in which lay the front line held by the left of the 2nd Buffs (Geddes' Detachment), the 1st Royal West Kents and 2nd K.O.S.B. (13th Brigade), and, passing through it, ascend the gentle slopes of Mauser ridge, held by the enemy's infantry'. The *History* proceeds: 'Directly the leading lines crossed Hill Top ridge they came under heavy artillery fire and were badly mauled between the support and front lines of the 13th Brigade, particularly by 5·9-inch howitzer shell, which knocked out whole platoons at a time, British and Indians falling literally in heaps'.

The next hour's fighting is difficult to describe and can only be pieced together from the Brigade Reports and accounts given later by the survivors. In the *Official History* the whole action is so compressed that one merely sees a rather weak wave surge forward and then recede, as had so many before them. Even the Brigade Report leaves one to guess most of what one desires to know, while the Regimental Diary merely records that at 2.15 p.m. 'the Brigade moved forward to attack and assault enemy's trenches', while at 3 p.m. 'attack fell back with heavy loss. Enemy used gas which affected the French first, who were on the left of the Brigade. They fell back followed by the Ferozepore and Jullundur Brigades who had got inextricably mixed up. Occupied trench for night'. But there is no doubt that the attack was made with great determination and vigour, and in spite of the men being tired already, of the complete ascendancy of the enemy in the air, and of the overwhelming preponderance of both enemy artillery and machine-gun fire, 'our men went forward splendidly'. Major Holbrooke writes of his company: 'It is beyond me to describe the enthusiasm of my own company; they were advancing to attack and kept up a great pace and perfect alignment, also frequently cheering and yelling for all they were worth. I dare not check them although we were getting in advance of other companies. A check in such a case might possibly have stopped their splendid *élan*. Our losses were great: every time we topped a rise a hail of bullets swept into us: also very heavy artillery fire. One of my havildars was blown to pieces by my side, but we could not stop. How far I got is a little doubtful. I saw the Germans standing up firing at us, so I may have got within 200 yards: then I got bullets through both legs and was crocked over completely. The last I saw of my own company it was still advancing heroically'. The other companies were in no way inferior. It was recorded that Lieut. O'Neill and his machine-gun crews did excellent work with the machine guns which had taken up a very exposed though useful position in a farmhouse.

For some reason little was said of the regiment in the reports: the *Official History* mentions only the Connaught Rangers and units in the Jullundur Brigade. Yet it advanced as far as any other unit and lost as heavily. Casualties were heavy, though fortunately the number killed was relatively light: 61 per cent of its officers, British and Indian; 58 per cent of the men.

It is necessary to go back again, however, if one wishes to get the setting of the story. Punctually at 2 p.m. the French attack had been launched and some little progress was made. There seems to be some confusion as to the exact time when the gas was released. The *Official History* mentions 2.20 p.m., while the Report of the Ferozepore Brigade says that at 2 p.m. the Connaught Rangers reported that the French appeared to be checked, as well as our own leading line, by gas. This discrepancy in the time may be neglected, as the watches of the various units had not been synchronised. Moreover, as the gas was released first on the French front and had to drift across the Ferozepore Brigade front, a certain amount of time must be allowed for.

In the meantime, owing partly to the severe machine-gun fire which they encountered, the attacking units of the Jullundur Brigade slightly lost direction and bore too much to the left, thus compressing the 129th front and driving them over to the left. Eventually the Connaught Rangers were forced across the road on to the French. The Report continues: 'Advance was made steadily and in good order up to the road across C 21 *c* and *d*. After proceeding north of the road some bunching occurred behind farmhouses owing to the effect of the enemy machine-gun and rifle fire'. After reaching Hill Top ridge the casualties were very heavy, but 'the front line continued to push on beyond the farm side by side with the French attack on our left, and eventually portions of all three regiments of the leading line of my Brigade reached the farm road running north-west by south-east in C 15 c and d'. By this time, owing to the loss of direction already mentioned and the heavy losses in officers, the various units had become considerably mixed.

At this critical moment the Germans released gas opposite to the French regiment on the right. Drifting from west to east across the front of the Brigade the cloud broke the advance everywhere and forced a retirement. Major Hannyngton, who was commanding the 129th, records how he saw a cloud of dense yellow smoke rising from the German trenches. This rose and spread, with the result that the leading line of the French 'turned about and came back through French farm buildings, their supports and reserves following suit'. The attack of the Ferozepore and Jullundur Brigades was also broken and the men driven back. The Lahore Division had failed—to do the impossible. In the attempt the men had suddenly to face a new horror, poison gas, for which they were prepared neither psychologically nor in material equipment, as they were not yet equipped even with the most primitive of respirators. 'The most they could do was to cover their noses and mouths with wet handkerchiefs or pagris and, in default of this poor resource, to keep their faces pressed against the scanty parapet. It was of little avail, for in a few minutes the ground was strewn with the bodies of men writhing in unspeakable torture, while the enemy seized the opportunity to pour in a redoubled fire.' The Ferozepore Brigade being on the left suffered more severely from the gas than did the Jullundur, as it had begun to thin out by the time it reached the latter Brigade.

This retirement 'was not checked until the troops had withdrawn behind our front line', but it was not universal; many devoted groups, both British and Indian, still clung on to their positions until early morning of the 27th. Certain mentions are worthy of record:

'Sepoy Raji Khan earned the 2nd Class, I.O.M., by his

bravery in carrying an urgent message under heavy shell and rifle fire. A shell burst only about 3 yards from him during his progress, wounding and almost putting him out of action, but he managed to struggle on and delivered the message.

'Later in the day, at a critical moment, when the troops were labouring under the tortures of gas, Major Holbrooke was wounded and lying in the open. Sepoy Ghulam Hussein, attached from the 124th Baluchis, dashed out and carried him under heavy fire into a safer position. He then collected a number of men and set them to work at a trench to form a rallying point. For his splendid example of bravery and coolness he received the I.D.S. medal'.

Major Hannyngton, who was in command of the regiment, received the D.S.O., and Lieut. Griffith-Griffin was awarded the M.C. for 'conspicuous bravery in action'. He was wounded.

Orders were issued at 12.30 a.m. on the 27th for the relief of the Jullundur and Ferozepore Brigades by the Sirhind Brigade, and this was effected by 3 a.m., when they moved back to La Brique. But not to rest. The Diary reports: '6–10 a.m., reorganisation of regiment into two companies', which does not indicate an excess of sleep. After this at 10.30 a.m. there was a conference at Brigade H.Q. at which it was decided that the previous day's programme would be repeated, with the slight modification that the Sirhind Brigade would now be slaughtered while the remnants of the Ferozepore Brigade would be in support. According to plan at 1.20 p.m. the attack began, went through the same dance of death and failed; only to be renewed at 6.30 that same evening, when once more the shattered remnants of the Sirhind Brigade and those who were co-operating with them again recoiled. The *Official History* devotes six pages to this second day's fighting—chiefly criticism. It is hardly a pleasing story, though no doubt illuminating and interesting to those engaged in the study of how not to do it. 'Nothing, however, but a carefully prepared offensive requiring much time to organise could—as Neuve Chapelle had indicated —possibly dislodge the Germans from the ground they had gained and had been steadily fortifying for several nights.' It is but one example of the price that will always be paid when there is an absence of unified command combined with political suspicion and friction. And the result: 'The British counter-attacks, unfortunately, had hardly done more than pass the front line', while the Lahore Division— one among many—had been completely shattered.

On the 29th the regiment, or what remained of it, was in trenches in reserve. At 11 a.m. as a last flutter it was ordered to form the reserve to the Ferozepore Brigade which was again to co-operate with the Sirhind Brigade operating in support of a French attack, 'which did not mature'. Finally, orders were received to march back to Ouderdun, at which place it arrived at 12.45 a.m. on the 30th. Having rested it marched about 10 a.m. to Meterem some three miles away, but returned in the evening to Ouderdun. Finally, on 1 May the Brigade with the Division marched back again to rejoin the Indian Corps via Meterem and Noote Boom, and bivouacked at Doulieu for the night of 2 May.

The only comfort in the whole affair was the small number of killed as compared with the wounded. The casualties were: killed and missing, Subedar Karam Dad and 51 other ranks; wounded, 6 British officers (Majors Holbrooke and James, Captains Money and MacMahon, Lieut. Griffin and 2nd Lieut. Culverwell), 8 Indian officers (Subedars Zerghun Shah and Turkestan, Jemadars Rahim Ali, Rahim Dad, Sher Jang, Didan Khan, Dadin and Ghafar Khan), 209 other ranks. The total killed, wounded and missing was 275.

The Division was thanked for its work and sacrifices by

General Sir Horace Smith-Dorrien, Commanding the 2nd Army, and by General Sir Herbert Plumer, Commanding Plumer's Force. Also by its Commander Major-General H. D'U. Keary and by Sir James Willcocks. It had deserved it.

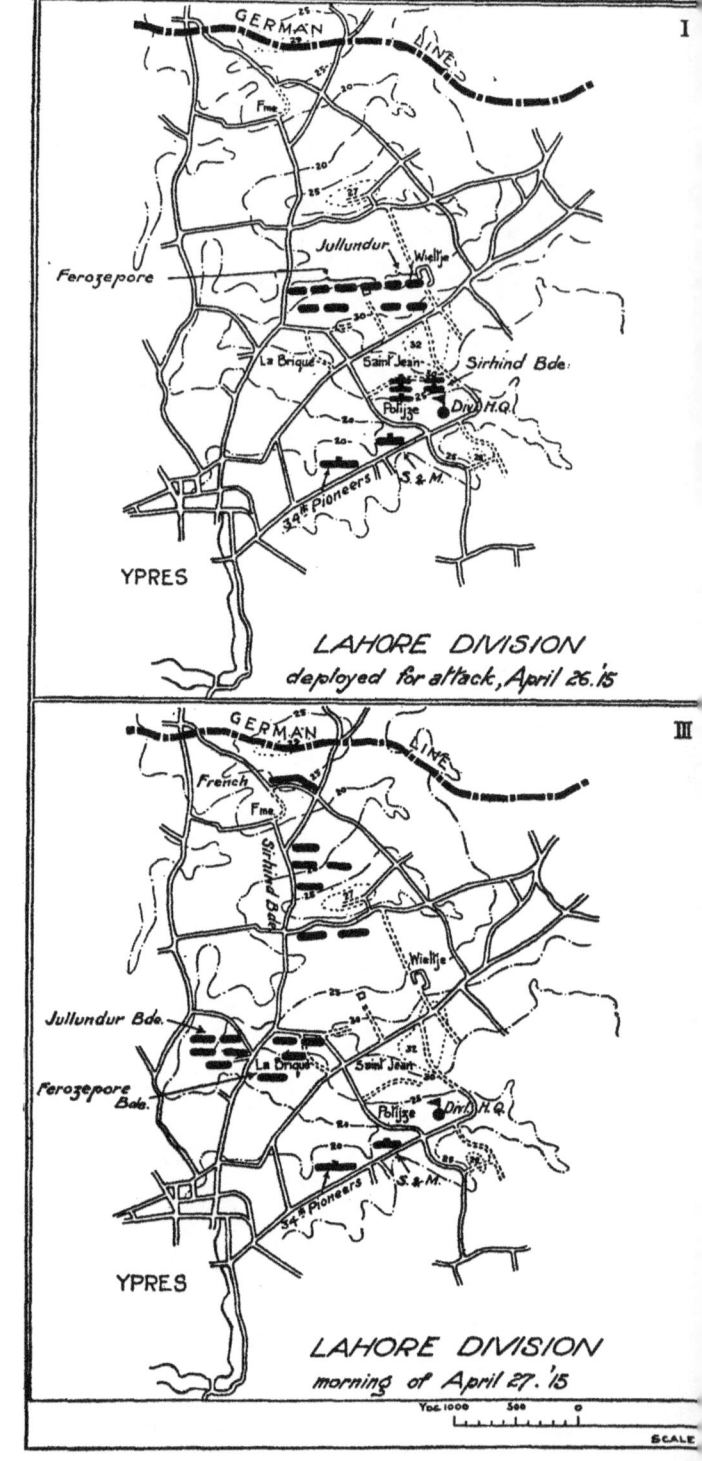

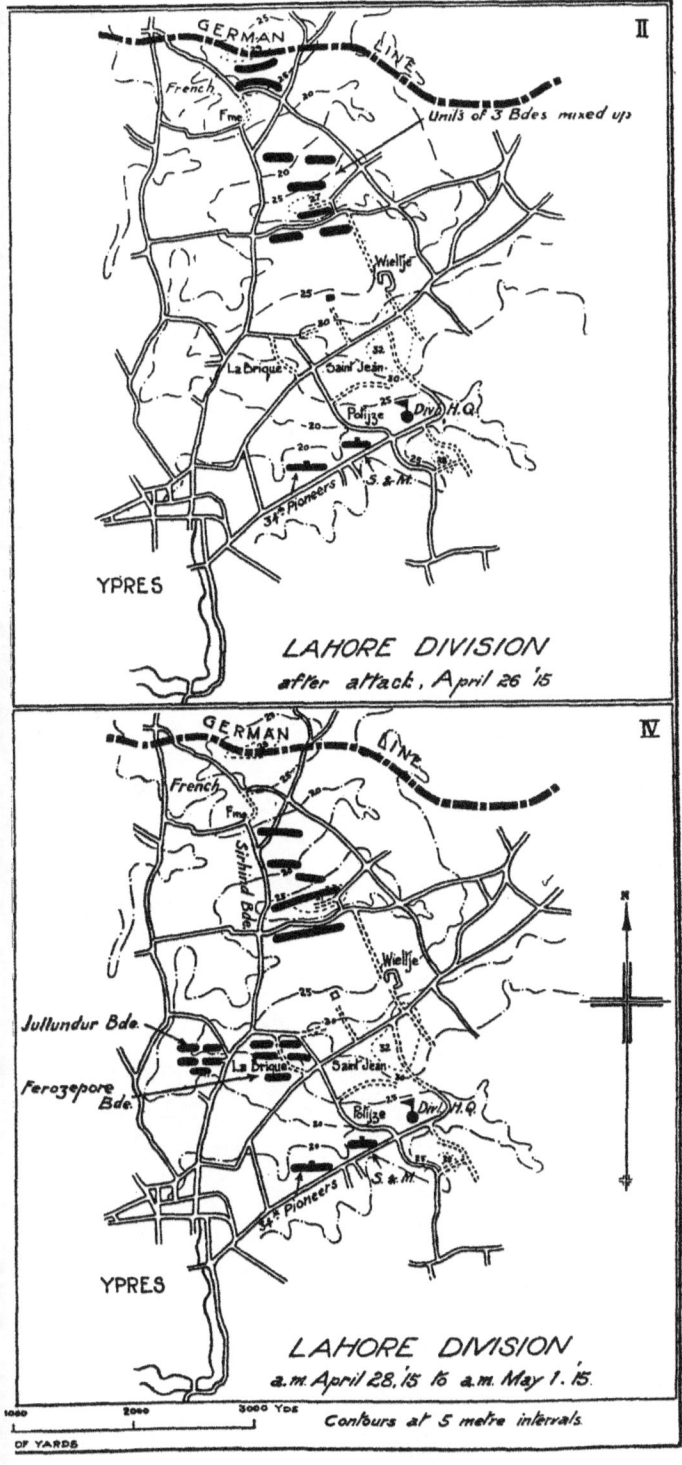

# CHAPTER VI

2 MAY–25 SEPT. 1915: In billets; Reinforcements; In line again; Ayub Khan's exploits; Trenches and billets; Reinforcements; Preparations for the offensive 25 Sept.; Withdrawn from trenches

SECOND Ypres was the last battle in France in which the 129th took an active part. The Indian Corps had still work to do, but for the time being the much weakened Lahore Division returned to the routine of trench warfare, while the heavy fighting during the month of May 1915 fell to the Meerut Division and the other Divisions of the Corps.

On 1 May the recorded strength of the regiment was: 6 British officers, 8 Indian officers and 233 other ranks. Of the British officers, Lieut. Lewis had rejoined on 28 April from hospital. The next day the regiment was reinforced by a draft of 1 Indian officer and 41 other ranks from the 84th. On the 4th Lieut. Browning also rejoined from the sick list.

The 3rd once more saw them in Paradis, no doubt more appreciative of its amenities than before, though no grateful note is sounded in the Diary. There Major Hulseberg went sick, as a result of the poison gas at Ypres. The immediate task was the reorganisation of the depleted companies. This was soon effected, and on the 6th it is recorded that the strength is 5 British officers, 8 Indian officers and 226 other ranks; 'this total includes about 50 men of Headquarters and Machine-Gun Sections, leaving about 176 other ranks to man trenches'. Late at night on the 6th they marched to close billets at Bout Deville, and on the 7th were placed at the disposal of the Meerut Division for the purpose of conducting prisoners. Not until the 18th did they go into the trenches. The interim period is of no interest. Various parties were detailed to 'conduct prisoners', but there seem to have been few to conduct. On the 13th Major Mitchell, who had rejoined on the previous day, left to join the 40th Pathans. Their tour of the trenches was uneventful. The usual things happened and there were the usual alarms. On the 27th they were 'warned to be ready for enemy attack to-night', which did not materialise. On the evening of 30 May they were relieved by the Worcesters and marched to Bout Deville, where next day they were detailed to Brigade Reserve. This was cancelled 1 June, and the regiment was attached to the 57th Rifles and went back to trenches. No. 1 Company, under Lieut. Browning, went into trenches and support on the right of the 57th. No. 2, under Major Crawford, went into the 'Gridiron' as local reserve. Headquarters were at Croix Barbée, as the Commanding Officer and Adjutant were for a time detailed for other duty, the former commanding the Brigade Reserve. The regiment, under Major Crawford, continued under the orders of Lieut.-Colonel Grey, 57th Sikhs, until relieved on the night of 5–6 June, when they marched to billets at L'Épinette, where they arrived at 4 a.m. During this turn in the trenches Jemadar Shah Zada was wounded. Casualties were slight. Their late arrival did not prevent them marching at 9 the same morning to Merville, where they bathed—a luxury well worth the loss of sleep, as one also parted with many intimate friends at the same time. Until the 12th they passed the usual life, 'resting'. On that date Lieut.-Colonel Hannyngton left them for a short time and proceeded on special duty to Marseilles, while the regiment with a strength of 155 rifles, excluding Headquarters and the Machine-Gun Sections, marched back to trenches, where they remained in local reserve under the command of the Officer Commanding 89th Punjabis. The tour lasted until the 23rd and was wholly uneventful but for Naik Ayub Khan's adventure, which will be described shortly. Few events call for record. On the 16th they 'stood to for an attack which did not come off'. There is also reference to reorganisation in system of sniping. Sniping had been carried on fairly systematically for some considerable time, but now the men were supplied with telescopic sights. On the 18th there is a cryptic record in the Diary: 'Work at night continued removing the end of right whisker of Port Arthur redoubt'. Two decorations were notified on the 20th: No. 471 Sepoy Raji Khan, 129th, received the I.O.M. 2nd Class, and No. 4321 Sepoy Ghulam Hussain, 124th, the I.D.S.M., both for their distinguished conduct at Ypres. Lieut. Bickford of the 59th was attached for duty, while Lieut. Thornhill went to Corps H.Q. Lieut. Bickford's attachment, however, lasted for only 2 days when he was replaced by Captain G. A. Phillips, I.A.R.O. Lieut.-Colonel Hannyngton returned on the 21st, and on the same day 'Naik Ayub Khan went out on patrol and did not return'. General Willcocks is reported to have visited the sub-section on the same day. On the 23rd the regiment was relieved and went into billets at Loretto Road. The next day they took over trenches in Rue du Bois as local reserves. On the 25th it 'rained all day'. While the regiment is sheltering we can return to Naik Ayub Khan and relate the story of how he disappeared and how he returned. This is best given in his own words as reported by Lieut.-Colonel Hannyngton to the Brigade:

'At 10 p.m. on the 21st instant I started, with one other man, to patrol the country in front of our trenches. I left our trenches at point S. 5, C. 3/2.

'The grass for about 100 yards this side of the German trenches has been cut. Their wire is about 15 yards wide and is composed of loops of barbed wire. I arrived at the nullah on the left of the road close to the barricade near point 62 about 1 hour before dawn. I waited till it was light and till the Germans stood to arms and then stood up and held up my arms, saying, "Germany, main India Mussulman". The Germans immediately called an officer who signalled to me to put down my rifle by the barricade. I then gave up my bayonet and ammunition and climbed over the barricade.

'The time was about 2 a.m. There were many Germans in the trench, all wearing the number 15 on their shoulders. They wore grey uniforms and soft forage caps with a stiff and black shining band, made of the same material as the German helmet. The trench was very deep and strong, the parapet about 9 feet high. It was revetted entirely with boards held up with stakes. The firing step was about 4 feet high also covered with boards, as was the floor. Steps were cut and boarded about every 10 yards up to the firing step, which was about 2 feet broad. The bottom of the trench was wide enough to allow two men to pass with difficulty. In the parados were well-built shelters for about eight men, the officers' dug-outs having doors and windows. All shelters were covered with about 2 feet of sandbags. About 5 yards behind their front trench and parallel to it runs a communication trench connected with the firing line in every traverse. This trench was about 6 feet deep and not boarded. There are from six to eight men in each traverse.

'Until the sun rose I stayed with the officer who called me in, and then he took me along the trench to a senior officer about 500 yards towards the German right. I saw four machine guns on this front. The machine guns were placed in dug-outs roofed with continuous beams, very strong uncut trees meeting one another. Above these beams was corrugated iron about as thick as three of our sheets, and above this about 4 feet of sandbags. The guns were about 1 to 2 feet above ground level and fired through an iron loophole. There was room in one of these dug-outs for some five men besides the machine gun.

'There were iron loopholes for day sentries only; wooden loopholes were, I suspect, used by extra sentries at night.

'The senior officer had no marks on his shoulder-strap except the number 15 in brass. The shoulder-strap was covered with silver braid. This officer talked to someone on the telephone, and I was sent off under the charge of one N.C. officer and two soldiers.

'The soldiers in the trench gave me cigarettes.

'I left the fire trench at about 8 a.m. The communication trench was winding, revetted towards the enemy, and with boards to walk on. The support trench was about 100 yards behind the firing line. The floor and parapet were boarded; the parados was unboarded. There were no dug-outs and the trench was absolutely unoccupied. It was just broad enough for two men to pass one another. I saw no third line of trenches.

'The course I followed was, as far as I can describe, as follows: points 65, 130, 131, 133, then by communication trench back to the wood. Thence I left the communication trench and went through the wood by a kucha road. This may have been point 72 or 73. On leaving the Bois I turned to the left on another kucha road and went on about 200 yards, with the wood on my left. I then turned to the right by another kucha road and was taken to the second of two bungalows on the right, quite close to the turning. This would be bungalow No. 76. The first of these two bungalows was half destroyed; the second, to which I went, had got no tiles on it.

'A trolley line ran along behind the wood and turned to the right by these two bungalows. I saw no Germans either in or behind the wood. I saw no trolleys.

'I was taken into the bungalow and saw two officers. The younger had no coat on; the senior, who saluted me and gave me cigarettes, had silver braid on his shoulder and a brass crown and a number, which I cannot remember. I think they were the C.O. and the Adjutant.

'The Major wrote a letter and sent me on with the same escort. I stayed there only about 5 minutes.

'I started off along the trolley line which continued till it reached a main road.

'On the road running from this city to the rear I saw about three companies of infantry, dressed like those I had seen in the trenches. I could not see the number. I was taken to the verandah of a large house. While I was there several soldiers came to look at me. I saw about eight men with No. 55 on their shoulders, and about ten men with No. 13 on their shoulders.

'An officer who spoke a little Hindustani came out with a General whose shoulder-strap carried thick silver braid, as thick as my finger. The interpreter brought a map and asked me what trenches I knew. I told him I could not read. He asked me why the 9th Bhopals had left. I told him they had been engaged for a long time and had lost heavily'.

He was then asked a number of questions relating to the regiment, its numbers, losses and general conditions.

'The senior officer then said that, if I would come over to the Germans, I should get very good pay, and that he would give me Rs. 300 if I brought over 20 men.

'These questions were asked at about 12 noon on the 22nd. I was then sent to sit in an orchard. They brought me milk and bread on three occasions. I saw, while I had been waiting before, about three companies of infantry, dressed like the men I had seen in the trenches, but I could not see their number. A number of soldiers came to look at me; I saw about eight men with the number 55 on their shoulder-straps, and about ten men with the number 15.

'I sat in the orchard until about 9 p.m. with some German soldiers. They all had a crown on their shoulder-straps and another mark I could not understand. They wore an ordinary black German helmet, with a black board on the top, raised up a little. One man took the grey cover off and showed me his helmet; it had a big white badge in front. (N.B. This appears to be the 16th Uhlans.)

'At about 9 p.m. the interpreter, one of the officers and I returned to the same trenches in a motor-car. The officers in the trenches did not want to let me go. However it was arranged that at dawn I should bring over the 20 men and call out my own name. The men were to bring rifles with them, but leave them in the grass. I then left the German trench and arrived back in our own trenches about midnight the 22nd–23rd instant.

'I brought back my rifle, belt and bandolier. They took my ammunition and bayonet.'

Ayub Khan was recommended for the V.C., but was eventually awarded the I.O.M. and promoted to Jemadar. This adventure was not undertaken on the spur of the moment, as Ayub Khan had spoken of his plans both to Major Holbrooke, his Company Commander, and to Lieut. Lewis. It had been forbidden by the Commanding Officer as being too dangerous, although the Division had been urgently demanding information such as was obtained.

At Rue du Bois they dug trenches, while the enemy in an equally routine way shelled them. Meantime it rained. Such briefly was much of their war experience. It is dull to record: it is more dull to read of: but it is infinitely more dull to experience day after day and month after month. It needs much discipline to dig trenches for ever and maintain a high morale. On the 29th they went into billets at L'Épinette, arriving at 3 a.m. Here Lieut. Griffin rejoined, while Lieut. O'Neill went to Brigade H.Q. and Captain Dickson, I.M.S., relieved Major Kukday, I.M.S., who proceeded to Bournemouth on duty. Next day there was an equipment inspection, while the regiment was 're-organised into one company'. After which they marched to Merville once again for a bath.

So 1 July found the regiment as one company with 7 British officers, 8 Indian officers and 195 other ranks, 'including men on detached duty'. During the whole of the month they were at 'rest' while the war still raged in front of them. July brought a new article of equipment, and it is recorded of the first day, 'Gas helmets tried on. Methods of wearing them explained'. Let it also be recorded that these were not the pattern so well known by 1918, but the primitive ancestor of doubtful value. Fortunately the gas-filled shell had not yet appeared, at any rate in the Indian sector, nor were the 129th ever called upon to use their gas helmets. The time was filled in with the usual fatigues, marching, bomb-throwing and inoculations. On the 8th they were inspected by the Corps Commander, when Jemadar Ayub Khan was congratulated publicly, presented with 500 francs (not yet depreciated), and told that he had been recommended for the I.O.M. As usual there were changes of billets. On the 14th they marched to Caudescure, about 3 miles north of Merville. There life was as before: the only change in the monotony being the difference in the name of the place, which after all did not make sufficient contrast to warrant any great enthusiasm. On the 21st, having exhausted the amenities of Caudescure or more probably for some more sufficient reason, they moved to Maraisse, half a mile north of Haverskerque, on which date it is recorded: 'there were 123 rifles available for the trenches, exclusive of the Machine-Gun Section'. On the 22nd the much-delayed reinforcements began to appear. Major C. G. Woodhouse, 126th, and 2nd Lieut. W. S. Thatcher, I.A.R.O., reported for duty. Major Woodhouse brought with him a complete company of his own regiment—263 men and 5 Indian officers. As a result of these additions the regiment was again reorganised and expanded into three companies:

   No. 1 of P.M.'s from the 129th, 127th, 124th, 84th, 66th and 62nd.

   No. 2 of Pathans from the 129th, 127th and 124th.

   No. 3 the newly arrived company under Major Woodhouse.

On the 27th the Corps Commander inspected the new draft, and on the 29th the regiment marched to billets half a mile east of La Gorgue. Two promotions are recorded: Jemadar Abdullah Khan to Subedar, and Havildar Ghulam Jilani to Jemadar and Jemadar-Adjutant. Lieut. Griffin left the regiment for a time to act as Staff Captain to the Brigade. On the 31st they moved into Brigade Reserve near Pont Logy, and on that night relieved the 4th Suffolks in the reserve trenches at Neuve Chapelle.

The recorded strength on 1 August is 9 British officers, 15 Indian officers and 480 other ranks. From this date until they were finally withdrawn from the trenches after 25 September, they were constantly in the front line or in that immediate neighbourhood. It is a very typical example of 'peace-time warfare'. Turns in the front line, then in reserve with the endless monotony which such an existence implies. Fortunately the weather during the early part of this period was moderately good, though it began to break up as September progressed. It was also a typically busy time, although there was no great pressure or strain. On 4 August Lieut. Griffin rejoined from duty as Staff Captain, but Lieut. H. V. Lewis went instead to Brigade H.Q. to a similar appointment. Captain E. P. Burd, 93rd Burma Infantry, joined for duty. It is recorded on and about these dates that parties were detailed to collect empty cartridge cases of which vast quantities were to be found everywhere. Salvage had not yet been much developed, though it was obviously becoming necessary. To the sepoy who had been trained to regard the loss of a clip of cartridges as an offence against God, Flanders was one continuous blasphemy, so that such fatigues must have been a great spiritual consolation. On the 7th they went in Brigade reserve trenches at Sign Post Lane, and while there began the construction of Baluchi Road—a communication trench which occupied much of their time and labour until the 17th. This ran for the greater part of a mile from Rue Tilleloy between Sign Post Lane and Chimney Crescent to sub-section Headquarters on Gurkha Road. It was a great work, worthy of note. Thus on the 20th it is recorded, 'Work on Baluchi Road day and night'. In this way did regiments become immortal, by giving their name to trench systems and ditches! Thus Ludhiana Lodge was a lasting memorial to the 15th Sikhs: Gurkha Road needed no explanation. Now, Baluchi Road would bring fame to its makers, while it brought safety from stray bullets and shrapnel to those who availed themselves of its shelter.

On the 11th Captain Stewart reported for duty, bringing with him a company of the 124th. So also did Major G. M. Morris, who brought 80 men from the 84th. The next day Lieut. R. B. Wilson, of the 7th Battalion Dorset Regiment, also reported.

At 8 p.m. on the 17th they were relieved by the 1/1st Gurkhas and went into billets at L'Épinette, whence they moved the next day to Croix Marmouse. The following day 'all men in the regiment bathed at Pont Riqueul', after which they went back to trenches at the junction of Sign Post Lane with Rue Tilleloy, taking over Hill's, Church and Château Redoubts. There they suffered from the Royal Engineers, who ruined their nights with working parties. It is recorded that on the 26th a 'Zeppelin passed overhead', but few were aware of the fact, and in any case an odd bomb or two more did not really matter. On the 27th three awards for gallantry and distinguished service were conferred by H.I.M. the Emperor of Russia, Sepoys Nek Amal and Fateh Haider receiving the Cross of St George, 4th Class, and Havildar Wasim Khan that of the 1st Class —the first two as an additional decoration to the I.O.M. won when bringing help to Captain Vincent when wounded, the latter for his courage and good work during the retreat on 20 December, 1914. On the 28th Jemadar Wali Dad of the 124th was killed while out on patrol. On the 30th Captain

Burd took command of No. 4 Company, as Captain Stewart had gone sick with fever.

September saw the regiment in the trenches with their full complement of British officers, 20 Indian officers and 685 other ranks. The section held lay between Bond Street and Plum Street, Nos. 2, 3 and 4 Companies being in the firing line and No. 1 Company in local reserve. During this month there was a fair number of casualties, as the regiment was in the line most of the time and the enemy was not inclined to leave one entirely alone. On the 1st they were reported to be firing Minenwerfers all day, though hardly a day passed without some coming over, a tedious affair for those in the front line, as it always entailed considerable damage to the trenches and also to the men from time to time. But chiefly it was annoying, as after the first explosion, which came generally as a complete surprise, everything had to cease in order that one could spot the next arrival, make a rapid estimate and walk in the opposite direction. The time chosen was often lunch time, and this added much to the bitterness of life. There was also considerable registration by the enemy in anticipation of events. All of this meant ceaseless work at night to rebuild the destroyed and damaged sections. Gradually also the weather began to break up, and with the rain came the inevitable mud and wretchedness. Duckboarding, if invented, had not yet reached this particular sector, so great efforts were made to pave the bottom of the trenches with broken brick, of which plenty could be obtained if the necessary fatigues could be arranged, but generally the men were already heavily worked.

Three Indian officers, Subedar Abdullah Khan, Subedar Azam Khan and Jemadar Sher Baz, were wounded early in the month as a result of the usual routine shelling and machine-gun fire.

On the 3rd 'Captain Phillips went to St Omer for instruction in German bombs', presumably in the hope that the coming offensive would be so successful that our own dearth would be amply made good by German supplies left behind in the hasty retreat. Otherwise most of the regiment knew quite enough about German bombs. There is no indication that this instruction ever bore fruit, so it is hoped that the said officer combined a little pleasure with his business at St Omer. Next day Subedar Zerghun Shah was wounded, while on the 11th Jemadar Sundar Ali became a casualty.

As the month passes one notes a growing interest in the direction of the wind. Thus 'easterly wind all day', or again 'wind north-east to east'. A visitor, had one been so foolish as to call, would have found little weather-vanes distributed along the trenches, which knowing ones pondered over continually. An east wind now meant more than a drop in the temperature. Also there was a great and growing activity along the communication trenches. The entry on the 13th is typical: 'Communication trenches reconnoitred and repairs undertaken to all trenches and ditches running between Forrester's Lane and the Rue du Bois'. This activity was by no means confined to the 129th, nor even to the Division, but was universal. Everything was working up for the great offensives of the 25th.

Meantime the routine trench life went steadily on. On the evening of the 20th the regiment relieved the 1/4th Londons, taking over from Plum Street inclusive, to the La Bassée Road exclusive. They also took over Orchard, Mole Hill and Pioneer Keeps, while they themselves were relieved in Copse Keep, Hen's Post and Edward's Post by the Connaught Rangers. Here they remained until withdrawn from the line on the evening of the 25th.

The British offensives of the 25th formed part of a more elaborate plan worked out together by the Allies. The main attack was to be made by the French in the Champagne, while the British were to attack in the neighbourhood of Lens and Loos and thus prevent the enemy from sending reinforcements further south. The attack by the Indian Corps was itself only one of several subsidiary operations planned to assist the major British operation. The assault was to be delivered by the Meerut Division at a point just north of that held by the Lahore Division, whose function was to protect that Division's right flank. Should all go well there were further plans for an advance on La Bassée, but it is hardly necessary to detail them here.

Of all this the regiment knew nothing but for a few of the senior officers, and even they were informed of very little save that which affected them immediately. What everyone did know was that they had been in the trenches for six weeks continuously and would welcome the opportunity of getting out of them, preferably over the parapet, for the spirit of the men was still good and the newly joined companies were eager for some 'real' fighting. Six weeks tends to make one dirty, as running water is rarely found in the trenches, save round one's feet. Moreover, the weather had been moderately warm in the daytime and there had been much heavy work to do. Added to the dirt and filth, moreover, were lice and vermin, which made life less pleasant than it might have been. Further, this particular region was not such as a sanitary inspector would have approved. The whole place was a charnel house and stank of rotten flesh, which was ever being resurrected by the continual shell fire, for the dead had been buried very lightly and were ever obtruding themselves. Little mounds in the trench bottom had a spongy feel, as one walked over them, while twenty yards in front was a recently drained ditch piled with putrefying corpses, until then 'missing' after the unsuccessful attacks of 9 May. Rats were as the sand of the sea; more numerous still were the mice. All were grossly overfed and cannibalistic. Not that one minded these things too much, provided the rations arrived to time and it did not rain.

Though the regiment knew little there was a growing expectancy, while as the time drew near it became obvious to all that great events were soon to happen.

Already the guns had been booming away in the south, when on the 21st began the four days' bombardment on the Indian front. Naturally it was more intense and more sustained on the Meerut front, but even on the Lahore front it was heavy enough to keep the enemy very quiet. For four days there was comparative peace and rest from enemy attentions. On the same day smoke bombs were issued, while ladders were distributed. But from time to time the enemy would reply, when the whole front would break into 'one continuous roar of guns and exploding shells'.

All went well until the evening of the 21st when 'five Sepoys left the trenches and disappeared'. Their desertion being reported, the Adjutant, Lieut. Griffith-Griffin, M.C., went with a search party into 'No man's land', where for nearly four hours he searched for them without success. This patrol was far from being a joy-ride, as the whole area was humming with rifle and machine-gun fire, which did not die down for some very considerable time, while the enemy flares made concealment difficult. Their desertion was serious, as they took with them a new pattern gas helmet which had only been issued a few days before, and it was feared they would supply the enemy with a certain amount of information. It was more serious still for the regiment, as it brought it under suspicion, so that after the 25th it did not go into the front line again. Thus can a few men dim the honour of a whole regiment. The company to which the deserters belonged was at once withdrawn into reserve and Major Woodhouse's company took its place.

Rain had now set in and continued to fall off and on until and after the 25th, making the whole trench system once more into a bog. Meantime the bombardment continued. On the 23rd it is reported 'field guns cut wire opposite our left front', but this entry is erroneous. The wire was never effectively cut in front of the 129th in spite of assurances to the contrary by those who knew better but who lived further back. On the evening of the 24th the patrols had reported the wire intact, while the enemy machine-gun emplacements were untouched. Thus it was that when those who occupied the front line and who would be destined to 'go over', should all go well with the Meerut Division, were informed of the possible attack, they laughed at the wisdom of their betters and, remembering the dead men in the ditch, ate up all their food, drank such drinks as they had, and made merry so far as the mud and their never-ending duties allowed.

The night was wet and cold. The enemy, knowing that something was in store for him next day, was very active with his machine guns and with rifle fire. All night he kept up a steady hail of bullets which just skimmed the parapets, beat against all the sally-ports and machine-gun emplacements, and swept the communication trenches. It was a night of considerable casualties, fortunately mostly of a light nature, but unfortunately largely arm wounds, which made those in authority more suspicious, especially after the desertions. These suspicions were entirely unfounded, as the company officers who were with their men all that night can affirm. There was no rest that night. Gradually and reluctantly the wet and chilly dawn emerged, and with it came the great day.

Zero time had been fixed at 5.50 a.m. for the Meerut Division. For the Ferozepore Brigade it was 5.58, at which time the smoke bombs were to be thrown out, while the artillery were to open a rapid fire and the machine guns were also to come into action as if an assault were about to be launched. This demonstration aimed at attracting the enemy's attention and immobilising his troops. Unfortunately for all, the wind had veered round before dawn and was blowing away from the enemy, so that the smoke bombs were worse than useless and merely helped to complicate matters. The enemy, however, was quite prepared for whatever might come, be it feint or real assault. The instant the British guns opened up, so also did those of the enemy. The noise was tremendous, as the enemy trenches were only a hundred yards away, so that the British shells were very low down, while the enemy shrapnel was bursting in salvoes over the front and reserve trenches, and the heavier shells were destroying the communication trenches and searching the roads behind. Some eight 9-inch shells fell very near the Regimental H.Q, in the Rue du Bois. The bombardment lasted for about an hour, while at the same time the enemy machine guns lashed the whole front. The casualties among the men in the front line were considerable, as the trench was a wide one and the men were standing-to on the fire-step in case of attack, as nothing could be seen through the blinding smoke blown back from the smoke bombs. In all this the conduct of the men was admirable: their one question being when they could go over. By the time the bombardment was over, the whole of the front line and the support trenches had been very badly damaged, while very large sections of the communication trenches had been obliterated. There is no doubt that the enemy was well prepared for anything in this sector, just as he was for the Meerut Division further north. So ended the last testing of the 129th in France. The casualties, all things considered, were light, 207 for the month of September, of which the greater percentage were incurred in that last stand-to on the 25th, when for over an hour they were on the fire-step with little or no cover, in readiness to repel the enemy should he attack, or equally ready to climb out should the order come to do so.

# CHAPTER VII

25 SEPT. 1915–1 JAN. 1916: Behind the line; Decision to withdraw Indian troops from France; Departure from France and arrival in Egypt

THE regiment was relieved soon after noon on 25 September by the 57th and took over garrison duty at Lansdowne Post. The wounded had been evacuated already, among them being two British officers, Captain Burd and Lieut. Thatcher, and one Indian officer, Subedar Mehdi Khan. On the 29th they marched to billets between Richebourg St Vaast and Croix Barbée where they remained in Brigade Reserve, and also supplied two small garrisons for Cats Post and Factory Post.

They were in need of a rest, having been in and about the front line for eight weeks. Meantime, while they were resting, decisions had been made involving the whole Corps, which was to be withdrawn from France. There is no need to discuss the reasons for this transfer, which was eminently wise and very urgent. The relief of the two Indian Divisions began on 4 November and was complete by the night of the 10th. The troops began to entrain immediately, but it was not until 10 December that the 129th left for Marseilles.

Meantime they followed the usual routine of those behind the line, and for the first time since their arrival their numbers were almost up to strength. On 1 October they numbered 10 British and 18 Indian officers and 645 other ranks, while by November they were well over 700. There is little to record. On the 1st they were in Brigade Reserve along the Rue du Bois, filling in the time with rifle exercises and grenade throwing. On the 3rd they handed over their two posts to the 7th Gloucesters and marched via Croix Barbée and La Gorgue to billets a little west of Estaires. On the 4th they were inspected by the G.O.C. Brigade. The next day they were reinforced by 2nd Lieut. M. I. L.

Smith, I.A.R.O., Subedar Mir Kambir Khan and 83 other ranks from the 127th and 108th. The rest of the month is but a repetition of drills and fatigues. So also is November, but the weather was not so good, though bad weather meant comparatively little to them now. On the 6th they marched via Robecq and Busnes to new billets a little way to the north-west of Lillers at Cornet Bourdois where they had been once before. There they remained until the 18th when they moved on to Mametz. On the 29th they marched to Beaumetz-les-Aire where they remained only a few days. Thence to Amettes on 1 December where Lieut. V. G. Robert, 13th K.R.R.C., joined them. Finally, on the 10th, they marched to Lillers and entrained for Marseilles. Of this return journey there is nothing to report. On the 12th shortly after noon they embarked on H.M.T. *Arcadian* together with the 40th Pathans and other units. The strength had now reached the abnormal figure of over 800, not including followers. Two days later, about noon, they sailed to Toulon to join their escort, and the following day sailed for Alexandria via Sardinia and Malta.

They had been in France roughly fourteen and a half months, and if one takes the date when they detrained at Arques (19 October, 1914) until 3 October, 1915, when they finally marched to billets, they had been in the fighting zone almost a year. During that time they had fought at First Ypres, Givenchy, Festubert and Second Ypres: they had suffered considerably on 25 September, while they had served very long spells in the front line. There had served with them 41 British officers, 48 Indian officers and 2547 other ranks. Of the British officers 8 had been killed and 15 wounded; of the Indian officers 8 were killed and 25 wounded; of the rank and file 146 were killed, 119 were missing (they were nearly all dead) and 944 wounded[1]. Of the original regiment there remained 4 British officers, 5 Indian officers, with less than a couple

[1] See Appendix VII.

To face p. 72.

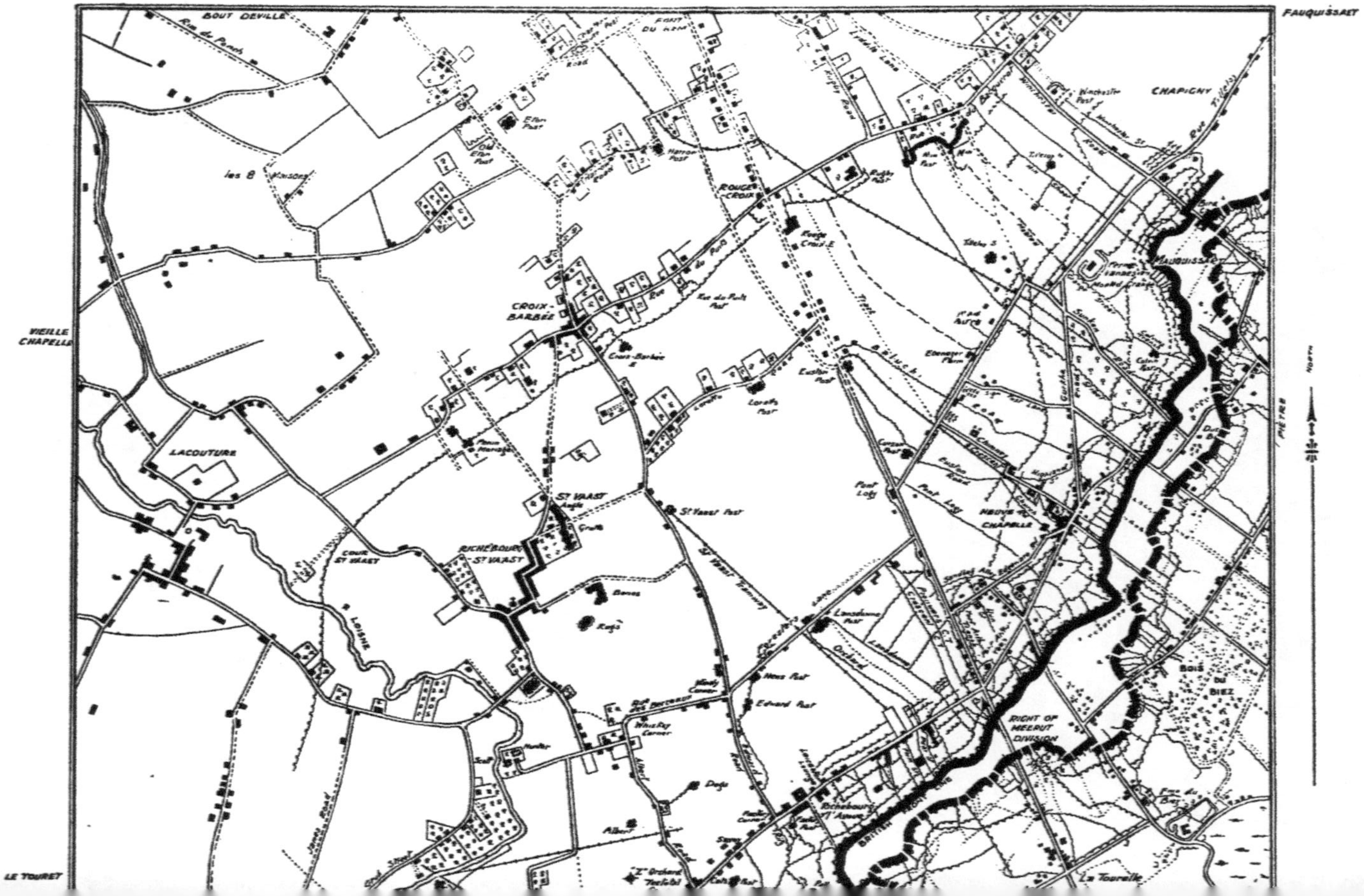
FAUQUISSART
VIEILLE CHAPELLE
LE TOURET
BOUT DEVILLE
Rue de Paradis
CHAPIGNY
les 8 Maisons
CROIX-BARBÉE
ROUGE CROIX
MAUQUISSART
LACOUTURE
ST VAAST
RICHEBOURG-ST VAAST
COUR ST VAAST
R LOISNE
NEUVE CHAPELLE
BOIS DU BIEZ
RIGHT OF MEERUT DIVISION
La Tourelle
Richebourg l'Avoué
PIETRE
NORTH
St Vaast Post
Lansdowne Post
Edward Post
Whiskey Corner
Orchard

Indian Corps Front in Flanders.

of dozen sepoys. No mean record. The King's words in his farewell message to the Indian troops were literally true of the 129th, as they were of the other units:

'The confidence which I then expressed in your sense of duty, your courage and your chivalry, you have since nobly justified.

'Yours has been a fellowship of toils and hardships, in courage and endurance often against great odds, in deeds nobly done in days of ever memorable conflict. In a warfare waged under new conditions and in peculiarly trying circumstances you have worthily upheld the honour of the Empire and the great traditions of my Army in India'.

The sea voyage was wholly uneventful. Alexandria was reached on the 21st. There they stayed but a few hours. Next day they reached Port Said. Here Major Hulseberg, Major Woodhouse and Lieut. Lewis rejoined. They unloaded ship, and on the 24th disembarked and entrained for Suez, where they embarked on H.M.T. *Bandra* for Aden, sailing on the afternoon of the 26th. Christmas Day is unrecorded. On the early morning of 1 January they reached Aden where they were welcomed by a former C.O., Brigadier-General C. H. U. Price in command at Aden, and by Captain C. E. Borton of the 129th, who was shortly afterwards killed at Aden. Here Major Woodhouse and his company disembarked. That same evening they sailed on their new adventure to Mombasa.

# CHAPTER VIII

JAN.–4 MARCH, 1916: Regiment leaves Mombasa for Voi. Training for new type of fighting; Arrival at Kajiado; Part of 2nd East African Brigade, 1st East African Division; Headquarters move to Longido West; Changes in composition of regiment; All ready

NO greater contrast can be imagined than that between Flanders and East Africa. If the men had suffered from too much rain and mud the average was now to be evened up by an excess of drought and dust, except in the rainy season when the floodgates of heaven were opened. In Flanders they had been confined to a narrow sector of country where they had alternated between trenches and billets. Now they found themselves in a great country, twice the size of France, where roads were practically non-existent and which at first was almost entirely unknown, fighting a highly mobile enemy, so that for long periods of time they were on the march daily. Flanders may have been dull and uninteresting, but it was not unhealthy, while the medical services were astonishingly efficient. East Africa had more to show, and has even been known to delight the visitor with its magnificent scenery, though the soldier is apt to be soured in his appreciation when the scenery gets mixed up with machine guns, short rations and long, weary marches: but it is exceedingly unhealthy for campaigning, and produces a variety of diseases which inflicted greater casualties than the enemy.

There has also been a tendency to underrate the sternness of the actual fighting and to contrast the casualty lists with the magnificent slaughters in France. It is true there was no artillery worth mentioning—about sixty guns of all calibres—while the ammunition supply was small, but the enemy was amply supplied with machine guns which he handled equally well as in France. Moreover the enemy troops were excellently trained and led; they were all either natives who were largely immune to the diseases of the country, or whites who had been in the colony for some time and were well salted. They were fighting on interior lines and were conducting a defensive war to which the country lent itself well. Encircling movements were excessively difficult to carry out, as there were never sufficient troops to stop all the gaps. Again and again the enemy passed through our lines by routes hitherto unknown and by breaking up into small parties. Lines of communication were long, and this meant that considerable forces had to be strung out over great stretches of country.

When the 129th landed in Mombasa hostilities had already been in progress since August 1914, but in spite of small gains in the west the enemy had definitely had the best of it, while the smaller British forces were pinned down on the defensive. General Smuts writes:

'During the nineteen months which had elapsed since the outbreak of the war before my arrival in East Africa, the enemy had on the whole been superior to us both in strategy and effective striking force, and it says much for the tenacity of our defence that during that period British East Africa was not overwhelmed. The enemy, while entrenching himself in our territory and successfully striking minor blows at us in many directions and unceasingly threatening our long railway communications with the coast at many points, wisely foresaw that the real struggle would come later and devoted his attention mainly to the recruitment and training of a large native army under German officers. The word had gone forth from Berlin that East Africa, the jewel of the German Colonial Empire, was to be held at all costs, and the German Commander, Colonel von Lettow-Vorbeck, was the man to carry out this order to the bitter end. The initial stocks of guns, machine guns, rifles and ammunition were from time to time very largely augmented by several blockade runners, and heavy artillery was supplied by the *Königsberg* and other warships on that coast. When, therefore, I arrived in February 1916, with South African reinforcements to take the offensive, I found opposed to me a very large army in effective strength not much smaller than my own, well trained and ably commanded, formidably equipped with artillery and machine guns, immune against most tropical diseases, very mobile and able to live on the country, largely untroubled by transport difficulties, and with a morale in some respects higher than that of our troops, who, in inferior strength, had borne the heat and burden of the defence for the last eighteen months'.

But all this was very soon to be changed. General Smuts landed on 19 February, and on 5 March the offensive began which was to drive the enemy out of his carefully prepared positions in and around Taveta. The 129th were a unit in the reinforcements which were being sent to East Africa to make the offensive possible. Between the date of their landing and 5 March they were busy shaping themselves once more into a regiment and learning the new type of warfare.

The journey to Mombasa took seven days and was wholly uneventful. They arrived early in the morning of 5 January, 1916, and immediately proceeded to disembark. This was completed very expeditiously, so that at 5 o'clock in the evening they entrained for Voi, except No. 1 Company which, being detailed for detached duty, entrained at Kilindini for Maungu. Voi was reached at 4 a.m. next day. It was, and probably still is, a dreary place, with nothing to be said in its favour except that being a junction one might hope for a more or less speedy departure elsewhere. The war had brought it into prominence, as it became the base for operations against the enemy forces occupying Taveta. From it a crazy line had been pushed forward toward Taveta, and in it were assembled the various forces which had so far managed to hold the enemy in check. It looked its best in the dusk when darkness obscured most of its ugliness, but doubtless, like most base camps, it was the Paradise for which the more advanced troops sighed. For in it were to be found food and comforts which seemed to collect there chiefly for the use of the large base staffs, whose main function at times seemed to have been obstruction. Voi was, at the moment, in a turmoil of preparation for the heavy reinforcements shortly due for the new campaign. Having spent the day in shaking themselves down, the 129th next day began their training for the new offensive very shortly to be commenced. The Diary records that next day at 6 a.m. they 'paraded for bush-fighting instruction', while the officers had lectures on the same subject from the Commandant. And so they did for several days until split up into separate companies and sent on patrols and outpost duty. These company movements are of little interest except to those who carried them out, nor were they of importance from the point of view of the campaign shortly to be launched. But they served a purpose beyond that of watching the enemy, for they taught all ranks how to march and to live in their new environment. Captain Lewis writes of this period: 'The utmost advantage was taken to train the regiment to the new conditions of fighting', and here it had the inestimable advantage of the previous African experience of the Commanding Officer who had commanded a K.A.R. battalion in 1910. The country from Kajiado to Longido provided an excellent training-ground, and the time spent there, with no enemy actually encountered but with the possibility of an encounter any day, benefited the battalion throughout its long stay in Africa.

The days, in spite of much hard work and some long marches, passed pleasantly, and training was carried on at every opportunity. 'We learned how to march through long grass and bush with screens of flankers, ready to shake out at a moment's notice into artillery formation, and then, at a quick command, into that for attack. We learned how to settle down quickly into a perimeter camp, and how to protect it efficiently from sudden attack. We learned the vital importance of always, even when the chance of meeting the enemy was remote, taking as thorough precautions against surprise as though an immediate attack was expected; and the principle that the commander of every unit, however small, was responsible, without orders, for the protection of his unit was impressed on everybody. Lastly we learned how to protect the feet from the "dodu"[1] and how to remove him should he, as he later often did, get inside.

'Nor was this training without its excitements. One day near Namanga the battalion was practising an attack in three extended lines through grass. Two lines had passed when, between the second and third, a huge panther, with a deep growl, sprang from a thicker patch of grass and came down between the lines. Men appeared to be everywhere but no one could fire. The angry and frightened beast, seeking escape, passed like a flash down the line, jinked and dodged like a snipe, while all one could do was to wave one's hands and "shoo" at it, as one would do to a goose. Finally, and inevitably, he met a man and knocked him down and sank his teeth in the sepoy's shoulder. Then, urged by shouts from everyone, he was away and into the grass, followed by three ineffective shots. He was followed up but never found.'

The various movements may perhaps be recorded. On 13 January Headquarters with Nos. 2 and 4 Companies entrained for Kajiado, which formed the railhead of the branch line from the main line to Lake Magadi, whence

---

[1] The dodu or jigger flea is a minute parasite which burrows into the skin particularly under the toe-nails, though it is not particular where it gets. The female then begins to lay her eggs and gradually the spot begins to fester. If the egg sac is not removed whole, the eggs begin to hatch out and the process is repeated until all the flesh is eaten away. It is exceedingly painful and very soon makes marching impossible. I have seen cases where all the toes have been eaten away or removed, while the rest of the foot resembled a mass of dirty putrefying rags.

watch was kept on the enemy who had once occupied Longido. No. 3 Company was left at Voi, where it was joined the next day by No. 1 Company which had been drawn in from Maungu. These two companies were further reinforced on the 15th by the arrival of Lieut. MacIvor with 149 other ranks from the depôt in India. This arrival of reinforcements calls for comment. It was the first draft to reach the regiment from its own depôt after seventeen months of war: witness of how completely unprepared was the Indian Army for war except for small frontier expeditions. Much of the weakness of the Indian Expeditionary Forces in Flanders and elsewhere was directly due to this breakdown in the depôts and also of the reserve system.

At Kajiado they came under the command of Major-General Stewart, commanding the 1st Division. It might be well to point out here that the term 'Division' in East Africa did not connote the same thing as in Flanders. An East African Division might and might not be up to standard strength and equipment. Generally it fell lamentably below standard in every respect. They were inspected, for at that time it must have added greatly to the morale of the Commanding Officer and his Staff to see and inspect his troops. In this way one came to realise that there were still troops in the field. Having been inspected the regiment immediately broke up again. On 16 January No. 2 Company, under Captain O'Neill, marched to Namanga where it arrived on the 21st, while No. 4 Company went to Kedongai, arriving on the 20th. On the 25th the two companies, plus the new draft, rejoined Headquarters. Four days later they moved out to Bissel which was reached on the morning of the 30th. It is recorded that it rained all night and that the men were wet through. From Bissel they marched to Olekenoni where they arrived the same evening. There they bivouacked in fine weather.

February found them 'part of the 2nd East African

Brigade commanded by Brigadier-General S. H. Sheppard, D.S.O., of the 1st Division'. Brigaded with them were the 29th Punjabis, 25th Royal Fusiliers, and a battalion of the Cape Corps. The strength was high: 13 British officers, 14 Indian, 730 other ranks. The month was uneventful: few movements took place except when one company relieved another on outpost duty. On the first the Diary records 'No. 2 at post Namanga: No. 4 at Kedongai: remainder on road between Bissel and Manga'. And so they remained until the 29th when one reads 'Battalion H.Q. with Nos. 1, 3 and 4 Companies and 3 machine guns left Manga for Longido West and camped for night at Elephant's Skull'. But internally some very important changes were taking place. Simla was awaking to the fact that there was a war on and not a frontier punitive expedition. The complete breakdown of the regimental depôts, from which reinforcements should have been fed to the regiments at the front, had gradually been made good, and attention was now being turned to the very mixed composition of the regiments on service. Already Major Woodhouse's company had been detached at Aden, and now on the 14th Captain Stewart with all the P.M.s of the 124th left, *en route* for the Persian Gulf, while Major Morris left three days later to rejoin his own regiment in India, whence he, too, found his way up the Persian Gulf. Major Morris's departure was sincerely regretted by all who knew him and had campaigned with him. It was comforting, however, to know that he had gone East instead of 'west'. On the 28th a new draft from the 127th joined at Manga. The Brigadier also was naturally interested in these changes, which resulted in the loss of some 250 seasoned sepoys and their replacement by recruits, but after discussing the changes wrote: 'I do not, however, consider that this will unfit the 129th for service with the 2nd East African Brigade.... The regiment, though weakened of so many old soldiers, cannot fail to gain valuable experience whilst it (the campaign) is in progress; while the spirit of the regiment appears to be excellent'. Certainly the rest from constant fighting had done much good and had enabled the officers to improve the efficiency and discipline, so that they were now ready for the campaign about to be opened.

It had been suggested that the whole regiment should be sent to Nairobi for training, but this counsel of perfection could not be carried out. In the meantime the Brigade was slowly getting together, so that on 4 March it could be recorded 'Brigade now ready to go forward on light scale of baggage without tents'.

# CHAPTER IX

5 MARCH–25 MARCH, 1916: Review of general situation; Offensive begins; March from Longido round south of Kilimanjaro; Arrival at Moschi; Advance from Moschi; Attack on Store; Enemy night attack; Van Deventer's flanking movement; Smuts's general plan; Attack by 2nd East African Brigade on Ruwu; Enemy withdrawn during the night; Kahe occupied

THE task before General Smuts was the invasion and occupation of East Africa. This of course implied the destruction of the German forces, no easy task, as they were well organised and well led. Their strength was estimated at about 2000 whites and 14,000 Africans with 60 guns and 80 machine guns. They were organised into companies of 150–200 strong, of which 20 per cent were white. Each company had two machine guns.

At the beginning of the year the position was briefly as follows. The front was nominally some 600 miles in length, stretching from the sea to the Victoria Nyanza, but was only held at certain points. Small forces watched each other near the coast. The next and most important point was Taveta, lying in the narrow gap between the Paré Mountains and Kilimanjaro. Here facing each other were the main forces of the combatants. North-west of Kilimanjaro on the boundary was Longido, which had been occupied originally by the enemy, but which was now in our hands. This point was watched by both parties but few forces were massed there. The rest of the front was not held except near the Victoria Nyanza.

The German position was a strong one. Taveta was the door into German territory. Actually it was British, but the enemy had occupied it immediately on the outbreak of hostilities and since that time had greatly strengthened it. It was further protected by Salaita and an entrenched camp at Serengeti about 13 miles further forward. There were also outposts at Mbuyuni and at Kasigao, from which points the Uganda railway was constantly threatened.

Prior to General Smuts's arrival a beginning had been made for the advance. On 15 January Major-General Stewart had been ordered to occupy Longido. A week later Brigadier-General Malleson had advanced from Maktau to Mbuyuni and had occupied Serengeti camp. The railway was immediately pushed on to this new point, while the enemy had been forced to evacuate Kasigao. Arrangements were immediately made for a large concentration at Mbuyuni, an excellent site, but which lacked water. This deficiency was made good by a pipe line from Bura, but the supply was insufficient and had to be supplemented by supplies carried in tanks on the newly built line. Early in February the South African troops began to arrive, and on the 12th the new troops began to learn wisdom, the first lesson being at Salaita. The despatch dealing with this attack on Salaita is a model which might well be adopted by the Staff College when training its future Generals how to gloss over unpleasant defeats: 'The enemy was found to be in force and counter-attacked vigorously. General Malleson was compelled to withdraw to Serengeti, but much useful information had been gained and the South African infantry had learned some valuable lessons in bush fighting, and also had the opportunity of estimating the fighting qualities of the enemy'. It might have added 'and of the 130th Baluchis who saved them from a disaster', but prejudice is strong in South Africa so the 130th were forgotten in this model despatch.

Such was the position when General Smuts took over. General Smuts accepted the main idea of his predecessor's plan but greatly modified the details. Briefly it was to make the main attack towards Taveta but at the same time to threaten the enemy's rear by an attack from Longido, which, coming in south of Kilimanjaro, would strike at

Moschi and Kahe and so cut his railway communications. With the Taveta attack we are not concerned as the 129th formed part of the Division which operated from Longido. All that need be said is that it was a brilliant piece of work which succeeded in its immediate objective, though not in its ultimate one, with the minimum of casualties. The Longido operation, which was an integral part of the campaign, was equally successful though not so spectacular.

The attack from Longido was to be made by the 1st East African Division under Major-General J. M. Stewart, C.B. In actual fact the Division consisted of the 2nd East African Brigade under Brigadier-General S. H. Sheppard, D.S.O., and the Divisional troops, as the other two Brigades were taken away to reinforce the main attack on Taveta.

The Division was to advance across the waterless bush between Longido and the Engare Nanjuki River—some 35 miles—occupy the latter place and then advance between Meru and Kilimanjaro to Boma ja Ngombe, an important road junction. Thence on to Moschi and Kahe with a view to cutting the enemy's line of communication on the Usambara Railway. The advance was to begin on 5 March, two days before the main attack. Everything depended upon the accurate timing of this operation.

At 8 a.m. on the 5th, therefore, the Brigade with the 129th in the main body marched out followed by the rest of the Division *en route* for Sheep's Hill and Ngasserai, while a squadron of the 17th Cavalry, the East African Mounted Rifles and other mounted troops circled round via the Kampfontein road towards Ngasseni. The regiment marched out with its full complement of officers and men. Lieut. MacIvor with 70 other ranks remained at Longido as post garrison. It was expected that the first objective, Ngasseni, a hill of some importance, would be defended, and as the only water-supply was at this place there was considerable anxiety on that score. Strict orders were issued, therefore, against drinking water without permission. At 6.30 p.m.

the Brigade reached a point within 3 miles of Ngasserai and halted while the hill was reconnoitred. Fortunately it was held by an enemy patrol only, and this withdrew before the advance of the 29th Punjabis, so that by 11 p.m. the whole Brigade was bivouacked.

This first day's march in the campaigns which were now opening deserves notice, both for itself and because it is typical of much of the routine campaigning which was to follow, and which will be recorded in this history. A history must be concise and cannot elaborate the scenes it records: yet a mere barren record of marches and battles is of no value and less interest. Soldiering is more than fighting in the narrow sense. Death and glory may appeal to the public and the very young, but it is not the soldier's ambition. Even in the Great War the percentage of time spent in battle was exceedingly small. The major portion of the time goes in preparation and manœuvring, which always means hard work and generally exhausting efforts. This march of some 30 miles over semi-desert country, in a tropical sun, in column and on a strictly limited water-supply, was an extremely exhausting task requiring good march discipline. All the troops, except a small number in the advance guards and on the flanks, were enveloped in a thick haze of dust from the moment the march started until the halt, at the end of the day. Only those who have done such marches know what they mean. It is one thing to picture war in terms of smartly aligned columns marching on good roads, it is another to see the reality—columns of filthy, sweating men, staggering with fatigue, at the end of such a march, and with parched mouths gasping for water. And to see these troops, in such a condition, pull themselves together for battle with an entrenched enemy, is to see real soldiers and to know the meaning of discipline. Long fatiguing marches such as this were to be the normal routine. Always the same monotony of bad dusty tracks, the same vigilance for an enemy equally determined and always alert, who could choose his own positions: always the same hardships. If one does not repeat these facts continually, but only records the events, the reader must use his imagination to elaborate the story. Further, the Diaries do not record hardships: they take them for granted, and thus constitute a truer record of the spirit of those who fought than novels written by neurotics and weaklings full of self-pity.

Though the Brigade only got in by 11 p.m. they were on the march at 2 a.m. next day, partly because speed was essential, partly because the night and early morning were the best times for marching. By daybreak they were on the west of the Engare Nanjuki marsh. The next day they were in Ngasseni. The same day at 2.30 p.m. the 129th with the Cape Corps and a section of the 27th Mountain Battery under Lieut.-Colonel Hannyngton marched to Engare Nairobi on a reconnoitring mission, but found little, as the enemy had withdrawn. Six prisoners—porters—were taken. Their losses were one mule killed by snipers during the night. Thence they marched the next day, leaving the Cape Corps behind, and joined up with the Division just before its arrival at Geraragua River. Geraragua was reached on 8 March after very slight opposition. On the 9th the Division halted in order to reconnoitre and let supplies catch up. It was found that the road as far as Boma ja Ngombe was impassable for wheeled traffic, as all the bridges had been destroyed. This necessitated another halt on the 10th while the exhausted ox transport should recuperate and while a new route was being found further to the west. At last a 'difficult but passable tract was found' and the march was resumed at midday. There is a certain amount of grim humour in such phrases as 'difficult but passable' which can only be appreciated by those who have assisted with the transport on such occasions—and then only some considerable time after the event. It was not only the animals which were exhausted on these occasions. Even the recording angel must have been considerably fatigued.

While the main column thus advanced, reconnoitring detachments of varying strength were being sent out to search the flanks and feel for the enemy. In these the 129th took their full share. Thus we read in the Brigade Diary for the 10th: 'One double company of the 129th went to second O in Olorungoti to help mounted troops'. They missed them, but it was hardly to be wondered at if one realises the nature of the country, which was a dense tangle of scrub intersected by native paths only. The maps too were grossly inaccurate. Another similar duty is recorded and exemplified about the same date, when a large fighting patrol of two companies and 100 K.A.R. were sent to attack and destroy a hostile camp, also near Geraragua. On their arrival they found the camp deserted, as so frequently happened; but they found some useful litter: 'Found useful maps and papers, green vegetables, picks and shovels, some dynamite, saddlery and some fowls which were taken back to the Division'. The inventory is useful in helping one to realise the scale of values current among the troops even in those early stages of the campaign. Maps came first and were always in demand, as those in use were quite inadequate. How bad were some of our maps in the opinion of the enemy was discovered from a captured enemy casualty list, where against a German officer casualty was pencilled the remark, 'Lost and shot through using a British map'. Last on the list came fowls. The Swaheli for a fowl is 'Kuku', sounded like 'cuckoo'. Like the English fowl of that name it is equally elusive. When ensnared it was in reality a poor thing, but after the endless tepid bully beef and army biscuit it was much coveted. It is to be hoped that Major Crawford, who was commanding this eminently successful expedition, kept at least a few for the regiment. Green vegetables also call for note. The African troops, who knew the country, generally managed to supply themselves with these, but the newly arrived troops did not know where to look, so that often they went for long periods without vegetables to the distinct disadvantage of their health. The rest of the inventory does not call for comment.

On the 10th the Division reached Mbiriri in some anxiety as to the fate of the cavalry, which should have been in the second O in Olorungoti but which were in actual fact on a hill-top elsewhere. Two days later the lost ones returned.

In the meantime the regiment with the Division had reached Sanja, and patrols had been pushed out to reconnoitre Greek House and Boma ja Ngombe.

On the 13th came news of the success of the main offensive and of the withdrawal of the enemy from Latema and Reata, and with it orders for the 1st Division to push on to Massai Kraal. Accordingly the Division marched at once for Boma ja Ngombe, while the Brigade, leaving the Division, marched *en route* for Moschi by the southern Moschi-Arusha road. With the latter went the 129th, though temporarily weakened by the detachment of Lieut. Wilson with 102 other ranks, left at Sanja to escort a convoy, and of Lieut. Stone with a similar force left at Boma ja Ngombe to protect the guns which had been left behind. Its strength was thus reduced to some 500 rifles. The Brigade pushed on as quickly as possible, fording many rivers. The Regimental Diary records little save the prosaic facts that a certain number of men were left behind at East Kware River to cook food; that it rained all night, and that the transport had to be helped across the fords. The Brigade diarist was, however, in better mood and was even loquacious: 'West Kware River was dry. Road excellent so far'. 'East Kware, which is a fairly fast-flowing stream about 20 yards wide at the drift and up to 1 foot deep, had some bad pot-holes, and drift required work to render passable.... There was great delay in crossing troops and transport in the light of a half-moon, so transport, 27th

Mountain Battery and one company of the 29th Punjabis left behind to come on in the morning. Rest after crossing, marched on at 10.15 p.m. for about 2½ miles. Rain came on and objective seemed to have been reached, so a halt was ordered for the night at 1.30 a.m. of the 14th (he probably meant that the troops were too exhausted to move further) alongside the road....March was resumed at 8.30, but now on Moschi.' These two records of the regiment and Brigade are illuminating as showing how the same facts affect different people. It depends largely on who has to do the dirty work. The day's march was very much a repetition of the previous night, save that it was in the daylight. More rivers were crossed with the same difficulty and toil. The bush through which they were marching was of varying degrees of density, but after reaching the Garangua it was almost impenetrable. The track was not too bad but was overgrown in places and cut up by the rain, while the enemy had blocked it in many places by thorn abattis.

Towards the afternoon the two British forces—from Taveta and from Longido—were drawing together so that caution had to be exercised to prevent a collision, especially as the K.A.R. were doing advance guard and their uniforms were almost identical with those of the enemy askaris. Just outside Moschi Station the K.A.R. were fired on and immediately the Baluchis were ordered forward while the K.A.R. stood fast. Such incidents as this were not infrequent, and often led to useless casualties unless handled with skill and coolness. Through the bush nothing could be seen, so that one had to get close up before recognition was possible, while the rule of 'safety first' tended to make one shoot first and apologise after. The advance was made, therefore, with great caution and 'two Union Jacks were sent out in front of our firing line'. The bearers of the flags are nameless but they deserve a passing tribute. Fortunately, the opposing fire was high and the enemy turned out to be the South African cavalry who were unaware of the Brigade's advance. The Diary concludes the affair: 'The mistake of the cavalry... might have led to more serious results, and it was mainly owing to the steadiness of our men that there were only about six casualties on our side'. Fortunately, the sepoys were all fatalists so that the casualties could still keep serene minds.

The regiment at the head of the Brigade then marched into New Moschi and proceeded to dig the usual perimeter camp, when after about a couple of hours digging in rocky ground they were ordered off a little south of New Moschi, where no doubt they were more fortunate with their digging. It rained hard all night.

They stayed at Moschi until the evening of the 18th but found no rest. Every moment was occupied. Those who were not on outpost duty were hard at work repairing roads and bridges which had been destroyed by the retreating enemy. 'The want of technical troops was felt.' There is also recorded a pathetic complaint about a certain wireless outfit, somewhere in their vicinity, 'making intercommunication on the line of defence very difficult, especially at night, owing to the numerous wires belonging to the apparatus'.

On the evening of the 18th the forward move began once more. This was part of a larger general advance ordered by Smuts, whose intention was to drive the enemy back across the Ruwu River and if possible to cut his retreat. The general plan was, roughly, that the 2nd South African Brigade should attack at Unterer Himo and the 3rd South African Brigade at Euphorbien Hill—advanced posts protecting Rasthaus Hill which itself covered the Rasthaus bridge, one of the enemy lines of retreat. The 2nd East African Brigade were to advance by the Mue Massai Kraal road towards their main objective, the wagon bridge at Kahe Kwa Ruwu, while van Deventer's cavalry, starting two days later from Moschi, were to carry out a turning movement further west, come in on the rear of the enemy at Kahe railway bridge and intercept the retreat by that route.

Meantime the enemy commander, in anticipation of some such offensive, had posted his forces very carefully in prepared positions and was keeping a large reserve of some eight companies at Kahe. He himself was not at Kahe, but was in a more forward position directing his front-line troops. The reserve was under one of his subordinates, who had orders to use his discretion should an emergency arise.

The country was exceedingly difficult to operate in, being covered in most places with dense scrub. It was this which made it impossible to attain the final objective. The enemy were driven back, but allowing for casualties got away intact.

Fighting began on the 18th on the British left where satisfactory progress was made. The next day the 2nd and 3rd South African Infantry Brigades attacked the Rasthaus position, while General Sheppard made a simultaneous advance with the 1st Division from Mue via Massai Kraal towards Kahe Kwa Ruwu. The 2nd East African Brigade with the 129th as rear-guard had already moved forward on the evening of the 18th, and after considerable transport difficulties had reached their destination by 12.30 a.m. It was a clear moonlight night.

At 9 a.m. the Brigade was ordered to attack the enemy's position near Store across the Kahe Kwa Ruwu road. This time the Baluchis were at the head of the Brigade with a company as advance guard under Major Hulseberg. The enemy were encountered at 3 p.m. about a 1000 yards south of Acacia and were easily driven back. Of this action one of the officers engaged writes: 'The regiment, accustomed to heavy fire to be met in France, took small count of the comparatively small number of bullets which whistled past them and came in for considerable praise for the pace at which it pushed the enemy's outposts through very difficult and bushy country. Far more serious was the opposition met from bees. The regiment, with Nos. 3 and 4 Companies deployed ahead, was moving along gaily enough when an aimed or stray bullet hit a bee-hive, a hollow log suspended from a tree. Bees were everywhere: and so, shortly, were the machine-gun mules. The road was impossible. Officers and men flung themselves on the ground, heads in the grass. A South African cyclist rode up in ignorance with a message from the Brigade asking the cause of the delay, handed his message to the scarcely recognisable C.O., and he too buried his face in Mother Earth. Gradually the bees lost their stings, and a message was sent back to the Brigade explaining the delay to the Brigadier who remarked, "Bees have stopped them: I thought the Germans couldn't have". Subedar Mir Bad Shah, who stood stock still muttering prayers, and Lieut. Lewis, who at the former's bidding also stood quite still, alone escaped unstung. With largely swollen faces the regiment resumed its march'.

Except that No. 4 Company, under Captain O'Neill, on the right of the advance line, temporarily lost touch—and themselves—no other incident occurred that day.

All this was but an affair of outposts, as the enemy were holding well-prepared positions further back; casualties were very slight. The real fighting was yet to come. Meantime the Brigade dug themselves in and spent a peaceful night. The next day, 20 March, General Sheppard was reinforced by three battalions of the 2nd South African Brigade from Unterer Himo in anticipation of more serious fighting the next day. The 20th passed peacefully. The usual patrols were sent out and were commended by General von Lettow for their good work—though at a later date. One little affair is worthy of record. 'At 11 o'clock No. 2 Company was sent to reconnoitre the enemy position covering the Ruwu River. The main position was found by suddenly bumping up against it. It was on the Soko Nassai River; Sepoy Alim Khan, a scout, found it first. Walking round a thicket he ran into a picquet, so knelt down and shot four: the fifth escaped. The Germans formed up to man the trenches, so after firing at them for a short time the company returned to Store with the four enemy rifles.'

The night was not to be so quiet. The enemy were at a loss to know what exactly was happening, so, to use von Lettow-Vorbeck's own words, he 'decided to drive the enemy's screen back on his proper position'. His account of the affair is of interest: 'It was bright moonlight when the leading company was fired on, apparently by a hostile outpost or patrol, which moved off. After that we encountered several patrols, but then, about three miles north of our own trenches, we came across a stronger opponent with machine guns. The very severe action which now developed proved that we had come up against the enemy's main position: to assault it seemed hopeless. Leaving patrols out, I withdrew step by step. Our casualties were not inconsiderable, and unfortunately included three Company Commanders who were difficult to replace'.

The Brigade camp was an entrenched perimeter camp of the usual type, constructed immediately the troops arrived at their destination. There was one company on outpost duty some 300 yards to the south. The night of the attack the 29th Punjabis were on outpost duty, but were reinforced as the attack developed by two companies from their own regiment and one-and-a-half from the Baluchis. Von Lettow does not say how many of his troops were engaged, and of course the estimates on our side are conjecture. The Brigade estimated 500–600. Another estimate goes as high as ten companies, which seems much too high. There may have been about 1000. The report goes on: 'They blew bugles and there was much shouting. In some cases individual men charged to within ten yards of the outpost trenches'. Attempts were made to work round our flanks but were unsuccessful. Finally, about 12.30 a.m. firing ceased and the enemy retired taking with them most of their dead and wounded. Some 11 dead and 5 wounded were found in the morning, while a few more bodies were found later in the bush. The enemy's casualties were admittedly considerable and were probably from 150 to 200 altogether. The repulse was a blow to the enemy and also a foretaste of what they might have expected if General von Lettow had counter-attacked the following day as he had intended. The behaviour of the sepoys was excellent. 'This night attack was carried out with extreme vigour by the enemy... the most noticeable thing, so far as the regiment was concerned, was the very good fire discipline which enabled the officers and non-commissioned officers to keep complete control, always a difficult thing to do on a dark night and under heavy fire.... The regiment fought with the greatest steadiness.'

The total casualties on our side were very small: 5 killed and 10 wounded, of which only 4 wounded belonged to the 129th. The other casualties fell to the 29th Punjabis. Among the regiment's trophies were three bugles picked up in front of the trenches the following morning.

While the 2nd East African Brigade was thus engaged in repulsing the enemy's night attack General van Deventer with his mounted Brigade had been making his way through the bush from Moschi with orders to proceed to the west of the railway, cross the Pangani to the south of Kahe and to come in on the rear of the enemy's position. By daylight on 21 March they were approaching the Pangani, having marched some 25 miles during the night, and they were now apparently within striking distance of their first objective, Kahe Hill, which was the key to Kahe. On receipt of this information General Smuts had ordered Sheppard to push on towards the Ruwu River with his two Brigades, while at the same time the 3rd South African

Brigade was ordered to attack Rasthaus and move south along the Himo until it established touch with Sheppard's left. Von Lettow's conclusion, therefore, that the attacks of the 21st towards the wagon bridge were the outcome of an undue optimism resulting from the repulse of his night attack, is shown to be incorrect.

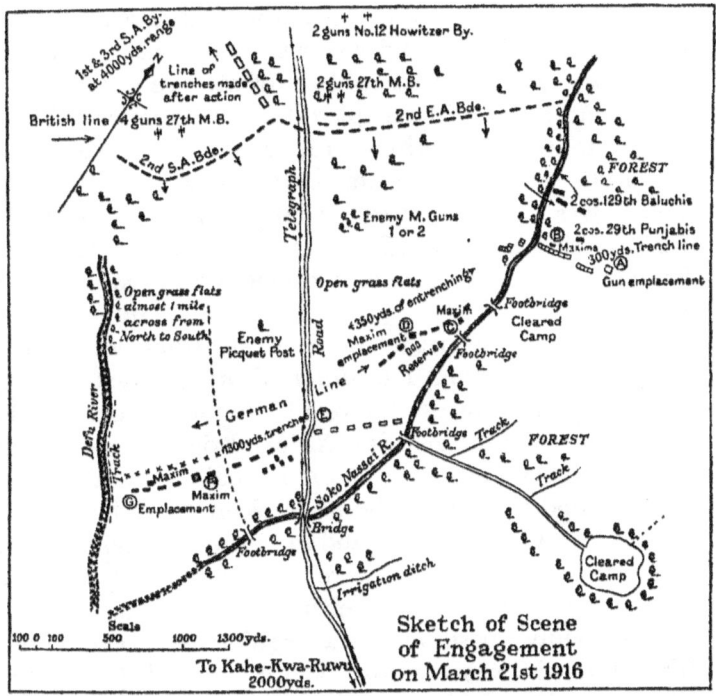

Sketch of Scene of Engagement on March 21st 1916

General Smuts's plan was a good one in its conception but failed to achieve all that had been hoped owing to the physical obstacles, which had not been allowed for. The 3rd South African Brigade never came into action, as the bush between Euphorbien and the Soko Nassai was so dense as to prevent their advance. Sheppard's intention of turning the enemy's right flank with the aid of this Brigade was nullified. Neither, unfortunately, was he able to get into touch with van Deventer and to know what was happening on his right, nor was he able to get news through G.H.Q.

Actually van Deventer had found a series of obstacles of a similar nature to those which had impeded the 3rd South African Brigade. When he reached the Pangani it was found that there was no bridge across at that spot and that the river was deeper and wider than had been expected. There was also a considerable current. Eventually it was swum and Kahe Hill occupied, but all attempts to sweep further south were entirely prevented by the denseness of the bush. As a result of this partial success at Kahe the enemy was forced to abandon his positions on the Ruwu River during the night of the 21st to 22nd, but the greater hope of surrounding him and forcing a decisive battle was not realised.

We can now return to the narrower front occupied by Sheppard's Division. The order of attack was: the 2nd South African Brigade, less one battalion, with its left on the main road; the 2nd East African Brigade, less the 25th Royal Fusiliers, with its right on the main road. They were to be supported by two South African Field Batteries, a battery of 5-inch howitzers and the 27th Mountain Battery, while two armoured cars were to operate along the road. The troops were to be in their positions at 9.30 a.m.

The enemy's position was a singularly well-chosen one. The almost impassable Soko Nassai guarded their eastern flank, the difficult Defu protected them on the west. In their immediate front was open plain varying from 800 yards to double that distance, while any advance over the plains was met not only by tremendous machine-gun fire from the main positions but by machine guns and rifle fire from the bushes lining the right bank of the Soko Nassai, thus taking any frontal advance in the flank. Machine guns and snipers were also most boldly placed well in front of the main position, in clumps of trees and grass; and these, being particularly well hidden, inflicted a considerable proportion of our casualties.

The attacking brigades were thus confined to a narrowing tongue of ground bounded by streams, which were not only wider and deeper than was thought but which were infested by crocodiles. Save for the open spaces already mentioned the bush was very dense, and this prevented accurate observation of the gun fire, so that the artillery support was very largely ineffective.

General von Lettow emphasises the care which had been taken to make the movement of reserve troops easy; roads had been cut in all directions. Further he was himself directing operations. General Smuts in his first despatch writes that it was Sheppard's intention to attack frontally, and with or without the help of the 3rd South African Brigade to envelop the enemy's right. For this he had not sufficient men, as a frontal attack could easily be held up by machine-gun fire. The enemy were well supplied with these, and the artillery entirely failed to silence them owing to inability to observe the effect of their fire in the bush. An enveloping movement might have met with initial success—as in fact it nearly did—but without a considerable weight of men it would soon have been stopped. Von Lettow had ample reserves which could have been thrown in rapidly at any spot. Actually he was on the point of counter-attacking when the news of the occupation of Kahe Hill decided him to withdraw from the Ruwu line.

The arrival of the 3rd South African Brigade would have supplied the weight required to drive home the Baluchi flanking movement on the German right, but as already mentioned the Brigade never came into action.

We are only concerned with the advance of the 2nd East African Brigade as the 129th formed part of this unit. By 9.30 a.m. the troops were in position ready for the advance, but they did not move forward until an hour later. The attack was led by the 29th Punjabis while the 129th formed the Brigade Reserve and advanced in the rear of the 29th. The preliminary advance of some one-and-a-half miles calls for no comment and was in reality a moving up into the assault positions. By 12.40 the 29th had reached the open space in front of the enemy's positions. Here the volume of rifle and machine-gun fire was so heavy that further progress was impossible. Another company of the 29th was therefore sent further to the left in support, but they too were held up by the Soko River and the thick bush. Meantime the first two companies were suffering from the enemy's fire, and casualties were beginning to mount up.

The Baluchis now came into action. At 2.20 p.m. No. 4 Company under Captain O'Neill was ordered to extend the line to the left and to find out where the enemy's right flank rested. What followed is best told in the words of Captain O'Neill's report made after he became a casualty: 'I posted my company as instructed on the left of the 29th and informed the Officer Commanding their left company that I was ready to advance. My orders were to try and turn the enemy's right flank. When the order to advance was given, the 29th on our right started rapid fire. Not being able to see anything of the enemy I advanced my company until stopped by the machine-gun fire. As soon as the position of the machine gun had been located, about 150 yards on our left front, I opened rapid fire into it and also turned my own machine gun on. This silenced the enemy, and I then gave the order to rush the position and capture the gun under cover of our machine-gun fire. Unfortunately our machine gun jammed as we were advancing, and by the time we were 50 yards from the enemy they had got their machine gun working again, and I was hit immediately and most of the men with me. The advance was through dense bush which made concerted action very difficult, and although we were in touch with the 29th throughout it was impossible to see how far forward they had reached.

'Had it not been for our machine gun jamming at the critical moment we stood a very good chance of getting through them with the bayonet, as when firing our machine gun completely silenced their fire'.

By 5 o'clock Nos. 1 and 3 Companies were entrenched in a line about 300 yards from the left of the 29th to a point on the right bank of the Soko. Meantime the Division had come to realise that they were up against the enemy's main strength, and orders were immediately sent out to withdraw the two companies east of the Soko and for the whole line to dig itself in. The casualties had been 16 killed and 53 wounded: of these the 129th sustained 5 killed and 14 wounded.

The intention was to renew the attack next day, but this was rendered unnecessary by the enemy withdrawing during the night. The South Africans had fared worse and had also been held up. Altogether the day had been a trying one. Compared with casualties on the Western Front the figures are trivial, but it must be remembered that the numbers engaged were also trivial: further, these pin-prick casualties mounted up as time went on and reinforcements were difficult to obtain. To have forced the issue by a frontal attack would have simply added to the casualties without any hope of success, as the artillery fire was ineffective.

Next morning the patrols, which had been feeling the enemy position, reported that they had gone. Immediately the 1st K.A.R. were ordered forward to seize the Ruwu bridge while the 29th and 129th came on later, about noon, having stayed behind waiting for their cooked rations. They marched to the railway bridge over the Pangani where they bivouacked. The rest of the month is merely a record of outpost duties and fatigues. Bridge building and repairing, road-making and block-house building, filled in the time of those who were not on duty watching and patrolling. Meantime the weather was rapidly working up to rain, and it was decided to withdraw the Brigade to New Moschi, leaving one regiment to hold the line of the Ruwu with Kahe as its main headquarters. On 25 March the Brigade marched back leaving the 129th to take first turn on the new outpost line.

# CHAPTER X

25 MARCH–21 AUGUST, 1916: On outpost duty along Ruwu; Rainy season begins; Havildar Zerdad's exploit; Relieved and withdrawn to Moschi; Malaria; New drafts; New general advance begins; March down Tanga railway; Arrival at Kwa Mdoe (Handeni); No longer fit for service owing to sickness; Recuperating in camp till 21 August

THE regiment remained on outpost duty until 11 April when it was relieved by the 29th Punjabis. This three weeks' duty ultimately caused more casualties, through malaria, than all the fighting had done, but its effects did not show themselves until some little time later. The exact line to be guarded extended from the Himo-Ruwu junction to about eight miles down the Ruwu Pangani River. All this front was low-lying and swampy, so that it was quite impossible to avoid infection.

It was an exceedingly busy and strenuous time. The fatigues were heavy and unending. Roads had to be made and repaired, block-houses built, bridges repaired and strengthened. All had to be done with the minimum of tools and material, and so demanded the maximum of labour. The normal routine of life went on as a matter of course while, in addition, touch had to be kept with the enemy, the country explored and mapped, and the strength of the enemy positions ascertained. To the men, but especially to the Mahsuds, these unceasing patrols were a godsend, as it enabled them to get away from the endless labour which otherwise filled their time, and helped them to remember that they were still soldiers and not merely coolies. Most of these patrols were, of course, uneventful, though they called for never-ending vigilance. Nevertheless they provided enough excitement and petty fighting to make men feel that life was still worth while.

Such an extensive sector could only be held at certain points. After the Brigade had been withdrawn Regimental

H.Q. moved to Kahe Railway Station, taking with them Nos. 2 and 4 Companies. No. 3 Company was left on outpost duty along the Ruwu, while No. 1 Company took over the defence of Kahe Kopje, about $2\frac{1}{2}$ miles south of the Kahe railway bridge. The two companies at Headquarters were occupied in repairing bridges over the Rau and Defu Rivers, in building a bridge to replace the destroyed railway bridge over the Ruwu, and in building the Ruwu blockhouse. On the 29th and 30th the companies at Headquarters relieved those on outpost duty.

On 1 April the Diary records a small patrol fight which may be taken as typical of much of the guerilla fighting that was to come and of the spirit of the Mahsud. Havildar Zerdad with a section of men who called themselves the 'jangian' (warriors) found the routine life in the Ruwu very monotonous and asked leave to go out on a long patrol. This was granted, and on his return he made a report which was received with considerable reserve by his Company Commander. 'Zerdad perceived this and resented it. He craved permission to be allowed to repeat his reconnaissance... and got his Company Commander's consent. He returned next evening somewhat tired but triumphant. He reported that when he approached the ridge covering the station (Kisangire Railway Station) he was certain that he would find a picquet, so he again extended his "jangian". He again advanced alone but this time keeping to the bush off the road. Creeping up the ridge, he hid behind a large tree and peering round saw a German officer inspecting the picquet. "So", he reported, "I just shot the officer, then the sentry, then a naik, then the bugler; and here is the officer's revolver, the naik's stripes, the sentry's rifle, and the bugler's bugle. So now you will perhaps believe my first story."'

For this, Havildar Zerdad was complimented by the G.O.C.s of the Division and Brigade. No. 35 Lance-Naik Zerim Gul also distinguished himself. It was a very good piece of work.

On 4 April the effects of living in such an unhealthy locality began to appear. Forty-three cases of malaria were reported by the Medical Officer. On the 5th and 6th the company reliefs were again carried out. Patrolling still went on, and again on the 5th there was a brush with the enemy near Kisangire Railway Station. This time the patrol was supplied by No. 1 Company. Enemy casualties, if any, were unknown. Our patrol had one man missing. His mutilated body was found and brought in two days later. Between the 9th and the 12th they were relieved by the 29th and withdrawn to Moschi.

Immediately after the arrival there the Diary records, 'About 300 men down with malaria'. As the bandas in which they were supposed to live were considered unhealthy they were burned and the whole regiment went under canvas. At Moschi they found life easier when not running fever temperatures, but there were a considerable number of fatigues to be undertaken, such as guards to the transport camp and for prisoners. Opportunity was taken of this comparative leisure to carry out company training and instruct the newly joined drafts in shooting and handling rifles. A few days later 250 men are reported with enteric fever though probably it was dysentery. On the same date is recorded that the 'rains broke'. That must have been because the Adjutant was too busy to notice the weather before. The Brigade diarist, having less to do, noticed that it was wet some days previously. Thus on the 13th, 'Rain made country round Kahe Hill a swamp'. It is curious that the Baluchis, who had only left Kahe Hill and its neighbourhood on the 12th, had not noticed the swamp. True they left on the 12th and the Diary only records the swamp on the 13th, but swamps are not formed quite so quickly even in tropical Africa. Probably having lived in a perennial swamp for three weeks they had got used to it, while the Brigade, knowing it was raining, and finding a swamp, connected one with the other as cause and effect. But there was no doubt that the swamps rapidly grew.

On the 14th it is recorded, 'Heavy rain most of the day; roads impassable for cars all day'. On the 17th the Defu River was flowing two feet above the bridge near Kahe. The following day 'rations very short', but the Defu, and in fact all the other rivers and streams, were making the best of it. On the 19th the Defu had risen another foot. On the 24th the Defu was still rising, after which date no one seemed to notice what had happened to the bridge over the Defu, or rather now well under it. After this the deluge, making transport almost impossible in the low-lying districts for some five weeks.

Until 19 May, when they were again on the march, there is little to record. The time was filled up with company parades and musketry courses, with instructional parades of various kinds, and with fatigues such as escorting prisoners and with combating sickness. Certain internal changes should however be noted. On the 18th, 97 Indian ranks of the 84th were ordered to join the 62nd Punjabis up the Persian Gulf, while their place was taken by a draft from Marseilles of 106 ranks under 2nd Lieuts. L. Brilliant and W. S. Goldsmith. With the draft came Jemadars Sikandar Khan, Dasin Khan, Sirdar Shah and Rahim Ali. A week later another draft arrived from the depôt in Karachi under Captain C. A. G. Money, while on the 17th Major A. G. Crawford, who had been with the regiment since February 1915, left to rejoin his own regiment in India. The regiment gave him a great send off, and he had earned it.

During this period also a certain amount of leave was opened for both officers and men to Nairobi. A few days before the regiment marched out again the G.O.C. Brigade, Brigadier-General J. A. Hannyngton, who had commanded them until just before the fighting at Kahe, visited them and presented ribbons to five men decorated for gallantry in France. At noon on the 19th they were again on the move and marched out at the head of the Brigade to Mue crossing, on the Taveta road, leaving behind them some

90 sick who were evacuated to Maktau. The following day they marched to Ruwu village, where they were again reinforced by a draft of 138 other ranks under Lieut. G. A. T. Cox, I.A.R.O. On 21 May they reached Kahe Kopje ready for the new offensive against the enemy. Even on the eve of a fresh campaign they did not waste time, but passed their leisure in practising bush fighting for the good of the newly arrived drafts. The advance really began on the evening of the 22nd when Captain Phillips, with No. 1 Company, was sent forward as advance guard to the column. Advancing to Kisangire Railway Station he found the place empty except for a few Indian traders. Ngata Hill was also found to be unoccupied. The column, with the regiment at the head, marched out the following morning, the 23rd, at 4 a.m.

It is now necessary to go back a little in order to consider the general situation. The period 21 March to 21 May marked a lull in active hostilities against the enemy save in the Kondoa-Irangi region, where the rainfall was less heavy and where in consequence active operations had been possible for a longer period. But it had not been a period of rest for anyone. The rapid advance from Mbuyuni and Longido, with the long marches under exceedingly trying conditions, had greatly exhausted the troops, while it had stretched out the lines of communication almost to breaking-point. When therefore the rains broke and the so-called roads disappeared the troops were threatened with almost complete starvation. There was no question of 'comforts' in East Africa at any time save for those at the base. Troops could consider themselves fortunate if they obtained their bare rations, which more often than not did not arrive, while to become a casualty, whether through enemy action or sickness, was to be condemned to purgatory. Every effort therefore had to be made to improve the roads and to link up the Taveta railway with the Usambara line.

At the same time the next phase in the campaign was being thought out. The data had to be collected and sifted and a definite plan arrived at. No easy task. How the decisions were reached is admirably and lucidly set forth in General Smuts's despatch dealing with this period. Here we are only concerned with the general plan and with the specific part which affected the 129th.

One of the first things to be done was to reorganise the very mixed forces under General Smuts's command. These were grouped into three Divisions. The 2nd and 3rd Divisions were composed entirely of South African troops, while the 1st, under the command of Major-General A. R. Hoskins, C.M.G., D.S.O., comprised the 1st East African Brigade under Brigadier-General S. H. Sheppard, D.S.O., and the 2nd East African Brigade under Brigadier-General J. A. Hannyngton, C.M.G., D.S.O. These Brigades contained British, Rhodesian, African and Indian units, and so were very mixed. The 129th found themselves still in the 2nd East African Brigade. Smuts writes in his despatch: 'The most important problem for consideration was the strategy to be followed in the coming campaign. As a result of the preceding operations we had just barely entered the enemy territory, which stretched out before us in enormous extent, with no known vital point anywhere, containing no important cities or centres, with practically no roads, the only dominant economical features of the whole being the two railway systems. Faulty strategy at the beginning, a wrong line of invasion once entered upon, might lead to months of futile marching and wasted effort. All our information credited the enemy with the twofold intention of conducting an obstinate and prolonged campaign in the Paré and Usambara Mountains and thereafter retiring to fight out the last phases of the campaign in the Tabora area, from which much of his supplies and most of his recruits were drawn'. After further discussion he proceeds: 'The direction of that movement (i.e. the campaign shortly to be described) was settled for me by the necessity of clearing the enemy from the Paré and Usambara Mountains before the further invasion of German East Africa could safely proceed. The general conception was to move eastward along these mountains, and at the point opposite Handeni to swing south and march toward the Central Railway in a movement parallel to that of van Deventer (who was to advance south from Kondoa-Irangi). The concentration of the enemy forces in front of Kondoa now made the occupation of the Parés and Usambaras comparatively easy, but the advance had to be rapidly executed to forestall any return movement of the enemy from Kondoa to the Handeni or Usambara area. Moving through the Massai Steppe along the old caravan route from Kondoa to Handeni, the enemy could reach the latter place in twelve days, and in two or three days more could be on the Tanga Railway at Korogwe. It was therefore advisable for my advance to reach the Western Usambara in a fortnight: further, if it could reach Handeni before the arrival of strong enemy reinforcements, I could have a second force almost the same distance from the Central Railway as that at Kondoa, and it would be impossible for the enemy to make effective resistance to the simultaneous advance of both columns situated 170 miles apart'.

Such was the problem. The enemy meantime had prepared for our main offensive coming via the railway, as this was the most obvious route by which the advance could be made. It was a route, moreover, which lent itself to easy and effective defence, while at the same time the defence would have the further advantage of the railway service. A direct attack along this route would therefore have been exceedingly costly in lives, while it would have been exceedingly slow. Smuts had neither the lives nor the time to waste. His plan was to avoid direct attacks against prepared positions, and to force the enemy out of these by threats to his flanks and rear.

The advance was planned, therefore, to be made in

three columns. The main body was to move down the left bank of the Pangani. With them went G.H.Q. and H.Q. 1st Division. A small column, consisting of the K.A.R. Mounted Infantry Company, the 3rd K.A.R., and a section of the 27th Mountain Battery under Lieut.-Colonel T. D. Fitzgerald, was to advance from Mbuyuni to the Ngulu Gap, while a third column, consisting of the 40th Pathans, 129th Baluchis, the 2nd Kashmir Rifles, with the 6th and 7th South African Field Batteries under Brigadier-General Hannyngton, was to move along the railway. Van Deventer was to remain where he was for the present and was not ordered forward until 21 July.

This combined offensive began on 18 May when Fitzgerald's column marched out of Mbuyuni for the Ngulu Gap. Hannyngton's column, as already recorded, moved forward on the evening of the 22nd and morning of the 23rd, while the main column under General Sheppard crossed the Ruwu bridge in the early morning of the 23rd.

We can now return to the 129th, already on the march since 4 a.m. General Smuts had emphasised the necessity for speed in the advance. This meant very long marches over a poor road purposely destroyed and obstructed by the enemy, who had been very thorough in their work. Throughout the advance there was little fighting, as Smuts's strategy had made it impossible for the enemy to hold their positions without the risk of being out-flanked by the main column, but nevertheless the advance was far from being a promenade. There was moreover always the risk of a fight and of being ambushed, so that the utmost vigilance was necessary. It was no mere route-march, but an infinitely laborious advance by troops searching the bush with flankers, protecting themselves with their advance guards always well ahead and continually on the alert. The strain imposed on all ranks by such an advance through thick bush was very great. For the advance guard there was the psychological and nervous strain of waiting to be shot, as often for great distances the bush was so close that mere alertness was of no avail. One knew the enemy was there after one had been shot at close range, often 10 to 20 yards. At least those in the rear knew. For the flankers there was the most exhausting toil of forcing their way through thorny scrub and high grass. Often it was a case of hacking their way with their pangas or long knives, specially issued for the purpose. For the main body it meant an infinitely slow march in dense clouds of dust and interminable waits in the glaring sun, for shade there was none. The toil and the tedium of these daily marches was beyond description, combined as they were with constant food difficulties. Nor was the day's work over when they had reached their objective. Each day on their arrival they had to construct the usual perimeter camp and go through the usual routine to prevent surprise, while in addition they were often engaged until the early hours of the morning making and repairing the so-called road for the transport to follow up. And day by day as they marched and toiled the fever caught in the Ruwu swamps began to show itself, until at length the greater part of the regiment was sick and lurching along dizzy and blind, till their burning bodies would stand no more. It cannot be emphasised too strongly that a fever casualty is just as much a casualty as any other, so that in reckoning up the regiment's toll the sick should be counted in with the killed and wounded. To be killed or wounded while assaulting the enemy is to fall nobly, but to march indefinitely, burning with fever or racked with dysentery, in a tropical sun until one dies or collapses on the roadside in a misery of pain and agony, is no whit less noble, though for this there are no decorations or mentions.

The first day's march brought them to Ngoya where they found water. This was seized and Laome Hill picqueted. This picqueting of hills was almost a routine procedure, as the road ran through hills all along its length. Small enemy patrols were met with, but retired after firing a few shots. Here they halted for the night. What they did next day is not recorded, but on the 25th they advanced towards Lembeni, finding the road constantly blocked. Great caution was exercised as they approached their destination, as it was thought that the enemy might defend it. The column was halted therefore about four miles out, while Captain Lewis was sent forward with two companies to occupy a position covering Lembeni. In addition, fifty rifles under 2nd Lieut. Jenkins seized Keili Hill. But the enemy had already gone, and by 6 o'clock they were all encamped at the railway station. Next day they marched within five miles of Same where they halted. Again it was anticipated that the enemy would make a stand, and plans were already made for a combined attack on the place in conjunction with Colonel Fitzgerald's column, which was approaching from the east. Again the threat to his flanks and rear was sufficient to make the enemy withdraw, so that shortly after 6 a.m. Same was occupied. Here the Brigade received orders to march via the Gonya-Mkumazi road, but found itself held up for lack of transport owing to the wastage due to the very bad state of the road. The difficulty was solved by dumping all superfluous ammunition, especially the artillery ammunition, and using the carrying capacity for supplies. Not that the gunners did not protest or point out that guns without ammunition were of little value. The inevitable retort was, of course, that soldiers without food were equally useless, and that there was more scope for infantry than for artillery. But the guns still went forward as a moral support! The march being resumed they left Same, and some ten miles east of it fell in with the 3rd K.A.R. The next day, the 29th, the Brigade was at Gonya. Thence they marched to Mikokani with two companies of the 129th doing advance guard, while the remainder of the regiment marched at the head of the column, a position coveted not so much as being the place of danger and honour as for its comparatively fresh air. The remainder of the column marched in their dust. On the 31st they were at Kalamba, whence at noon Nos. 3 and 4 Companies were ordered to march by road west of Lasa Hill to Bendela where they halted for the night, while the remainder of the regiment camped a couple of miles due east of Lasa. During this advance they surprised an enemy patrol, killing an askari whose rifle when examined proved to be the property of the 130th Baluchis. Such a recovery of lost property must have rejoiced all hearts, though there is no mention that Simla was informed. The Diary closes the month with an entry which gives much food for thought: '17.00 hours—enemy fired five or six shells which fell within a mile of the Brigade. Brigade then halted for night and all mules were sent back for water to Kalamba'. Was this the German way of dumping ammunition and is the entry to be read as cause and effect? Or was it the brevity of weariness?

The first of June came in unheeded, but found the regiment still in good strength with 17 British officers, including the Medical Officer, 19 Indian officers and 623 other ranks.

Before the month was out, fever on top of the endless hardships had reduced the fighting strength so greatly that almost for two months the regiment had to be left in camp, while only a machine-gun detachment marched with the Brigade. There is nothing to record but the itinerary to Korogwe, which was reached on the 15th, and the subsequent march to Kwa Mdoe near Handeni, which was reached on the 24th; after which date, until almost the end of August, they were really on the sick list.

Each day's march was much the same in its monotony and hardships. The retreating enemy showed very considerable skill in making the troops constantly deploy in order to advance against possible positions, so that a mere record of miles marched gives no indication of effort expended. On 1 July the regiment marched to Mkumazi, and there the Brigade halted until the bridge over the river should be repaired. Meantime there was patrolling to be done. On the 3rd they were sent to Langata where they bivouacked for the night. Next day they marched in the direction of Mkumbala with orders to find a camping-ground near a water-supply somewhere by the Ngoha River. Instead they found three companies of the enemy with five machine guns and one field gun in a well-chosen position waiting for them. There developed the usual bush fight in which one Indian officer and seven other ranks were wounded. But the fighting was not pressed, as orders had been received from the Brigade not to get heavily engaged. They got rid of a considerable amount of ammunition before returning to Langata. No. 4 Company, patrolling in the direction of Hill 620, had the pleasure of ambushing an enemy patrol who were trying to ambush them. They captured a wounded askari who 'gave very useful information'. But he was evidently somewhat of a raconteur. At least the Brigade thought so when summing up the veracity of his evidence. As a result of the enemy's presence there was much patrolling next day and some shots were exchanged. And so on until the Brigade was ready to march again. On the 8th the move forward began again. They marched with the main body to Mazinde: thence to Mombo, which was entered after very slight opposition. The roads about this locality were evidently worse than usual. After Ngoha River, black cotton soil was struck and made progress almost impossible. Having extracted themselves from its more than glue-like grip they found the road had converted itself into a watercourse, whence followed the sequence, 'Fatigue parties to help Pioneers—work not finished till dark'. It rarely was. Next day 'rocks in road and bad drift necessitated halting. Working parties out again till dark repairing road ahead'. As they approached Mombo they had the torture of seeing two trains puff away to Korogwe. It was certainly easier to retreat than advance. At Mombo they had a day's rest, but again pushed on, reaching the Vuruni River on the evening of the 11th, having left behind 2nd Lieut. Jenkins, Jemadars Durani and Nur Khan I with 110 other ranks to hold Mombo. Once more the road was impossible, so that the Brigade advance was held up for nearly 36 hours while fatigue parties worked day and night, without cessation, making the road and repairing bridges. By the afternoon of the 12th the road was ready and the Brigade marched to Makuyuni. The Diary makes dull reading during all this time, but they were feeling rather dull fellows. The Brigade found life more interesting. Thus when at Makuyuni, they received a visit from two German railway officials, who requested that they might be allowed to reside at Wilhelmstal 'to watch the interests' of the railway company. They had taken no part in operations 'except railway management'. Another time they received an 'intelligent Goanese' who gave them much information which seemed almost too intelligent. The advance still went on in spite of these diversions. It was expected that the enemy might put up a fight at Mauri, but again they withdrew, having very effectively destroyed the railway bridge. Finally, on the 15th they reached Korogwe at 11 a.m. after some resistance from the enemy, though there were no casualties. Again after a day's rest they moved forward crossing the Pangani by the bridge at Zugimoti plantation. This bridge had been saved from destruction by the foresight of the G.O.C. Brigade who had pushed forward the 3rd K.A.R. to seize and hold it. Having crossed the bridge their march was directed on Handeni. Marching at 4 a.m. they reached Zindeni at 10.30 a.m., having marched nearly 25 miles. Lieut. Jenkins's detachment which had been left at Mombo was again left behind at Korogwe. Next day, with Nos. 2 and 3 Companies under Captain Money as advance guard, they reached Kwa Mdoe (Handeni) where they remained for some considerable time, except for a two-days' excursion towards Ngambo, in which direction they were ordered, as Brigade had been informed that two enemy companies were advancing to burn Mgamba. As so often happened the enemy did not materialise.

By 24 June the regiment as such was no longer fit for service. The Brigade reported, 'The number of sick from fever very great. 129th Baluchis reduced to 158 rifles fit for work, and total infantry strength of Brigade reduced to 1115 rifles. The greatest sufferers were the battalions which did duty at Kahe'. There was only one wise thing to be done—to withdraw the entire regiment and send it to a really healthy place where it could regain its health. This for various reasons could not be managed, but they were allowed to rest and recuperate until 22 August. As the Diary puts it, it was 'decided to leave the regiment alone at Ndarema, give the men plenty of good food, and give every assistance for them to get fit'. After what they had gone through, these weeks of rest from strain and excessive labour and marching were indeed a time of relaxation in which they were gradually built up ready for fresh toils. But they were not days of idleness. To have allowed the men to do nothing, especially in such an environment, would have been merely demoralising. Those who could were given sufficient work building lines and block-houses so as to fill in the time, while company training went on systematically. Special efforts were directed to increasing the efficiency of the newly joined drafts, who came out inadequately trained.

Until 12 July they remained at Handeni, while the Brigade moved off again on the 8th taking with them a machine-gun detachment of three guns. This consisted of Lieut. MacIvor and 2nd Lieut. Goldsmith, 2 Indian officers and 77 other ranks. On the 12th they moved to Ndarema, a little to the north of Handeni on the Kondoa-

Irangi road, where they passed the month building a new camp for themselves and on various duties already enumerated. The new camp was rather a fine thing, and they almost became guilty of the sin of pride about it. 'At Ndarema the banda-covered camp grew into a really fine village. It was in a German rubber plantation, and the straight trunks and branches were exactly what was required for good building: bandas for barracks, mess-rooms and officers' quarters were constructed as well as roomy hospitals for the numerous sick.' But to prevent too much arrogance they were visited by a plague of 'dodus'. 'This was the worst place for "dodus" which the regiment occupied.' Foot inspections were held twice daily, and as many as 20 were sometimes taken from one man's feet. It was impossible to put a bare foot to the ground without picking up several. There were also lions, which were 'numerous and roamed round just outside the camp at night. Powerful block-houses, connected by V-shaped bomas, were constructed to protect the camp'. One is not quite sure whether the protection was against the lion or the enemy, probably both. Against the dodu there was none. One cannot but think that Moses's collection of plagues loses in artistic completeness by his neglect of the dodu. Even Pharaoh would have come to heel sooner with his toes full of dodus.

While the regiment was in Ndarema there was a certain amount of coming and going of officers and men. A few British and Indian officers had been on the sick list, but were not ill enough to be sent to the base hospitals, which perhaps was just as well, for evidently the South African nurses were not all they might have been, at any rate on matters of geography. One sick officer had cause to lament this defect, as his nurse would affirm daily—she was evidently a persistent woman—that Mount Everest was in Turkey. To have actually seen the mountain itself in the Himalayas, more or less in the direction of Tibet, and to be told that it had been moved, in these days of little faith is not good for malaria patients. On the 14th the Brigade arrived once more at Handeni *en route* to the Pangani. With it went Captain H. V. Lewis, who had been acting as Adjutant in the absence of Captain F. M. G. Griffin, away sick. Captain Lewis was attached to the 3rd Kashmir Rifles, and while with them won a bar to his M.C. Lieut. C. S. Browning also went with the Brigade as A.P.M.

And so the weeks passed while gradually the fever ran its course and the general health began, very slowly, to improve. The Diary records that 'every endeavour was made to make the men fit and to bring the effective strength of the regiment to its war establishment. Musketry, physical drill, rifle exercises, route-marching, etc., were carried out'. Meantime the trolley line from Mombo to Ndarema had been repaired so that supplies could be more easily brought through. Before marching out they were all completely refitted with clothes and boots. A few reinforcements also arrived. Finally, on the 21st three machine guns and two machine-gun teams arrived from the 5th Light Infantry, and with this hint came marching orders.

# CHAPTER XI

21 Aug.–28 Sept. 1916: Occupation of Tanga; March via Korogwe to Tanga; Embark for Bagamoyo; March from Bagamoyo to Dar-es-Salaam; Rest in Dar-es-Salaam; Re-embark; Detachments occupy Mikindani and Sudi; Headquarters return to Dar-es-Salaam

THE main tide of war had meantime swept south from Handeni in the direction of the Central Railway. Van Deventer's Division had begun their advance from Kondoa on 24 June, and by the end of the first week in August had cut the Central Railway at Kilimatinde and Dodoma. Everything was ready for a further advance, and once more an attempt was to be made to encircle the enemy. The 1st and 3rd Divisions were to resume their advance towards the railway through the Ngulu Hills. This was no easy task, as the enemy had massed here a great part of his troops, while he occupied very well-chosen and prepared positions. As usual, Smuts decided to get round the enemy, and for this purpose the 2nd Division was to move along the railway to Kilossa while the 1st and 3rd were advancing south. The hope was entertained also that if the enemy were not cornered in the mountains he would still be brought to bay at Kilossa. This hope was, as usual, frustrated.

Meantime there had been some very minor fighting in the Eastern Usambaras. Tanga had been occupied on 7 July and some small enemy forces dispersed, while on 15 August Bagamoyo was occupied and used as a base for further operations along the coast. It was now decided to occupy effectively the whole of the coast line, Dar-es-Salaam being the first objective. For this purpose a force of some 1800 rifles was assembled under Colonel Price. It was to form part of this force that the 129th marched on the 22nd.

On that date they 'marched with porter transport and camped for the night at Zindeni. The marching-out strength was 230 rifles, while about 90, who had just rejoined from hospital, were sent from Handeni to Korogwe in motor lorries'. Captain Phillips, with 50 men who were only fit for light duty, was left behind for garrison duty and had great difficulty in obtaining his freedom. He was first forgotten by the Post Commandant and then delayed, as the Commandant still thought he needed protection against the long-since-departed enemy.

Next day they marched to about 12 miles south of Korogwe, where they bivouacked in a rubber plantation. On the 24th they marched into Korogwe, where Captains Lewis and Browning rejoined them from the 2nd East African Brigade. Thence they went by train, a novel experience, to Tanga, where they received orders to embark on H.M.T. *Barjola*. This they did on the 28th, sailing at 5 p.m. for Bagamoyo. Here they landed during the morning, wading ashore waist deep, and were billeted in a school-house. They were still badly under strength, and so had temporarily attached to them 3 British officers and 200 Indian ranks of the 5th Light Infantry. A medical inspection showed as fit 12 British officers, 13 Indian officers and 328 other ranks. Of these 2 Indian officers, Subedar Abdullah Khan and Jemadar Durani, with 81 other ranks were left behind to form a depôt, while the rest marched on the 31st with 'B' column in the direction of Dar-es-Salaam.

The attacking force had been divided into three columns: 'A' column, consisting of the 40th Pathans, had marched at 2 p.m. for Ruwu railway bridge; 'B' column, consisting of the 129th, the Loyal North Lancashires and a naval detachment, marched at 2.30; while 'C' column, made up of the 2nd West Indian Regiment, set out at 4 p.m. along the coast.

Nothing very much happened. They marched to Singa and bivouacked but found no water. It was a 'quiet, clear night'. Next day they supplied the advance guards and marched at the head of the column, reaching Mapinga at 10 o'clock. Here they halted long enough to cook their food, and again pushed on in a heavy rain to Magoza where there was a good water-supply. On the 2nd the column marched to Gunja Peak, where Lieut.-Colonel Hulseberg and Major Money went sick with malaria. Next day, again supplying the advance guard, they advanced under the command of Captain Griffin, with Dar-es-Salaam as their objective. Great caution was exercised. A German gun emplacement, some five miles north-west of Dar-es-Salaam, was approached in fighting formation after a preliminary bombardment from the sea. But the enemy had gone with their gun, leaving only a dummy in its place. After this minor excitement they marched, less No. 3 Company, and bivouacked at Massassani. No. 3 was left behind as an escort to a wireless detachment, probably the same entanglement about which they had grumbled at Moschi. The next day at 6 a.m., at the head of the column, they marched into Dar-es-Salaam and civilisation. It was indeed a 'Haven of Peace' after so many months of marching and privation, with its beautiful land-locked harbour and white gleaming sand, with its well-shaded roads and its well-built bungalows. A place to rest the soul as well as the body after so many weary toils.

There they remained for a full week, during which the Diary records nothing at all, the surest indication of peace and rest. The week passed all too quickly, and on the 11th they embarked once more on the same transport, with a detachment of the 40th Pathans and the 5th Light Infantry, in order to complete the effective occupation of the remainder of the coast towns in accordance with General Smuts's plan. Next day they arrived outside Kilwa, which they were to know better very shortly, but passed on to Mikindani where, preceded by Marines and a naval detachment, they landed. There was no opposition and they bivouacked in the Customs House. Next day, the 14th, a detachment of 117 Indian ranks from Nos. 3 and 4 Companies, under Captain Browning, Lieut. Robert and 2nd Lieut. Smith, with Captain Dickson as Medical Officer, were posted as garrison. They were reinforced by three naval machine guns. The remainder of the force marched in the direction of Sudi. Halting at 5 p.m. they pushed on at midnight and reached Sudi at 1 p.m. on the 15th. Here Nos. 1 and 2 Companies were left under the command of Captain Lewis while Headquarters re-embarked on the *Barjola*, which sailed for Lindi with the 40th Pathans. This done the *Barjola* returned to Dar-es-Salaam, and Headquarters took up their residence at the barracks. Here they received two drafts, one under 2nd Lieut. Palin, of some 200 Indian ranks from Maktau, and the other under 2nd Lieut. Thatcher, who arrived a few days later, on the 24th. They remained until the 28th when once more they embarked, this time on H.M.T. *Edavana* for Kilwa and a fresh campaign.

Meantime the companies at Mikindani and Sudi passed the time pleasantly enough, though not in idleness. They were well fed, 'eggs, chickens and fish being available in large quantities'. What more could they want? With this diet and the general ease the men's health greatly improved, so that they were ready for the equally arduous days that were to come. Captain Lewis spent much of his time in teaching his men to swim. From Mikindani Lieut. Robert went further south into Portuguese territory, where he met and stayed with our noble allies and saw much that caused him to wonder. He was most hospitably entertained and returned full of glowing accounts of the abundant supplies of wine, without which our allies were unable to take the field. He also learned that the most comfortable way for an infantry officer to march was to be carried in a hammock. Finally, he was kissed by the General in command. After this he returned to the regiment and the realities of life.

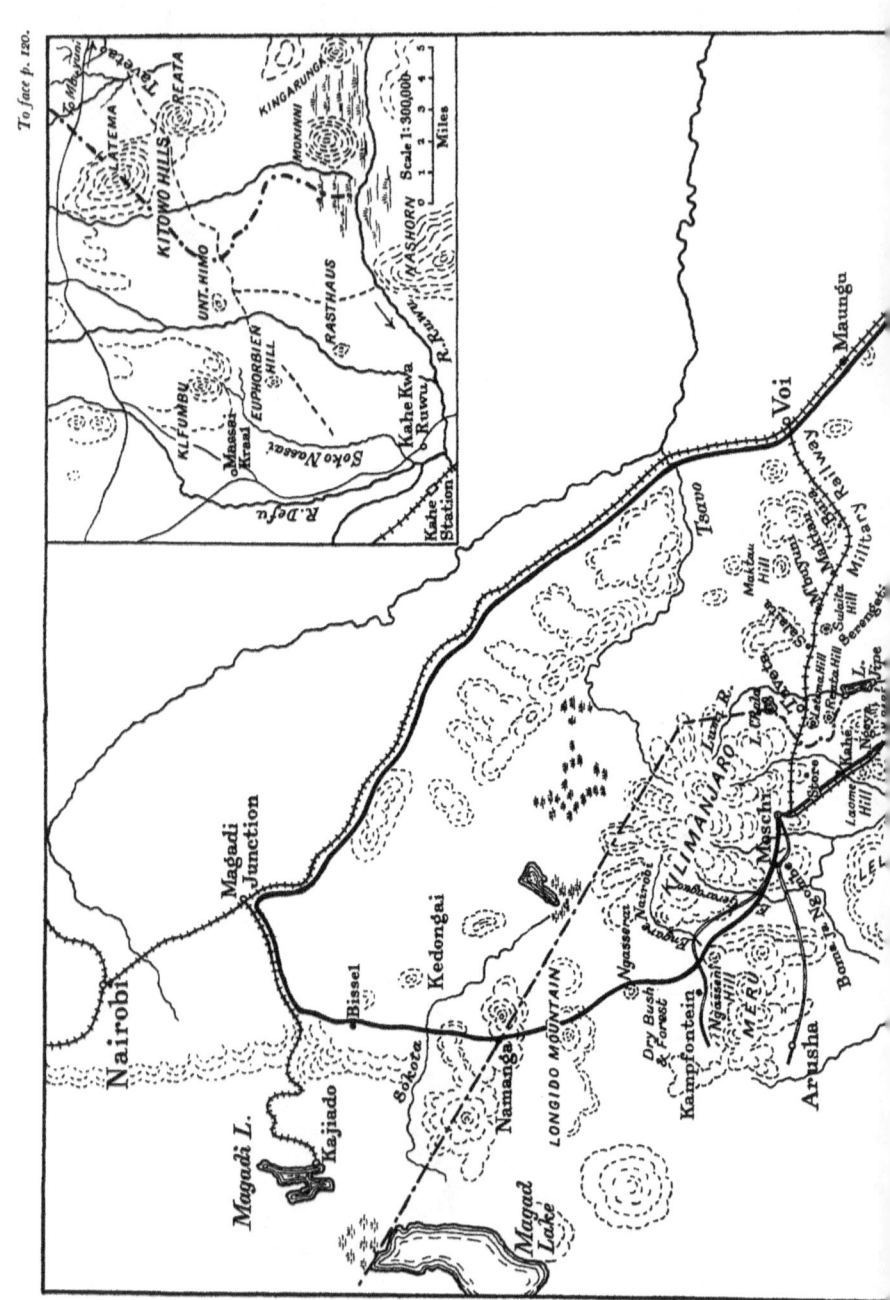

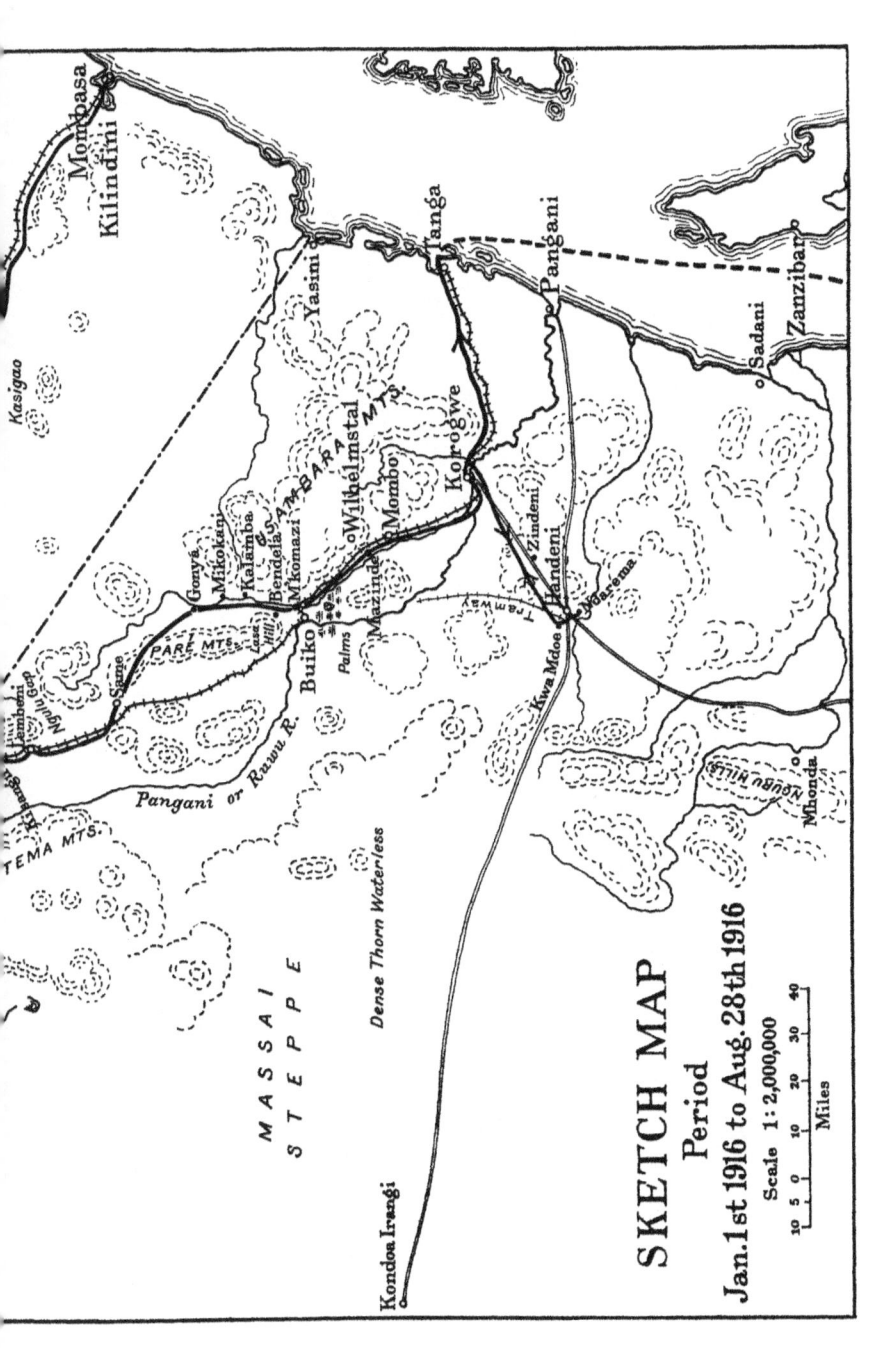

# CHAPTER XII

28 SEPT.–3 DEC. 1916: Transfer of regiment to Kilwa area; Occupation of Kibata; Patrolling

THE transfer of the 129th, together with the other units, under the command of Brigadier-General J. A. Hannyngton, to Kilwa, was part of a new plan of operations.

The fighting during the previous three months had failed to achieve General Smuts's primary objective, the complete defeat and capitulation of the enemy forces, but had succeeded in pushing them south from Handeni to a position some 30 miles north of the Rufiji River, along the Mgeta River.

It had been an excessively arduous campaign. The enemy had chosen his own line of retreat through the Nguru Mountains to the Central Railway and then again south through the Uluguru Mountains. He knew the country well and had prepared his positions beforehand. It was ideal country for defence and for rear-guard actions. Moreover the enemy was fighting on interior lines, and when compelled to fall back did so on to his supplies, so that each retreat simplified the problem of transport.

To have attacked these positions directly without a much greater artillery support would have meant a casualty list infinitely greater than that actually sustained without the promise of success. Apart from the waste of life which this would have meant, Smuts had not sufficient troops to throw away. He was compelled, therefore, to resort to turning movements, which, to be successful, entailed long marches under exhausting conditions, as speed was always essential to success. These marches were made over every kind of country by tracks so bad and difficult that the troops were almost always on short rations, as the transport could very rarely keep up with them.

By the time the Mgeta front had been reached the troops had almost outmarched the transport, which was operating over some 300 miles of track from the railhead at Korogwe on the Tanga Railway. Food-supplies were both precarious and inadequate. Horse transport had almost ceased to function, as the greater number of the animals had died from the tse-tse fly bite. The mechanical transport was in an equally desperate condition, having been shaken to pieces over the terrible tracks, misnamed roads. The greater part of the vehicles were in need of repair, but there were neither sufficient workshops nor spare parts for the work.

The troops, too, were utterly exhausted with excessive marching and fatigues, with constant underfeeding and exposure, and with sickness. Malaria and dysentery were universal, so that the hospitals were incapable of accommodating all the cases, while large numbers of those returned as fit were far from being so. No further operations were possible until the men had been properly rested and fed, and until there had been a complete reorganisation both of the forces and the transport. Finally, any new advance would lead into the swamps of the Rufiji, and the rains were imminent.

While the main drive had been due south there had been fighting on the other less important fronts. The Anglo-Belgian forces had been busy clearing the north-west of the enemy territory. Tabora had been occupied on 19 September, and the enemy forces from that district had made their way gradually, though with considerable losses, to the Mahenge Plateau.

The enemy were now confined to a comparatively restricted area. Smuts had written: 'The net result of all these operations... is that the Germans have been driven south over the Central Railway and are now disposed as follows: In the north-east, on the Rufiji River and about 30 miles to the north of it; in the west, along or south and east of the Great Ruaha River and Ulanga River. With the exception of the Mahenge Plateau they have lost every healthy and valuable part of their colony. In the east they are cut off from the coast, and in the south the Portuguese army have appeared north of the Rovuma'.

To attack along the Rufiji front would be to do exactly what the enemy desired, yet at the same time it was necessary to dislodge him from these positions. Once again the general idea was to encircle the enemy, to tighten gradually the circle and so compel a decisive action. At the same time every effort had to be made to prevent the enemy forces on the Rufiji and in the Mahenge Plateau from uniting. The execution of such a plan was difficult, as there were not enough troops to stop all the gaps had they been known, and our knowledge of the country was far from complete.

On 20 September it had been decided 'that Brigadier-General J. A. Hannyngton, C.M.G., D.S.O., should command a column which was to operate from Kilwa in the direction of Liwale'. Smuts at a later date describes this movement of Hannyngton's column to Kilwa as the first step in the formation of the 1st Division, 'which, after some reorganisation and transfer of units, was assembled later at the same place and was intended to take part in a great encircling move south of the Rufiji'.

The column was made up of the Loyal North Lancashires (who generally were too sick with malaria to supply more than some machine-gun crews), the 40th Pathans, the 2/2nd K.A.R., and the 129th, together with various technical troops. A nominal 2000 rifles.

The Kilwa area is about as attractive as other low-lying parts of German East Africa, which from the soldier's point of view is not saying much. The coastal area is low-lying, swampy in the rains and malarious, as is also the northern portion about the Rufiji. Lying not too far from the coast are the Mtumbi Mountains, comparatively low hills largely covered with bush of varying degrees of density and eminently suited to the guerilla warfare which soon developed. These hills are not too unhealthy. To the north they slope to the Rufiji swamps; to the south to the Matandu River; further west they slope away to the scrub-covered country bounded by the Luwegu River, a tributary of the Rufiji. In addition to being malarious the whole region, save some of the more elevated portions of the mountain area, lies in the fly belt, so that animal transport is not possible. This fact, coupled with the usual lack of roads and the breakdown of the transport elsewhere, made the Brigade Major record in the first paragraph of the Column Diary: 'It was realised that transport from Kilwa would prove a very serious question'. This prophecy was fulfilled. At the moment the only possible transport was by porters and the difficulty was to obtain sufficient of these.

The *Edavana* arrived in due course at the place of disembarkation facing Kilwa Kisiwani, not to be confused with the other and larger Kilwa Kivinje some few miles further north. Kilwa Kisiwani had been chosen as there was comparatively deep water inshore, whereas at Kilwa ships had to lie out a great distance. This was all that could be said in Kilwa Kisiwani's favour, otherwise it did not come up to expectation. Seen from the ship by the troops, who had already learned to expect nothing in Africa, it was nevertheless depressing. A slimy mangrove shore led gently up to firmer ground covered with scrub. Through this slime and its tangle of twisted roots the 61st Pioneers had already cut a way which had been continued some little distance into the bush, where it showed like an ugly red scar. Floating gloomily alongside this landing-place were a couple of dingy barges containing alleged drinking-water and food-supplies. Dotted along the shore and about the track were working-parties of the 61st Pioneers, groups of African porters and an odd assortment of humanity gathered from many continents.

The K.A.R. went ashore almost immediately after arrival, and being supplied with porters disappeared into the bush *en route* for Njinjo. Next morning the 40th Pathans disembarked and also marched off, together with four Machine-Gun Sections of the Loyal North Lancashires, for Matandu ford. The 129th, still composed only of Headquarters and the new drafts, were landed immediately afterwards, but were compelled to wait until the following morning as the supply of porters was exhausted. They made a camp, therefore, for the night, while Lieut. Palin with 20 men marched to Mtaba Hill to guard a naval gun against possible enemy patrols. They subsequently rejoined the main body, having met not the enemy but some of the local inhabitants—gorillas—with whom there were embarrassing encounters. That same evening a fresh convoy of porters arrived, so that the regiment was able to march at 6.30 next morning. The distance from Kilwa Kisiwani to Kilwa is some 15 miles over quite good road. The march was uneventful save for the fact that the regiment missed the water-holes owing to the map being faulty. This necessitated a long halt in the middle of the day, while search was made without much success. Eventually Kilwa was reached about 5 p.m. There had been a false alarm, *en route*, that Kilwa was being attacked, but fortunately nothing happened so that the new drafts were allowed to rest.

Kilwa possessed a few brick houses and some barracks, the front of which had been destroyed by shell fire. For the rest it was the usual collection of mud-built houses and huts. Its worst feature was the water-supply which was salty. For five days this was the only water that could be obtained. Afterwards a supply of sweet water was found several miles out of the town.

That night the men bivouacked in the town square facing the sea, but next day the regiment marched some mile and a half down the Liwale road, and there built a camp where it remained until 10 October awaiting orders. During these days little happened. The recruits were trained in bush fighting, while all ranks were occupied in the usual drill and rifle exercises. On the 6th Nos. 1 and 2 Companies under Captain Lewis and Lieut. Cox rejoined from Sudi, as also did Nos. 3 and 4 Companies with Lieut. Robert from Mikindani. The new drafts were distributed among the companies. On the 8th the regiment supplied an escort to a K.A.R. convoy proceeding to Njinjo. This on its return was attacked in the dark by a K.A.R. escort which mistook it for the enemy. One sepoy was killed before the mistake was discovered.

On the 10th the regiment, less 2nd Lieut. Graham and 43 men left behind to form a depôt, or because they were sick, marched out once more as part of a small column. The other unit was the 1/2nd K.A.R., one of the newly raised battalions. With them went the 139th Field Ambulance and the usual porter transport. Lieut.-Colonel Hulseberg was in command of the column, so that the command of the 129th devolved on Major Money.

The objective was Kibata, a stone-built fort occupying a position of some strategic importance in the Mtumbi Hills. The movement was made in conjunction with the Brigade plan for occupying the main strategic points in this district, and also as part of the general reconnaissance which had been going on since General Hannyngton's column had landed at Kilwa.

The whole position was at this time very obscure. An Intelligence Report, dated 7 October, purported to give what was then known of the general distribution of the enemy forces, but the information was scanty and not too trustworthy. General von Lettow states that there were five weak companies under Major Schulz, while two other companies with a 4·1-inch gun were at Mpotora.

Both sides were watching each other carefully. Von Lettow was chiefly anxious about his food-supplies, which had been jeopardised by the advance to the Rufiji. As this very fertile region was now within reach of the enemy he was forced to look for alternative sources of supply further south round Madaba and Liwale, while he played for time on the Rufiji.

Smuts on the other hand had temporarily 'reached the end of his forces', and was chiefly engaged until the end of the year in reorganising his troops and in preparing for his next campaign. It is probable that the best strategy would have been to seize the food-producing areas and so have starved the enemy into surrender or to have compelled him to attack. It is, of course, easy to be wise after the event, but there is no doubt that the enemy commander managed to do what he wanted and forced his opponents rather to dance to his tune.

The original objective of Hannyngton's column had been Liwale, and the enemy had been afraid lest this should threaten one of his alternative sources of supply. Gradually, however, Hannyngton had been drawn into the Kibata district instead. This change of direction was the more easily made as it held out to Smuts the tempting bait of an attack on the enemy's rear. The enemy knew this too but had calculated the situation rightly. Von Lettow writes: 'the Kibata country...was very mountainous and difficult for manœuvre, and as long as the enemy remained there I did not think it very dangerous'. He also had another reason for his confidence and this was his opinion as to the value of the troops opposed to him. For whereas most of his own troops were either natives fighting in their own country and so immune to disease, or whites who were well salted—and also well taken care of—his opponents were either largely whites who could not stand the diseases and hardships, or newly raised black troops who were inexperienced in fighting. He writes: 'At the end of 1916 I regarded the military situation in the Colony as remarkably favourable, for I knew that the South African troops were for the most part worn out with battle casualties and sickness, while a large proportion of the remainder were returning to South Africa at the end of their engagements. Prisoners had repeatedly assured us that they had had enough of the "picnic" in East Africa. The Indian troops also, who had been in the field in East Africa for some length of time, were reduced in numbers, while the late arrivals—we identified Indian Pathan Regiments in Kibata —consisted largely of young soldiers. Other regiments, like the 129th Baluchis, who had fought in Flanders, were without a doubt very good, but they might not be expected to stand the fatigues of African warfare for a prolonged period. The enemy's askaris were, generally speaking, new troops, and only a small proportion of them had at that time been in the field'. This estimate was a remarkably just one.

Such was the position when on the 10th the Baluchis marched together with the 1/2nd K.A.R. for Kibata. To those who had been in Africa for some time it was very much a repetition of previous experiences, though this time there was to be more than mere marching; but until the heavy fighting began at Kibata on 6 December there is little to record except continual marching and hardships, with occasional small fights from time to time.

The first day's march was short and easy, though dusty and hot, to the Matandu River, where camp was formed on the north side of the river. The 40th Pathans had been there for some time and were camped on the south side. Here was plenty of water, so that there was much washing and bathing during the remainder of the day. Next morning, helped by the moon, the column made an early start and was away by 4.30 for Kimbarambara, which was reported to be held by the enemy. The K.A.R. led, and by 7.30 a.m. had sighted the enemy on a ridge in front. The usual type of small action developed. In all these fights the enemy was merely fighting delaying actions and had no intention of defending his position indefinitely, as it did not serve his purpose to do so. His usual plan was to choose a good position for defence across the road of advance well defended on its flanks by thorn bush. This he held with a machine gun or two and with rifle fire from well-concealed trenches. To advance directly up the road on our part meant considerable casualties, as a frontal attack would be swept by the enemy's fire, which in the absence of any artillery was very hard to beat down. It was therefore necessary to work to the flanks while the centre engaged the enemy. These flanking movements were often prolonged and very exhausting, as the men had literally to cut and tear their way through the thorn bush. Finally, after some considerable time the flankers would begin to converge on the enemy, making it possible for the centre to move forward once more. Just when the attack was about to be pushed home the enemy would evacuate their position, having already sent their transport on when the fight began, and retreat quickly down the road, so that when the attackers made their final advance it was against an already evacuated position. All that was found, as a rule, were a few piles of still warm cartridge cases. Everything combined to help the enemy in these tactics of endless small rear-guard actions, but at the same time it must be admitted that he was exceedingly skilful in choosing his positions and in defending them. Occasionally he blundered either by counter-attacking at the wrong time or by holding his positions a little too long, and on such occasions we were able to get a little of our own back. But generally it meant that the attackers suffered the greater number of casualties and, what was equally important, were forced to exhaust themselves in laborious flanking movements so that the rate of advance was exceedingly slow.

Such was the nature of the attack which developed before Kimbarambara. By 8.30 a.m. the K.A.R. had pushed as near as was possible and the volume of fire was fairly heavy. At 9.15 a.m. the 129th was ordered to reinforce the right flank of the K.A.R. with one company, and No. 2 Company moved out accordingly. At the same time 'E' Company was sent to support their left flank, but by the time they were moving into position firing ceased and the enemy had retired. Whereupon the column advanced and encamped on the enemy's position. Two whites and one askari were taken prisoner. Other enemy casualties, if any, were unknown. The column lost one killed and one wounded, both K.A.R.

The same day in the afternoon a small patrol under Subedar Ghulam Jilani was sent out to capture some enemy askaris who were reported to be in some bandas, about one-and-a-half miles away. Shortly after they had gone heavy firing was heard, including machine-gun fire, so that No. 1 Company was sent to assist them if necessary. The patrol had found the enemy in position and had withdrawn. The remaining hours of daylight were spent watering and feeding the column and in making camp. The water-supply was very inadequate, as it was until Kibata was reached, so that the men suffered considerably from thirst as the advance continued. Next day the column was away again at 4.30 a.m. for Mianbondo with the 129th leading. This place was reached at 8.30 a.m. after a cool march, and a halt was called. Everybody was now congratulating himself on his good fortune and had already begun to think of food and perhaps a short rest, when suddenly there came a burst of machine-gun and rifle fire.

After the main body had halted, the advance guard, under Lieut. Robert and Subedar Mir Kambir Khan, had pushed on. The road led down into a valley which it crossed on a slightly raised track until it sloped up gently into fairly close bush. Here at the edge of the bush on the far side the enemy had placed two machine guns, hoping to inflict very severe casualties on any troops which should advance along the valley. The trap was an excellent one and worthy of success, but fortunately Lieut. Robert's bush sense had made him give the order to shake out into attack formation in case of trouble. The order had hardly been given when the enemy opened fire. Subedar Mir Kambir Khan also acted with great energy and resoluteness, pushing forward with his men into the thick grass. Here they were charged at very close quarters by the enemy, several whites with some askaris. Subedar Mir Kambir Khan with his men knelt down, and with the utmost coolness killed one white and mortally wounded another and captured an askari. The attack was stopped and the enemy retired as quickly as he had advanced. The skill and energy of these two officers certainly averted what might have been a very nasty little disaster. It might also be remarked that the men were mostly old sepoys who had been well trained to handle and use their rifles. One sepoy was killed. A tribute should also be paid to Ober-leutnant Steffans who so gallantly led the enemy attack and who was killed in so doing.

The water-supply at Mianbondo was very inadequate, so that the men were not watered till very late that night: many indeed got hardly any water at all. But if water was scarce, rats were plentiful. In the stillness which gradually fell they swarmed out in hundreds, running about in the moonlight among the sleeping men, searching for food, creeping into their clothes for warmth and biting the sounder sleepers, evidently thinking they were dead and therefore legitimate food, as did their brothers in Flanders.

Next day the column was on the road at 4 a.m. for Chumo. This day's march was by far the most trying and exhausting. The men were not properly rested from the strains of the previous day, and nearly all were very short of water and thirsty before the march began. The bush was fairly thick and the road in places very narrow, varying from a maximum of six feet to three. The enemy were known to be still in front, so that it was necessary to push out flankers who with the utmost difficulty made their way through the dense grass and bush. These naturally dictated the pace of the column, which marched for the most part in a haze of dust so dense in places that one could not see more than some 20 yards ahead. The men were crowded together and the day very hot, so that very soon they were drenched in sweat and parched and blinded with dust. The march was a succession of halts and slow advances which were also exhausting, as throughout the day there was no shade at all. Chumo was not reached till 3 p.m., by which time the almost total lack of water was making itself very severely felt, and many of the men were staggering along like drunkards with blackened lips and tongues. Every now and then a man would collapse, to be helped up by his almost equally exhausted comrades, who shouldering his rifle and kit staggered forward themselves with their increased burden. For the men with malaria or dysentery it was beyond endurance, marching as they did with temperatures of over 100°. These collapsed unconscious on the roadside, and were left until they could be succoured by the ambulance bearers and brought in later that night. So the interminable day seemed to prolong its weary hours for all, until suddenly, topping a slope, the column looked down on Chumo with its great grove of coconut trees laden with nuts and with its promise of water and shade. Almost in a moment the news had gone back and the weary were mustering their strength for the last effort.

Once arrived the temptation to obtain the nuts after the strains of the day was too much for the wretched porters, who had suffered more than any others from thirst. In an incredibly short space of time there was at least one man at the top of every tree, hurling down nuts to the grave danger of the struggling mass of men snatching for the prizes below. A few of the recruits, forgetting their recent training, joined in the scramble, so that for a few minutes there was a small riot. This was quickly quelled with the help of the older sepoys, who still maintained their discipline. The nuts were collected and distributed properly, while the Supply Officer was left to settle with the owners. But the day was not yet over. The water-holes were found to contain only a few inches of black mud, so that search parties had to be sent out while the remainder made camp. Eventually a good and plentiful supply was found about a mile back, off the beaten track. From this the men were watered, though the procession continued until about 10 p.m.

Though the day had been so exhausting the column was on the march by 4 a.m. next day with the 129th leading. The route was now over very hilly ground, and in some places was so steep and abrupt that the men could only pass by sliding and climbing down. Half-way a halt was called by a small stream, after which the final march was made. It had been anticipated that Kibata would be defended, and plans had been made accordingly. As the column neared its objective the fort could be seen standing out against the sky, but soon this view was lost as the road twisted and dipped among the hills. The approach was made with great caution, but the scouts found the place abandoned, except for a white missionary and a few women and children.

This peaceful occupation was duly appreciated, for Kibata is no easy place to attack as the enemy found to his cost some few weeks later. Properly held it could have caused very considerable casualties to the advancing column. The remainder of the day and the whole of the next day were given over to rest and washing, and on the 17th the column, less the 1/2nd K.A.R. left in occupation, started on its return march to Mitole, taking with them various odd prisoners and the women and children. They also took some two dozen fowls. This caused some correspondence with the appropriate official at the base, who issued his formal reproof and showed his righteous indignation at such an act. Being well fed himself he probably failed to realise that the column was not, and that for several days the officers' ration had consisted chiefly of inadequate supplies of bully beef and biscuits, so green with rottenness and so full of weevils and maggots that they could only be eaten with the eyes closed. The fowls were well worth the reprimand.

The return march was uneventful. Having no enemy to search for and knowing where water was to be found, the marches were merely dull. Matandu was reached on the 18th, and next day Lieut.-Colonel Hulseberg proceeded to Kilwa, while the regiment, less Major Money, 3 Indian officers and 126 other ranks left behind as a garrison in place of the 40th Pathans, marched under Captain Lewis for Kimbarambara, *en route* for Mitole, which was reached on the morning of the 20th. They at once proceeded to put it in a state of defence, and there the regiment remained until 5 November.

On their arrival they received a message from the G.O.C. thanking them for their good work. So far the Brigade could congratulate itself. Figures showed that whereas the enemy had lost 77 in casualties of all kinds, the Brigade had lost only 17.

The days at Mitole were occupied with the usual employments, but there was much patrolling, especially in the direction of Njinjo, Ndende and Kimbarambara. One of the many duties of these patrols was map-making and correcting, as the so-called maps were exceedingly sketchy and inaccurate. This is well illustrated in the confusion which resulted from an apparently simple order from the Brigade that the 129th should send 100 rifles from Mitole to Mtumbei Chini, where in a very short time they were to be relieved by the 1/2nd K.A.R. from Kibata. The Diary merely reports: 'On the 23rd Captain Lewis, 2nd Lieut. Palin, 3 Indian officers, 100 other ranks with a maxim marched at 15.00 hours to Mtumbei Chini via Ndende....' It does not repeat the sequel, which can only be pieced together from odd remarks in the Brigade Diary and in a record kept by the Adjutant of the 129th. Actually

Mtumbei is a district about the size of a medium-sized English county and is covered with bush, so that movement is only possible along so-called roads and native tracks. This was not realised at the time the order was given, the impression being that it was a definite spot. Hence when the patrols from the 129th, the 1/2nd and the 2/2nd K.A.R. set off under their guides to Mtumbei, and in due course reported that they had arrived, but that up to date they had seen and heard nothing of the other patrols, there was considerable anxiety in the various Battalion H.Q. and much perplexity at Brigade H.Q. Hence the laconic entry in the Brigade Diary, 'Misunderstanding about position of Mtumbei Chini'. This misunderstanding continued for a week, while African runners ran hundreds of miles with messages and sketch-maps to Battalion H.Q. and thence to Brigade H.Q. 'The last few days have been rather agitated. Everybody from Brigade H.Q. to the newest recruit in the regiment has been trying to solve the great question, where is Mtumbei Chini? The 2/2nd K.A.R. have found three possible Mtumbei Chinis. The 1/2nd K.A.R. have a special one of their own. Lewis has gone to our Mtumbei and is waiting for the 1/2nd to relieve him. The Brigade has sent us a composite map made up of three sketch-maps superimposed, one from each of the three patrols. It fairly bristles with Mtumbei Chinis. This, however, is only half the trouble, as there is a Mtumbei Juu, which also seems to wander at will round the country-side. This has got mixed up with the Chinis so that the maps simply dance with Mtumbeis, some Chini and some Juu. More letters, more sketch-maps are sent, and the runners send up the mileage covered to an unprecedented figure. Finally, it is settled beyond a doubt that the Brigade has been misinformed and that the Mtumbei Chini they mean, and which they wish to be held, is not an Mtumbei at all but an Abdullah Kitambi. So peace at last.' The incident closes with one of those majestic decisions so frequent and necessary in war time. 'Spot where main road from Utete to Kibata via Ngarambi crosses the Mtumbei River, to be known as Kitambi.' Meantime Lewis and his patrol were on one-third rations, and everybody had discovered that Juu meant north and Chini meant south. While in camp this patrol very narrowly escaped being burnt. 'We were attacked by a very serious bush fire which came down with the wind at a great pace in a wall of flame. Only by extreme exertion was a lane of grass cut sufficient to stop the main attack, while in places where the fire leapt the lane the men were able to beat it out.'

Gradually the various detached units joined up again, while two small drafts, one under Subedar Turkestan of 69 men and the other under 2nd Lieut. N. W. W. Johnstone of 51 men, also reported for duty.

Meantime the enemy was beginning to turn his attention to Kibata, and already there had been a reported move of several companies from the Rufiji front. The various units in the Brigade had been warned of this probability, so that as the month of November passed patrol work became more active while the Kibata garrison was ordered to strengthen its defences. Captured despatches also revealed a threat to Njinjo from the German force at Mpotora. It was this latter threat which caused the rather sudden move from Mitole to Njinjo on the 5th and thence to Lunguani, while the larger movement against Kibata eventually drew the regiment to that place. There is a constant coming and going, sometimes of the whole regiment, often of companies and patrols, which is rather wearisome to record and read but which is typical of the East African fighting.

On the 5th the regiment marched to Njinjo, having left a garrison at Mitole. There they bivouacked on Chemera Hill, which is stony and hot. Meantime the supply column had got lost so that all were on short rations, that is shorter rations, as very rarely did the regiment ever get full rations and never at this period. While there, came news of an enemy attack on Kibata held by the 1/2nd K.A.R., with orders to send a company to Kitambi to relieve a company of the 1/2nd which was being drawn in to Kibata. No. 1 Company under Lieut. Cox marched at 5 a.m. on the 6th after having denuded the rest of the regiment of all their food-supplies. A little later the regiment, less No. 1 Company, marched to Lunguani with orders to halt where the Mpotora road met the Nambanji road. The road junction proved to be a myth, so after considerable delay they bivouacked near the 2/2nd K.A.R. on a stony ridge devoid of vegetation or shade. There they grilled for the better part of two days till the necessary map correction had been made, after which they marched back to Chemera Hill on the morning of the 8th. The same day they marched again *en route* for Kitambi. The evening march in the cool of the moon was pleasant. A halt was made about 10 p.m., but after a few hours' rest they were on the march again for Kitambi which was reached at 10.30 a.m. Lieut. Robert and 2nd Lieut. Palin rejoined from Mitole, while No. 1 Company was already there. There the regiment remained until the evening of the 12th awaiting further orders and patrolling in the direction of Ngarambi and Nambanji. By this time everybody was feeling very tired, partly with the marching, but chiefly owing to the exposure to the full sun at Chemera and Lunguani. The continued shortage of food and complete absence of any fresh food or vegetables was also beginning to affect the general health, while malaria and dysentery were increasing. But the next five days were to be equally fatiguing. On the 12th Kibata reported that an enemy patrol was at Mtumbei Juu near the Mission. Orders were issued to the 129th to march at once for that place. This they did, setting out at 8 p.m. and arriving at 2.30 a.m. The road is hilly and not too bad, except in one place near Tawa where it rises in three almost perpendicular ramps which had to be climbed. As usual the patrol had departed long before the regiment arrived. All that was found was a gramophone which sang patriotic German songs in a loud voice until it was silenced by direct orders from the Commanding Officer. On the morning of the 15th the regiment again marched for Kitambi, leaving a garrison at Mtumbei Juu, but next day were ordered back again to Kibata, 'upon which there was much swearing'. Before marching out, a detachment of the 5th Light Infantry, which had been with the regiment, received orders to rejoin their own regiment at Kilwa. As it was anticipated that there would be trouble getting the mules up the ramps an early start was made and Tawa was reached at 8 p.m. It is recorded that 'great difficulty was experienced in getting the mules over this stage' and that they 'were very exhausted'. So was the whole regiment, which hated those mules that night more than ever mules have been hated before. Major Money with Lieut. Johnstone and 100 rifles were left at Kitambi. Major Money was and had been really ill with malaria for several weeks and was not fit to march. Lieut. Robert, who was also ill, was sent to the Field Ambulance.

In spite of the strenuous march of the previous evening the regiment was away at 4 a.m., and after rationing Lieut. Cox at the Mission reached Kibata at 8.30 a.m. in time for breakfast, which contrary to all expectations was awaiting them, thanks to the hospitality of the 1/2nd K.A.R.— sausage, bacon and coffee. A meal still remembered, and which made even the mules appear in a new light.

Kibata was well worth all the toils to reach it. Situated at a considerable elevation it was healthy and cool. There was plenty of water and a good supply of fresh vegetables. Here the regiment was to remain until well into January. There was plenty to do, as it had to be put into a state of defence in anticipation of an enemy attack of which the Brigade had vague warnings. As there were now two units present Lieut.-Colonel Hulseberg took over the duties of

Officer Commanding the Post, while Captain Lewis was in command of the regiment.

On the 18th the regiment relieved the 1/2nd K.A.R., and took over various posts which had been established on the surrounding hills, while the 1/2nd went into reserve. Patrolling also went on to the east and north in the direction of Pungatini and Mwengei. After five days of this they were in turn relieved by the 1/2nd K.A.R., and in turn went into reserve. On the 24th Captain Browning, Lieuts. Wilson, MacIvor, and 2nd Lieut. Goldsmith, with 2 Indian officers, 34 other ranks and two machine guns rejoined for duty, having been absent from the regiment since 1 August, when they marched with the 2nd East African Brigade.

Captain Browning brought with him a well-filled chop-box, as also did the others. He also brought with him an African *chef* of whom he was inordinately proud and who, it was asserted, could cook a real dinner worthy of a French menu—provided of course that the Supply Officers at the base were willing to send up a few raw materials to work on. Patrolling still went on as a routine affair but provided little excitement or news. The Diary has little to say, and the patrols certainly less, about the coming storm, so that everything went quietly until the 6th. On 3 December Nos. 2 and 4 Companies under Lieuts. Palin and Smith relieved the 1/2nd K.A.R. in Picquet Hill, so that the 129th were in the line when the attack developed.

# CHAPTER XIII

6 DEC. 1916–13 JAN. 1917: The fighting in and around Kibata; The enemy retire north; Action at Mbindia

THE fighting at and around Kibata stretched over a period of almost six weeks, beginning on the morning of 6 December and continuing until 13 January, 1917, when the action near Mwengei may be said to mark its close. It was one of the most important series of actions in which the regiment took part in East Africa, though it could not compare with the spectacular slaughters of Flanders.

Kibata, as already mentioned, occupied a very important strategic position, for it was the main junction and switching point for the troops of the 1st Division as they faced north and watched Utete and Mohoro. It should never have been abandoned by the enemy in the first instance and, if recovered, would have checked any advance north from Njinjo via Abdullah Kitambi and the Mission, while the whole line of communications from Kilwa would have been in danger.

Von Lettow had at first been too preoccupied with the problem of his food-supplies to pay much attention to the British forces at Kibata, and knowing the nature of the country he could afford to take risks and wait. Gradually, however, the slow but steady advance of these forces made it necessary to take action. He had already dealt with the Portuguese to his very considerable gain in stores and equipment, while at the same time the front north of the Rufiji had stabilised temporarily. He was therefore at liberty to move a considerable body of troops against Kibata. He writes: 'I considered it necessary to transfer strong forces from the neighbourhood of Kissingere towards Kibata. No opportunity had presented itself of fighting a decisive successful battle north of the lower

Rufiji, as I had expected. I was obliged to proceed to a prolonged operation in the mountains of Kibata, which offered but little prospect of leading to a decision'.

One cannot agree that he thought the Kibata offensive so unimportant as he makes out. To a General of his experience Kibata must have held out considerable hope of success and, in fact, he almost succeeded. He ought to have done so had his troops really pushed in to the final attack on the day they captured the 'Lodgement'. Had he taken Kibata he would in all probability have annihilated the whole of the British forces there and could have rolled up the Kibata front very completely. It might not and would not have finished the fighting, but it would have had very important results for the Germans, and would have greatly strengthened their position in all this part of East Africa. He failed because his troops, though excellent in defence and in bush fighting, had not quite enough nerve for a real assault such as the situation required.

On the other hand the British forces had little to congratulate themselves upon save that they were willing to take punishment and to face hard fighting. The element of surprise when the attack opened on the 6th should never have been there, as the enemy offensive had been expected for a considerable time. The trenches and strong posts were inadequate and hopelessly exposed to gun fire after more than five weeks, during which there had been time to construct them. They had been made on the assumption that it was impossible for the enemy to bring up guns. As so often happened, the Germans did the impossible. Finally, food and medical stores were lamentably short. What saved the situation at the moment of crisis was the fact that the 129th had been well trained in Flanders to a tradition of heavy gun fire, to being slaughtered patiently, and to the necessity for pushing home assaults. Bush-fighting tactics will not win a war, though they may prolong one.

Kibata has been described as 'an inverted cup standing in a high-rimmed saucer, the rim in some places, as at Picquet Hill, overlooking the top of the cup'. The writer continues: 'The main defences were on the rim, which it was essential to hold, as it can be easily imagined that, were one part of the rim held by the enemy, the sides of the cup and any part between the cup and the rim would not only be exposed to fire, but in many cases to close-range enfilade fire, besides affording a perfect Observation Post for gunner-officers. The Fort was in the centre of this inverted cup.

'The defences had, unfortunately, been prepared under the assumption that the Germans would not bring up guns over the abominable country which they would have to cross. Bush was cleared away, and the redoubts on Picquet Hill, the highest point of the rim and the key of the position, stood out clearly for anyone to see from the next ridge.

'So thick was the bush and so precipitous the hills beyond Kibata that neither our own patrols nor those of the K.A.R. reported definitely the coming of artillery, and its presence was not known until the first shot was fired'.

On the morning of the 6th when the fighting began the garrison at Kibata consisted of the 129th Baluchis mustering 8 British officers and 240 Indian ranks; and the 1/2nd K.A.R. with 17 British officers and 563 African ranks. There were 7 machine guns. All the picquets and posts were found by the 1/2nd K.A.R., except on Picquet Hill which had been taken over by the 129th on the 3rd. Here there were 150 rifles. In reserve there were the remaining 90 rifles of the 129th and one company of the 1/2nd K.A.R.

The offensive opened about 1 o'clock on the afternoon of the 6th, but the heavy fighting began the next day. The enemy's advance 'was observed commencing with the occupation of Ambush Hill by 60 rifles with 2 machine guns. This was followed shortly afterwards by the occupation of Cocoa Nut Village, our picquets at both these points being driven in'. Both these positions lie to the north of Kibata, where the outposts were located on the second ring of hills which surround Kibata Fort. After this the fighting

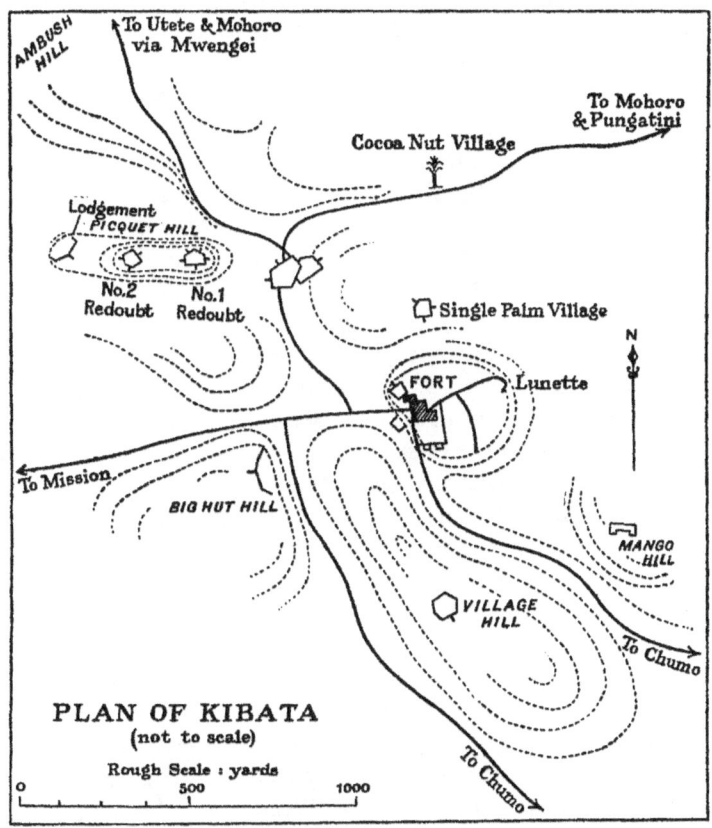

took the form of heavy machine-gun firing and rifle fire until about 6 p.m., when the enemy were driven temporarily from Cocoa Nut Village by long-range machine-gun fire from the Lunette near the fort. With the darkness the fighting died away except for occasional firing and some sniping. Picquet Hill came in for little attention, but already, in anticipation of trouble, Major Lewis had taken over command. The next morning at 6.30 the enemy attacked Palm Village and Single Palm Village, posts on the inner rim of hills, both held by the K.A.R. The attack was in considerable force, but was held up. Its object was twofold, to encircle Kibata if possible, but also to pin down the garrisons of these places and to divert attention from the main attack upon Picquet Hill. This hill is a long narrow ridge on the north-west side of Kibata, separated by a valley from the fort and by another valley on its west and north sides from a higher ridge occupied by the enemy on the previous day. Originally it was covered with thorn bush, as were all the surrounding hills, but as already mentioned this had been cleared away by the K.A.R. when they had begun fortifying it some weeks previously. It was defended by two redoubts rather like the strong-posts in Flanders in size though not in strength, as it had not been anticipated that the enemy would employ artillery. Hence there were no real dug-outs, but only shelters, while the trenches themselves were not deep enough. Communication between these redoubts was effected by paths on the southern slope of the hill; there were no communication trenches between them on the top. No. 1 Redoubt defended the eastern portion of the ridge and looked out towards Mwengei, Palm Village and towards the Mohoro road. No. 2 Redoubt occupied the western portion and faced the higher ridge across the scrub-covered valley. Below this redoubt was a slightly lower feature, later called the Lodgement, held by a small picquet. The ridge, with its cleared top, made an excellent target for artillery and the Germans were good gunners.

Had this position been captured, as it ought to have been, the enemy would have commanded all the roads leading into and out of Kibata, while at the same time it would have enabled them to observe the slightest movement on the part of the garrison, and so direct their gun and machine-gun fire with complete accuracy. Also it completely commanded one of the two water-supplies and enabled machine-gun fire to sweep the road leading to the other. Its capture would have meant the fall of Kibata, with the complete defeat and possible capture of its garrison.

The actual attack was not delivered until the evening, as the enemy evidently hoped to blow the garrison off the hill with artillery fire. They began therefore a long bombardment about 8.30 a.m., which was directed chiefly against No. 2 Redoubt, although No. 1 came in for a fair amount of attention. Three guns were employed, a 4·1-inch naval gun, an 88 mm. howitzer and a field gun. These steadily increased their fire until between 9.30 and 11 a.m. it became very severe, almost 100 shells bursting into or over this small redoubt, which measured some 40 by 20 yards. Casualties were considerable, as all the men could do was to crouch down at the bottom of the trenches while the storm lasted. Many were buried, but were rescued by their comrades. All the time the enemy machine-gun bullets whipped the parapets, making observation very difficult and hazardous. But the expected attack did not come: instead the shelling died away into a desultory fire supported by bursts of machine-gun fire, which lasted until 5.30 p.m. Meantime the garrison laboured to repair their shattered trenches and parapets, but little could be done in the daylight. Once again at 5.30 p.m. the barrage fell with even greater intensity for half an hour, during which time even more shells fell upon them and completely destroyed what remained of the redoubt. But the garrison still hung on, led by their officers both British and Indian. Parched with thirst, burnt with the sun, they crouched among the dead and the wounded, still waiting for the expected assault. Still the trenches fell in. Major Lewis was buried once, Lieut. Palin three times, Lieut. Smith shot in the head, and these experiences were but those of the sepoys. At 6 p.m. the guns lifted and the long-expected attack was delivered, only to be shot to pieces and brought to a standstill by the survivors. During this phase Captain A. Caldicott, who with a platoon of K.A.R. had been sent to reinforce the 129th, was shot dead. The Baluchis had justified von Lettow's high opinion of them: Punjabis and Mahsuds of No. 2 Company vying with each other in endurance and courage.

The enemy, however, had established themselves some 80 yards away on the edge of the ridge, the Lodgement. There they entrenched and made life more difficult and unpleasant for Kibata than it had been before, as it put one water-supply out of action and made movement in and about Kibata more difficult.

So soon as night had come the survivors were relieved by 'C' Company of the 1/2nd K.A.R. This relief was completed by 9 p.m., while the wounded were finally evacuated towards midnight.

The following morning the attack was again renewed against the K.A.R. Supported by shell fire and machine-gun fire the enemy assaulted three times. At 9 a.m. the position was considered serious as the attackers had reached the obstacles in front of the redoubt, though these were not very formidable, as barbed wire was rare and the enemy guns had been too effective. Captain Browning was sent with 60 rifles of the 129th as a reinforcement, but before he arrived the danger had been averted and the enemy driven back.

While this second attack was being made on Picquet Hill the enemy had also been attacking elsewhere with the same objects as before. Heavy machine-gun fire was directed against Plain Hill and Big Hut Hill. On the former was a Baluch machine gun under Jemadar Fateh Haider, I.O.M. During the fighting the enemy got a direct hit on this gun, killing Jemadar Fateh Haider and wounding two of the crew. The gun was wrecked. Another machine gun in No. 1 Redoubt was also put out of action in this way. Jemadar Fateh Haider's death was a great loss to the regiment. He had been with it from the first and had shown great bravery on many occasions, especially when at Givenchy on 20 December, 1914, he fought his machine gun until his sap-head was literally surrounded by Germans.

The 9th was a day of comparative calm, though it was not to end so peacefully as it had begun. The enemy had abandoned his assault tactics and was confining himself to gun and machine-gun fire. The Brigade writes: 'He occupied points of vantage from which he fired on all movements, gradually extending these round our positions. From his observation points he directed gun fire at any point that was likely to cause us loss, so moving his guns that if possible no portion of the position should remain safe'. The effect of this was that in a remarkably short time Kibata and the neighbouring hills rapidly became a rabbit warren, and for a time trench warfare developed. The most annoying and dangerous enemy position being the Lodgement, it was decided that it must be recaptured. This was to be effected by a night attack, to be led by Captain Browning with No. 4 Company and two platoons of the 1/2nd K.A.R.

Meantime the gravity of the position at Kibata was beginning to react upon the distribution of the remaining troops in the Kilwa area. Though the Kibata garrison had repulsed the first attacks, they had lost considerably, and, under the increased strains coupled with very inadequate rations, fever was making itself felt. Reinforcements were necessary to make the situation secure, but more especially if the enemy were to be forced to retire. At 2 a.m. the 2/2nd K.A.R. arrived from Mitole, having covered a distance of 40 miles over difficult hilly country in drenching rains in 34 hours. With them came a section of the 27th Mountain Battery as a reply to the enemy artillery. The

Brigade had also decided that the best way to relieve the pressure on Kibata 'was to act with a force against the enemy's right flank from the direction of the Mission at Mtumbei Juu. The Gold Coast Regiment was accordingly ordered to proceed to Kitambi, while the 40th Pathans were temporarily drawn in from Ngarambi to take over from them'.

Though calm, the day was not without its alarms. Thus the Diary records, '7 hours, heavy firing heard from direction of Mikurumo. This proves to be an enemy party firing at battery mules going to water...9 mules reported lost or killed'. At 10.15 a.m. the enemy are reported 'to be digging in on their lodgement on Picquet Hill. We unable to hinder this as they have excellent covering fire from snipers and machine guns'. At 11.30 a.m. the two mountain guns opened fire on the enemy digging party, and so the day passed.

Captain Browning's attack was ordered for 10 p.m. and was to be 'preceded by two rounds of gun fire' and covered by machine-gun fire from No. 2 Redoubt. It was duly launched, and the first line led by Captain Browning reached the enemy trenches, where he was shot at point-blank range on the enemy parapet. A few of his men penetrated the trench but were immediately counter-attacked and driven out, and the attack broke down. Captain Browning's loss was very deeply felt. He was one of the original cadre of officers who had sailed from India with the regiment in 1914 and had been with them practically all the time. When the attack on Kibata began he was in hospital suffering from dysentery, but immediately insisted upon rejoining his men and continued with them until his death.

From now onwards the fighting was essentially of the trench-warfare type, with its monotony and occasional excitements. The regiment took its turn in the trenches and at the various posts and occupied its so-called leisure moments building more and better trenches, constructing dug-outs and eating what meagre rations were available. The weather also began to break up, and there were a number of wet days which did not add to the brightness of life. But the garrison was far from dull and by no means dejected. Owing to the hilly nature it was possible to walk about if one chose the correct places, and the dangerous ones soon became known almost by instinct. While in reserve, except near the fort one could live in the usual 'banda'. Even the trenches had a friendly feel for those who had been in Flanders. The position resembled in some respects a siege, as the enemy almost encircled Kibata. The two roads which still remained open were for a time constantly threatened, so that the arrival of convoys was a difficult and problematical business. A few enemy patrols on the Chumo road might have precipitated a food crisis. Food was indeed a constant difficulty, and for most of these six weeks everyone was on very short rations. The worst fed of all the troops were the British officers. The commissariat catered in a grudging way for the sepoys, but generally went on the principle that the few British officers were not worth the trouble. Hence the totally inadequate supply and the rotten biscuits. Of fresh food there was none.

Other conditions were equally bad. The hospital arrangements were always very inadequate; now they were hopeless. There was a very complete lack of equipment of all kinds. Bandages were so scarce that dressings could only be changed sometimes once a week, and this in a tropical climate. There was no operating table, hardly any hospital orderlies. Captain Dickson, I.M.S., did all that was humanly possible, and the regiment will remember him with gratitude. But no devotion on his part could make up for this complete lack, and a great number died who would never have done so if properly looked after. On the whole it was better to be shot dead in the Kibata area than to be badly wounded.

For the British officers, when not on duty, the doctor's

tent was an unofficial rendezvous. After visiting one's men and other friends one looked in on the doctor, though one rarely saw him as he was generally too busy. The hospital was situated in a steep narrow ravine on the south-eastern side of Kibata, the only safe position during the fighting. Even then an enemy party machine-gunned it, causing six casualties, until Captain Dickson rushed out waving a Red Cross flag.

Here one foregathered and ate from the doctor's table, a door torn from its hinges, which was used both for meals and for operations. The ravine was a well of heat, in which the lifeless air rarely seemed to circulate, but lay stagnant and heavy. Here, on either side of a central track, were the few tents and the many grass huts full of wounded and sick men. As a result of the first five days' fighting, there were more than could be handled of wounded men: later, when the casualties due to fighting diminished, those from dysentery and malaria kept up the numbers.

The scene appeared to be astonishingly ordinary—the heat, the crowding, the dirt, the vermin all seemed to fit into a picture one had known for a lifetime. The doctor's tent was jammed between two sick bays, so that from it could be seen, heard and smelt all the suffering, death and decay due to comfortable inefficiency long miles away. On the opposite side of the track facing the tent was a small open space where the fresh cases were dumped awaiting the doctor's examination. They all came if one had time to wait, African, Indian, British, some very still, some tossed with fever and pain, though most not too serious but to feel content to be there. Sometimes there would be an urgent case when the cups and biscuits would be quickly cleared from the table while the doctor prepared for an operation. If necessary one assisted in odd ways: if not wanted the ejected guests would sit outside eating and watching.

The actors changed, but the scene maintained its essential sameness as the guests sat eating and talking. On the other side of the tent wall maybe a Loyal North Lancashire machine-gunner, who had had his throat shot to ribbons, choked slowly, interrupting the talk with his moans and gaspings. In front a demented Kaffarondo porter, tethered by a piece of string to the ground, but convinced he could not get away, mouthed and grimaced, making uncouth noises; while on the other side of the tent lay an officer, slowly dying of gangrene. He had fallen into a lion trap while on patrol and the poisoned stake had impaled him. So when an amputation case arrived, which demanded the table, the visitors would depart to their posts, having gathered all the news and refreshed themselves in each other's company.

Clothes, too, presented a constant and unsolved problem, as officers were allowed but 40 lbs. of baggage. Boots wore out only too quickly, while the thorn bushes tore one's clothes to ribbons. The solution lay in auctioning the kit of the dead, the money being credited to the dead man's estate. If one was outbidden for anything one really coveted, there was always the consolation of hinting to the fortunate purchaser that there might be another auction in the near future. Nor would he hesitate with an appropriate reply.

After the failure to take the Lodgement the 2/2nd K.A.R. took over the whole of Picquet Hill, relieving 'C' Company of the 1/2nd K.A.R. and the Baluch garrison. The regiment then went into reserve and had a quiet time. On the 11th Nos. 1 and 3 Companies under Major Money arrived from Kitambi, where they had been relieved by the Gold Coast Regiment. Their arrival was not without excitement as the enemy shelled the road where it topped the crest of the hill into Kibata. There were no casualties. Later in the day Captain B. de L. Brock with 2 Indian officers and 42 other ranks also arrived. Next day Nos. 1 and 3 Companies under Major Money took over Picquet Hill from the 2/2nd K.A.R. The following day, the 13th, Major Money was killed by machine-gun fire, while Jemadar Mohamed Sadiq was dangerously wounded and died next day. Jemadar Mohamed Sadiq, a gallant Mohmand, had been with the regiment from the start. He received his promotion to Jemadar on his death-bed as a recognition of the great services he had rendered. He was a great loss. Major Money's loss, too, was much felt as he had served the regiment well. Only his indomitable will had kept him going for several weeks, as he had been very ill with malaria. On the 14th the Picquet Hill garrison was in turn relieved. The 15th began quietly, except for some slight shelling. One shell penetrated a room in the fort where Captain Brock and two other officers were breakfasting, with the result that they lost their breakfast, while Captain Brock was wounded, though not seriously. The remainder of the day passed uneventfully, as the enemy was too busily engaged with the Gold Coast Regiment near the Mission to have any spare ammunition for Kibata.

The fighting near the Mission was part of the plan to relieve the pressure on Kibata. Since the 9th the enemy had confined himself to shelling and machine-gun fire, but he was known to have sufficiently large forces around Kibata to make the situation serious. The idea was 'to push on from Gold Coast Hill towards the Mwengei road so as to get in rear of the enemy entrenched at Kibata'. The Kibata garrison was to strengthen its position by the capture of the Lodgement, which was not only a thorn in the flesh, but a real danger spot, as the enemy might at any time renew the attacks on Picquet Hill from this place.

Late on the night of the 12th the Gold Coast Regiment arrived at the Mission, but owing to the heavy rains and the fatigued condition of the men they were allowed to rest the next day. On the morning of the 15th they attacked Gold Coast Hill where they were held up by the enemy artillery and lost heavily. The sound of the fighting could be heard at Kibata, where the garrison listened eagerly for signs of an advance. While the enemy was thus occupied plans were matured for a night attack by the Baluchis on the Lodgement.

The Diary records on the 13th: 'Brigadier-General O'Grady arrives from Chumo at 21 hours and takes over command. Convoy consisting of food, 100 hand grenades and ammunition, escorted by 40 rifles 129th Baluchis from Chumo comes in during the night. Major Farfan and 1 Section 27th Mountain Battery arrived midnight'. The arrival of this interesting miscellany, under cover of an ink-black night and a deluge of rain, was an important factor in the proposed attack, though the convoy little thought so as it crawled and slipped from Chumo to Kibata, losing battery mules down the hill-side and a complete train of donkeys which took the wrong turning.

The attack was planned and arranged by Major Lewis for about 11 p.m., when there would be a slight moon to help some ten minutes after the trench had been taken, while the assault would be made in complete darkness. The 27th guns were to shell an under-feature of the Lodgement called the 'Bump', where the enemy kept their local reserves: there was to be flanking fire from machine guns, but the main reliance was the 100 Mills bombs which had just arrived. With the help of these it was hoped to bomb the defenders sufficiently to have time to pull up the obstacle of pointed stakes which protected them. This obstacle was about 6 feet broad and 4 feet high. In front of this again was a 'boma' of bush covered with long sharp thorns.

The bombers were mostly young Mahsud recruits who had arrived with Captain Brock. Most had never seen a bomb before, but they took kindly to them. Also they were led by Naik Sahib Jan who had earned already an I.O.M. for outstanding gallantry. There was no time for much practice, so they were not told much more than: 'This is a Mills bomb; you pull out the ring and throw it'. The bombs were to be detonated by some of the Loyal North Lancashires who had arrived in Kibata some days previously. Actually they detonated only about 60 of them and sent the 100 back as ready for action.

About 9 p.m. the assaulting troops made their way across the valley up to Picquet Hill and were in the trenches facing the enemy by 10.30 p.m. Creeping out quietly they cleared away their own obstacle, after which 10 pioneer bombers, under Jemadar Ayub Khan and Naik Sahib Jan, crawled forward barefooted towards the enemy trenches, along the razor-backed ridge at the end of which was sighted a German machine gun in the Lodgement. The glow of a cigarette in the mouth of the German sentry behind the gun showed that the garrison though unsuspecting was alert. These were followed at about 20 paces by the first line of assaulting troops, also with bombs, under Lieut. Thatcher and Subedar Muhammad Afzal. Behind these came a second line, while Major Lewis in No. 2 Redoubt directed the action and had control of the reserves. Punjabis and Mahsuds in about equal numbers participated in the attack.

It was a perfect night for such an attack. A gentle breeze was blowing away from the enemy's trenches through the tufts of grass and scrub, helping to minimise the small sounds of the moving men, though this was almost nothing as Mahsuds move silently. In front, the Lodgement, backed by a clump of small trees, could be discerned dimly against the skyline. Everything was dead quiet. The pioneers crept forward in absolute silence and reached the enemy obstacle without being detected and immediately threw their bombs, not all of which exploded. This was the pre-arranged signal and instantly there was pandemonium. Yelling like fiends, the second and third lines rushed forward hurling their bombs and screaming with excitement. Machine guns, waiting for the signal, clattered and rattled into action, to be answered by the enemy machine guns which swept the

The flag at Kibata during the bombardment

The flag after the enemy had withdrawn

whole of their front. Our shells shrieked over, spraying the Bump with shrapnel, and were immediately answered by the enemy artillery fire which crashed down on No. 2 Redoubt, while a wild rifle fire added to the noise. Picquet Hill suddenly leapt into flames as the firing grew more and more intense, while from all around anxious eyes strained into the darkness, made doubly so by the flashes, waiting for the end. For 15 minutes the attackers were held up by the obstacle. Jemadar Ayub Khan was badly wounded in the face as he strove to force his way through, but the men got down on their bellies and pulled the stakes out one by one, all the time firing, bombing and yelling. A few inches over their backs the enemy machine-gun bullets streamed harmlessly into the night. It was found afterwards that the gun was firing through an emplacement with a steel shield, and that this had been so placed that the gun could not be depressed enough to do any damage so long as one remained quite flat. Suddenly the gun ceased fire as a well-aimed bomb exploded over the emplacement. Immediately, the attackers were through the remaining stakes and into the trenches shooting and stabbing. Once in, the affair was soon over. A feeble attempt to counter-attack melted away immediately and the Lodgement was permanently won. The casualties were remarkably small. Jemadar Ayub Khan badly wounded, Subedar Muhammad Afzal wounded in the shoulder after he was in the trenches and where he did stout work, Lieut. Thatcher slightly wounded in the head by a bomb which conveniently decapitated a German askari, some 10 feet away, who being a bad shot missed him five times while stuck in the entanglement, and 10 other ranks killed and wounded. The enemy lost much more heavily. Five whites and 8 askaris were taken prisoners. Allowing for the usual proportion of wounded to killed, the attack must have accounted for about 40 of the enemy. General von Lettow mentions this attack, but is mistaken when he writes that 'several companies' attacked. There were certainly not more than 80 men all told, but they were out to win and would have taken a good deal of stopping. He also asserted later that the attack found his men in the midst of a relief and so in a certain state of confusion. That may have helped, but does not detract from the belief that nothing would have stopped the men that night. The loss of the Lodgement was fatal to any hopes which the enemy may have entertained of taking Kibata. After this he confined himself to the defensive.

The captured position was taken over by the 1/2nd K.A.R., who consolidated it during the night. The attackers marched back to their quarters and slept. For this action Lieut.-Colonel Hulseberg, who was commanding the regiment, received a bar to his D.S.O., Major Lewis the D.S.O., 2nd Lieut. Thatcher the M.C., Subedar Muhammad Afzal the I.O.M. (2nd Class), No. 3151 Havildar Mirza Khan and No. 436 Sepoy Mir Jan the I.O.M. (2nd Class). It is on such occasions as this that decorations seem invidious, and those who received them felt that they were but held in trust for all who had taken part in the attack. All ranks had behaved splendidly.

On the 16th the regiment was in reserve near the fort, but on the evening of the 17th they took over the whole of the picquet line from the K.A.R. There was at this time a considerable amount of sickness among both officers and men. On the 18th Lieut. Cox collapsed after having carried on for two months with severe malaria. Lieut. Goldsmith went to hospital sick with dysentery, while Subedar-Major Mir Kambir Khan, and Subedar Mir Bad Shah, I.O.M., had also to be evacuated. Both these Indian officers had served with distinction and had in every way maintained the very high traditions of their regiment. They only went to hospital when they were so weak they could not even stand. The regiment had lost altogether 7 British officers and 7 Indian officers in a fortnight. On the 23rd

Captain Dickson, I.M.S., was relieved by Lieut. A. H. Brown, I.M.S. Captain Dickson had been with the regiment since the end of June 1915, and was certainly in need of a rest. Since his arrival in East Africa he had always been desperately short-handed both as regards assistants and material. He had served the 129th well.

After five uneventful days the regiment was relieved in turn by the K.A.R. and went into reserve in Reserve Valley and Plain Hill. On the 24th Lieut. R. B. Wilson and 2nd Lieut. V. G. Robert rejoined from hospital, bringing with them 2 Indian officers and 47 men. Once more patrolling began—along the old Chumo road and Mission road, to Harman Hill and towards Gold Coast Hill, but there was nothing to report. Christmas Day passed quietly, and was made the more pleasant by the contents of the chop-boxes of the recent arrivals. These contained, in addition to the more solid foods and drinks, luxuries such as pâté de foie gras and two bottles of champagne brought up by the far-sighted Lieut. Robert. The very sight of such foods raised the morale of the British officers enormously. Later in the day an aeroplane flew over the fort and dropped a large parcel of cigarettes for the men. On the 26th, in order to work off the effects of this excessive living, there was much patrolling, while at 6.30 in the evening Nos. 2 and 4 Companies marched under Major Lewis for Chumo 'to rest'. It is recorded that they 'marched all night and arrived in about 4 a.m. dead beat. Up at 8 a.m. and all over the hills again, choosing sites for trenches which kept us busy until the evening'. The remainder of the regiment moved the following morning to Water Picquet on the Chumo road, relieving the 1/2nd K.A.R., and took over the various picquets in that place. Here they were joined by Captain Phillips, 2nd Lieut. Jenkins (who left the next day *en route* for England), 1 Indian officer and 83 other ranks. From Water Picquet patrols were sent out regularly to Mikurumo and up the Hanga Valley, while on the 29th Captain Phillips with Lieut. Palin, 67 rifles from Nos. 1 and 2 Companies, 3 machine guns and 1 gun of the 27th Mountain Battery marched for Chumo with orders 'to proceed with five days' rations via Mingumbe and Hanga towards Minjumbe, to operate in that district and return'. This he did, while a smaller patrol of 50 rifles and 1 machine gun under Lieut. Thatcher pushed up the coast road to Samanga. But the enemy had already left these places so that both patrols had little to report. Captain Phillips did, however, bring back a report which reminded one of the information brought by the spies to Joshua. 'Minjumbe is a fertile place. There are large numbers of mango trees all weighed down with mangos.' Like a true Scot, however, he qualified his praise: 'the mangos are not up to the standard of the Bombay grafted mangos'. Nevertheless they were good.

On the 7th the regiment was back again at Kibata ready to take its part in the final phase of the operations. Ever since the night of 15 December, when they were turned out of the Lodgement, the enemy had been on the defensive, but their positions were too strong to assault without very considerable loss on our part. Nor was such a course necessary as Smuts had bigger movements pending, which would force von Lettow to turn his attention elsewhere. On 22 December G.H.Q. had moved from Morogoro to the Dothumi in anticipation of this larger offensive, but the heavy rains delayed the advance until 1 January. By the 6th General Beves was across the Rufiji and had seized Mkalinso. Sheppard's Brigade had crossed at Kimbambawe on the night of the 5/6th. Further west van Deventer and Northey were also moving. It was as part of this large co-ordinated movement that the 1st Division began to push northwards with Mohoro and Utete as the immediate objectives.

Already the German commander was aware of his danger

and had decided to withdraw his troops. Such a withdrawal was easy to effect without the Kibata garrison being immediately aware of it. It was, however, known to the Division by the 5th, and on the 6th Brigade had issued orders for a general movement against the enemy positions. On the 7th the 1/2nd K.A.R. occupied Platform and Observation Hills and Palm Tree Village. Next day they attacked Ambush Hill which was held very slightly by a small enemy force. On both occasions the 129th were in reserve. After this, they took over Picquet Hill, and at 2 p.m. attacked across the valley towards Ambush Hill, but the enemy had already withdrawn.

On the 9th Major Lewis with a company got in the rear of these retiring enemy forces on the Mwengei road, whereupon the 1/2nd K.A.R. attacked them from the south along three spurs of the ridge but they managed to withdraw to the east. There were nine casualties in this slight action. On the 11th at 4.30 a.m. the regiment, accompanied by a section of the 27th Mountain Battery, moved out from Kibata against the enemy rear-guard on the Mwengei road, which was now covering the retreat of the main body and also of the 4·1-inch gun, which was being slowly pulled away.

The road to Mwengei is hilly and closed in by thick bush. It is also commanded by several hills, which must be picqueted before any safe advance is possible. Progress was very slow therefore, as Lieut. Robert with No. 3 Company laboriously felt his way forward. The enemy opposition was very slight but enough to make caution necessary. By 10.30 a.m. the column was within sight of the village, which was defended by a low ridge commanding the road. The two mountain guns began to shell this ridge as the infantry worked their way forward. Lieut. Robert was to make a frontal attack, while Lieut. Thatcher with No. 4 Company made his way through the bush to turn the enemy's right flank. Both attacks were pushed home at the same time, but as usual the enemy had withdrawn and the village was found to be evacuated. Casualties had been slight. By this time it was dark, but the troops had still to be watered and fed, while the usual perimeter camp had to be constructed. It was a long and tiring day.

As touch had been lost temporarily with the enemy, two patrols were sent out at dawn the following morning. A small one of 20 men under a havildar was to reconnoitre towards Limbanguku, while a larger one of 100 men with two machine guns under Captain Phillips proceeded towards Mbindia. Both patrols were to have native guides, but as one of these did not arrive the smaller patrol set off without, and mistaking the road proceeded along that to Mbindia. The larger patrol was slightly delayed in starting.

The small patrol had only proceeded some mile and a half down the road when they were ambushed, 3 machine guns opening fire at 150 yards. Ten of the patrol were killed, seven wounded, while four escaped into the bush. Meantime Captain Phillips had come on, thinking that the firing came from a K.A.R. patrol on the hill-side, but very shortly his patrol came under fire and one man was wounded. At the same time one of the survivors rushed up and warned him of the situation and also asked for help for the wounded men lying in the road. This unfortunately could not be given, so the wretched men had to lie out in the sun until after dark, when the doctor, with stretcher-bearers, went off at very considerable risk and brought them in.

Captain Phillips at once began to feel his way up the hill-side in the direction of the firing, sending out patrols to get touch with the enemy. One of these almost immediately came under machine-gun fire at close range and lost two killed and four wounded out of twelve: the others were also held up. Very gradually as the day went on he worked his way on to the ridge and entrenched within 150 yards of the enemy.

This ridge was exceedingly narrow, being only some 60 yards wide. It had been practically cleared of vegetation by the enemy, who had used it as a gun road when bringing up their guns against Kibata. The sides were excessively steep and covered with dense bush. Here the enemy had constructed two lines of trenches, the front trench being slightly to the left of the direct line to the second. These were defended with 4 machine guns which swept the whole top of the ridge.

Further progress for the time was impossible. About 4 p.m. Lieut. Robert was sent up to reinforce with 50 rifles and 2 machine guns of the Loyal North Lancashires. There was a good deal of heavy firing on both sides, while from time to time the 4·1-inch gun sent over a reminder of its presence. This gun also shelled the Headquarters and reserves, but did little damage beyond killing and wounding a few porters. In reply the 27th Battery sprayed the enemy trenches, while one shell, bursting short, just missed Captain Phillips and Lieut. Robert.

The night was exceedingly cold, and the men, without blankets and with little food, felt it very much. Many of them had malaria. The casualties for the day were 12 killed, 11 wounded and 2 missing. These were afterwards found dead.

The following day orders came to assault the enemy position. Captain Phillips accordingly made the preliminary arrangements, 'sending 2 machine guns and 30 rifles to a ridge east of the enemy's position whence they could, and did, bring effective fire to bear on the left flank and rear of the enemy's position. Two other machine guns had been placed to fire on our first objective and two more to keep down the fire of the enemy in the second objective while the first was being assaulted'.

The attack was to be made in two stages. At 2 p.m. came torrential rains, drenching and chilling everybody, so that the men could hardly grasp their rifles. At 2.30 p.m.

the two guns of the 27th Mountain Battery opened fire on the second objective, while at 3 p.m. two bomb-throwers of the Loyal North Lancashires opened fire on the first and second objectives. 'The range was too long for the second objective, but the bombs bursting high had a most demoralising effect'—on the assaulting troops who ran into this bomb barrage. Fortunately one of the bomb-throwers burst from its holding-bands and stunned the gunner operating it, much to the joy of the assaulting troops: the other received orders to cease fire.

About 3.5 p.m. the assault was made by No. 1 Company under Lieut. Thatcher and Jemadar Sikandar Khan. As the front was so narrow the attackers had to advance from their trenches in file and then deploy. This took time and prevented any very rapid attack. Fortunately the covering fire was very effective and kept down most of the enemy fire, though they brought two machine guns into action. Twice the attackers had to take cover as the fire became too heavy, but gradually they made their way forward till within 30 yards of the enemy trenches when again they were forced down. Waiting their time they made the final assault and captured the first line of trenches. Here Lieut. Thatcher was seriously wounded, but the men pushed on, led by Jemadar Sikandar Khan, towards the second line of trenches. By this time the attack was going forward well.

Major Lewis, seeing Lieut. Thatcher fall, immediately sent forward Lieut. Robert, while he himself brought up the reserves. Bomb-throwers and a machine gun were rushed up for action against the second objective, but before they could be got into position the men had already taken it. 'Then began a memorable hunt. The sepoys, their tails well up, chased the Germans along the ridge until they had driven them right off it. Machine guns were brought out as quickly as possible and placed in the position which had been occupied during the attack on

Kibata by the German 4·1-inch gun. Lieut. Palin, with 70 rifles and 2 machine guns, was immediately despatched to Mushroom Tree Hill to which the enemy had retired, and machine-gun fire was brought to bear at long range on the retiring enemy.' Unfortunately both guns, which had been firing very heavily, jammed just as the enemy were crowded on the road, and the best target of the day was lost. The pursuit was carried on by the K.A.R. The casualties were 2 killed; 1 British, 1 Indian officer and 12 other ranks wounded. So ended the fighting which had begun on 6 December. By the time it was finished the regiment had lost about two-thirds of its original strength in fighting or in sickness, but it had lived up to its high reputation.

Six recommendations for rewards were made: Captain Phillips for 'mention in despatches' for coolness and bravery under fire during the attack, and ability in conducting the operation of the 12th, culminating in the occupation of the commanding position whence the attack of the 13th was launched. Lieut. V. G. Robert for 'Military Cross for gallantry during the attack on 13 January. When Lieut. Thatcher was wounded he carried on the pursuit, and by his fine example led on the men until all our objectives had been attained'. Jemadar Sikandar Khan 'for daring disregard of his own safety during the attack on 13 January while keeping the attack moving forward and from becoming disorganised. Recommended for I.D.S.M.' No. 1436 Havildar Ghulam Kadar 'for gallantry in the attack at Mwengei. When moving towards the machine-gun emplacements one enemy gun opened fire. He shouted to his men to charge the gun and himself set the example'. No. 4493 Havildar Bagh Khan 'for conspicuous gallantry in leading his men during the attack at Mwengei on 13 January'. No. 4320 Lance-Naik Tor Khan, 'who three times crawled out in front of our trenches under fire to light smoke bombs as signals to aeroplanes on 12

January. The enemy were 150 yards distant and the bush was cut down'.

Throughout the fighting at Kibata a small Union Jack belonging to the 1/2nd K.A.R. had been kept flying in spite of every effort on the part of the enemy gunners to destroy it. This flag was taken away by the K.A.R. when they left Kibata. Sometime in May 1917 the Adjutant of the 129th received the following letter, together with the flag, from Major L. G. Murray of the 1/2nd K.A.R.:

'Dear P. M. C.,

The officers of my regiment very much hope that you will accept this flag as a small token of the esteem we all feel for your magnificent regiment.

We fought side by side at Kibata against considerable odds for a period of six weeks, from 6 December 1916 to 14 January 1917, on which date we finally drove away the enemy rear-guards.

During the first few critical days it was the bravery and devotion of your regiment which saved the situation and kept the flag flying.

I enclose a few photos to show how the Boche did his best to down the flag, which he only succeeded once in doing. It would be no exaggeration to say that between four and five hundred shells were fired at this flag.

Please remember me to Major Lewis and the other officers of the regiment, who are now, I hear, returning to India.

Yours very sincerely,

L. G. MURRAY, *Major*
1/2 *K. A. Rifles*'.

The flag is now in the regimental mess in India, and is a souvenir of a great fight and a great friendship.

## CHAPTER XIV

13 JAN.–18 JULY, 1917: Rainy season begins; Effect on general plan of campaign; Condition of troops; Regiment back in Kibata; At Ngarambi Chini; Floods; Very short rations; Back in Kibata; Concentration at Chemera; End of rains; Offensive reopens; Arrival of fresh drafts

ONCE again the main offensive had failed; partly because the rains broke before their usual time and were particularly violent; partly because there were insufficient troops effectively to close the circle; but largely because the enemy were still strong in numbers and morale and were in excellent positions. The Rufiji was crossed by the 1st East African Brigade at Kimbambawe and by General Beves at Mkalinso. The Nigerian Brigade had pushed the enemy out of Kibongo but had failed to dislodge them from Nyandote, 15 miles south of Mkundu, on 24 January. Colonel Burne's Column from Kisegesse advancing through Koge to the Rufiji was making slow progress. Operations in the west, while satisfactory, were not sufficiently decisive to affect the position in the eastern area. The impression given in Smuts's last despatch that the war in East Africa was now practically over, and that all that remained to be done was to round up a number of scattered and demoralised enemy parties, was entirely wrong. The back of the enemy opposition was not broken until the end of 1917. They never were demoralised.

The rains did not affect the whole fighting area to the same extent nor at the same time. Northey's forces were able to carry on a fairly vigorous offensive, while the middle section of the Rufiji held by the enemy was not seriously affected till the end of March. But on the front whence the big offensive had been launched they were very heavy. Both Generals Hoskins and van Deventer in their despatches of 1917 emphasise the severity of these rains and their disastrous effect upon communications and on the health of the troops:

'All seemed to be going well when on 25 January heavy rain began to fall, ushering in the wettest season known in East Africa for many years. By the 27th the lines of communication from Mikesse to Kimbambawe were interrupted by the washing away of bridges and the flooding of roads; and operations in all areas were henceforward seriously hampered by the untimely rain.... In the Mgeta and Rufiji valleys roads constructed with much skill and labour, over which motor transport ran continuously in January, were traversed with difficulty and much hardship a month later by porters wading for miles in water above their waists.... The valley of the Rufiji and its various tributaries became a vast lake.... Patrol work had to be carried out for some time in canoes, and the men found themselves making fast to the roofs of houses which had lately formed their quarters.... The conditions of the Kilwa area were equally trying, as roads became impassable for motor transport and animals died within a few weeks of being landed. An even more serious factor perhaps was the sickness among the troops. The coastal belt and the valleys of the Mgeta and Rufiji even in dry weather are unhealthy for all but the indigenous African; and during the rains there is a great increase in malaria, while dysentery and pneumonia strike down even the African. In 1916 many of our troops in East Africa spent the rainy season in high and comparatively healthy localities. It was impossible to do this in 1917...'.

The enemy forces in the eastern area about this time were concentrated largely in the neighbourhood of Utete or east of the Lugonya River. Some six or seven hundred were opposing the advance of Colonel Burne's Column from Kisegesse, while the southern bank of the Rufiji from Utete to Nyakisiki was in their possession. There was also a force in position 4 miles south of Mkindu facing the Nigerians and the Cape Corps. Gradually von Lettow withdrew from the middle Rufiji, though he remained there long enough to consume the available crops 'almost to the last grain'. The evacuation was carried out 'gradually and in echelon'. The greater part of the troops were assembled at Mpotora, whence they made their way to the neighbourhoods of Kilwa Kisiwani, Lindi and Liwale. Already, however, there were some 700 of the enemy about Lindi and westwards in widely separated detachments at Tunduru, Newala and in the valley of the Mbemkuru.

Now that the great drive had failed it was necessary to reconsider the whole position, of which the outstanding feature was the critical state of supply and transport. 'There was no reserve in the advanced depôts; the number of porters was insufficient; the animals in transport units were dying, and the drivers of the mechanical transport were falling sick so rapidly that the numbers of troops in the front line could not be maintained there.' The best line of supply was the Rufiji itself, so that one of the immediate objectives was 'to push the enemy off the Rufiji River and as far south as possible, so as to use the Rufiji River for transport purposes: and the operations of the Kilwa and Rufiji Columns had been conceived with this object'.

It was also necessary to evacuate the greater number of the South African units on account of sickness. The Indian troops remained, as did the African. The despatch records: 'The hardships of the campaign and the brunt of the fighting since 1914 had been borne by some Indian units and by the King's African Rifles. These had also suffered severely from sickness, especially the Indians; but units were so weak as to make it impossible to withdraw any of the K.A.R., and only certain of the Indians were able to be sent to healthier ground to recuperate'.

This evacuation of troops, together with the difficulties and obstacles already mentioned, meant that any vigorous offensive was quite impossible, so that for several months the whole of the campaign is but a weary and monotonous record of transport difficulties, endless sickness and ceaseless patrolling, with a certain amount of fighting on a limited scale. The Higher Command was waiting for the rains to cease, while at the same time it was reorganising the transport and the forces in the field. It was also trying to find out the enemy's intentions: no easy matter in a country such as German East Africa. Gradually the drift of the enemy forces towards Mpotora and then to the areas already mentioned was ascertained, but only as a result of never-ceasing patrolling on the part of the troops.

Such is the background against which the movements and actions of the 129th must be viewed during this period. From January until the middle of July the Diary is dull and tedious, being little else than a record of an endless series of marches and an infinity of patrols which, viewed by themselves, are meaningless and certainly not worthy of a detailed record. It is only when these activities are correlated with the larger ones of the Division and of the total forces that they have significance. Yet they must be mentioned, partly because it is necessary to do so if a true historical perspective is to be maintained, but chiefly to emphasise the fact that these dull periods demanded the same fortitude and singleness of purpose, the same determination to persevere to the bitter end in spite of sickness, lack of food and bad food and all the prolonged hardships, as is demanded to win a battle.

The recent advance from Kibata had been part of a general advance, in a northward and westward direction, of the 1st Division, which consisted of the 2nd and 3rd East African Brigades. The 2nd Brigade had occupied Mohoro on 16 January and was advancing against Utete through the Kitshi Hills. The 3rd Brigade was clearing the country immediately north of Ngarambi. By the end of February the Division was on a line Utete-Namatewa-Chemera. This last place with Mitole covered the tram-line which was in course of construction from Kilwa towards Liwale. From February until June this sector remained pretty much the same.

Immediately after the fighting on 13 January the regiment occupied Mbindia and formed a camp on a spur below the position which had been occupied by the 4·1-inch gun. There they remained until the 27th, when they marched back to Kibata 'as unable to do any more work in the district'. In the interim they were patrolling in all directions. On the 15th one of these patrols found the 4·1-inch gun minus its breechblock and sights, and was nearly ambushed, but got away with one man wounded. On the 18th Mbwara was occupied after the exchange of a few shots. Next day the number of British officers was reduced to four, as Captain Phillips and Lieut. MacIvor were both evacuated with malaria. On the same day came the award of the M.C. to Lieut. Palin for his services on Picquet Hill during the early bombardments and at Gold Coast Hill. The patrolling still went on, but the enemy were falling back so that most of the reports were negative. One patrol, wishing to be more positive, reported 'no enemy met with but an occasional footprint seen'. The K.A.R., however, found more than footprints at Kiurubi and were held up with a nasty jar. Here the enemy rear-guard made a stand for a few days and delayed the advance. Whereupon the Division wired the Brigade 'that from correspondence captured it was judged enemy are completely demoralised, and an immediate attack against Kiurubi is most desirable'. That is, one presumes, from a military point of view. The 129th were to reinforce the K.A.R. But on the 24th, the day selected for the attack, the enemy had gone.

They remained at Kibata until 30 January, when they marched to the Mission and the following day to Kitambi. This sudden move was due to orders from the Division to the Brigade that the 1/2nd K.A.R. and the 129th should strengthen the 3rd Brigade towards the west. They waited at Kitambi until the 4th, when they marched out in the early morning via Namatewa for Ngarambi Chini, situated on a tributary of the Lugonya, which was reached after a trying march. 'The road was bad, being covered with mud: had to ford river 2 feet deep.' It would appear almost that they were fussy, but such a remark must be interpreted in terms of East African mud. It meant that the men could lift their feet with difficulty as the mud was so deep and sticky. Fording a river meant more than wet feet. At Ngarambi Chini they came under the 3rd East African Brigade and took over the camp and picquets from the 40th Pathans.

They remained at Ngarambi Chini until 16 February and had a trying time, as the excessive rains were flooding all the country and making transport impossible. 'Ngarambi was the furthest point reached in the pursuit of the enemy towards the Rufiji, and here the utmost difficulty was experienced in feeding the troops.' Owing to the torrential rains and the impassable nature of the roads most of the transport could not be used any further than Mitole. Two bridges were washed away at the Matandu River, and there was great delay in getting ration supplies across. Beyond this, animal transport could not be used on account of the great mortality among the animals from sickness. The only possible form of transport left was porters. 'A porter eats what he carries if he has to march further than 7 days from the place where he gets his load. He only carried 14 days. Consequently the supplies left at the end of that march for the troops is practically nil. If the distance is more than 7 days there is nothing left, as the return journey has to be provided for. In addition ammunition and other non-animal commodities have to be carried. The consequence of this state of affairs was that we at the front were on the shortest of rations.' For two days, Major Lewis remembers, an officer's rations in his company consisted of a tin of sardines and a handful of mealie meal per diem.

'The sepoys were so exhausted that it was difficult for them to march a mile. The manner in which they carried on in these circumstances reflects nothing but credit on their spirit.'

There was plenty to do. Daily patrols were sent along the Ngarambi-Njimbwi and the Ngarambi-Kiwambi roads, while Lieut. Robert was sent a little further west with 100 rifles and 2 machine guns to hold Green's Post Crossing where the Ngarambi-Nangue road crosses the Lugonya River, and was similarly occupied. Shortly after arrival came a Brigade order to construct a bridge across the river, 'as Division is unable to send technical troops'. Neither could they send any material or tools, but in spite of these deficiencies and the state of the weather the bridge was built. Meantime Robert's detachment were being flooded out of their position. The bridge across the river had been swept away, and the picquets on the far side could only be reached by swimming. 'A porter swims across with their (the picquets') food, but it is usually wet when they receive it.' Finally, the camp was 2 feet under water and the post had to be moved back. One man was drowned in withdrawing the picquet.

On 16 February the regiment, less Lieut. Robert's company, marched for Namatewa on its way to Kibata. They rested for a day at Kitambi, leaving on the morning of the 19th for the Mission, passing, *en route*, the 8th Battery with its Baluchi escort: 'it was having great difficulty in getting its guns up the hilly road'. No doubt the Battery would have put the matter more picturesquely. One remembers the 129th mule transport on the same route some months previously. Kibata was reached in the early morning of the 20th. Here the men were 'properly housed' in the old K.A.R. lines, and here they remained until 8 April.

Until the end of the month they were allowed to rest, so that, apart from instructional parades, there is little to record. On the 23rd Major Lewis, Lieut. Robert, Subedars Abdullah Khan, Ghulam Jilani, Rahim Ali, Sikandar Khan, Sherbat Khan, Jemadar Nur Khan with 32 other ranks and 4 followers left for leave to India. It was well deserved, though it is doubtful whether many of them got any further than the coast. Major Lewis for instance went to hospital instead, and then was sent on duty at Morogoro to start a Lewis Gun and Stokes Mortar School. The Indian officers and men had not seen their homes since the outbreak of war in 1914. On the 27th Captain J. C. T. Gaskell of the 69th Punjabis reported for duty. On the 20th Lieut.-Colonel Hulseberg was appointed to the temporary command of the 2nd East African Brigade. Major Lewis took command of the regiment until he went on leave.

March was uneventful. It found the regiment with a strength of 6 British officers, 11 Indian officers and 386 other ranks, but these numbers belied its real strength. The hardships and the sojourns in the low-lying districts had brought on an epidemic of malaria, while the perpetually bad feeding and constant exposure had greatly reduced the vitality of the men. The Diaries almost entirely pass over the casualties due to ill-health, and one would know little but for two short entries. On the 10th there is the 'weekly medical inspection, 36 per cent men unfit for service'. On the 22nd a further and closer inspection reveals an even worse state of affairs: 'Inspection of 240 all ranks by S.M.O. Kibata. Of those on parade 16 men permanently unfitted: 60 unfitted for two months, and in addition 40 men were placed in regimental hospital and others temporarily unfitted'. Towards the end of the month the Brigade wired that 'all fighting ranks should be equipped with a blanket, waterproof sheet and mosquito net'. To which the reply was, 'ours mostly in Kilwa'. Given such conditions it was impossible that the men should not go sick. Patrolling started again along the old routes to

Mwengei and Mbindia, where Captain Gaskell and 50 rifles were sent to form a post and to patrol towards Kiruwiru and Mtavi. Longer patrols were sent out to Nkulu via the Mission under Jemadar Karam Dad and Jemadar Hasham Din. These patrols took several days, and in such rains and conditions were far from being picnics.

There were also the usual comings and goings. On 2 March Captain Brock arrived from Kitambi with a detachment, but left a fortnight later for Utete to take up the duties of Staff Captain to the 2nd East African Brigade. On the 3rd Lieut. Palin with three men set out for Morogoro for a signalling course. Next day Lieut.-Colonel Hulseberg went to Mohoro. On the 5th Captain A. C. Gover, 121st Pioneers, reported for duty. On the 16th Lieut. J. W. G. Steell, (S.A.) R.A.M.C., relieved Captain Newton.

It rained steadily and heavily all the month of March and went on raining for two months after that, but it was better to be in Kibata than the low-lying regions. That, however, is not saying much. The whole regiment, or what remained of it, suffered continuously from malaria, while food-supplies were so precarious that during the whole of this period they were threatened with actual starvation. Most of the time they were on less than half-rations, and even then what little they had was so bad that under normal conditions it would have been condemned. The atta for the sepoys came in sacks which were not waterproof and was as 'hard as concrete' when it arrived. Little else arrived. Letters also when they did arrive were mere pulp. 'Yesterday a gang of porters with mail bags came plodding along and we flung ourselves on them to find two bags for the 129th, the contents of which were shaken out on the ground, and what a sight! Great dollops of chewed paper pulp with here and there a letter more or less intact sticking out of it. You see these bags, which were not waterproof, have been wandering round through torrential rains for a month or two in the charge of primitive savages, at the mercy of anyone who thought they would like to have a look inside on spec....' But to show that their hearts were still right they held some regimental sports on the 30th. What were the events and what the prizes is not recorded, nor how many entered. Most of them were only capable of running temperatures.

Very gradually during the next month the Brigade was being dribbled south and concentrated in the Chemera area to meet the enemy concentration in the Kilwa district south of the Matandu River. The withdrawal of the enemy from the Uteenge Lake area went on steadily during April, and towards the middle of the month it became evident that considerable numbers were concentrating about 20 miles to the south-west of Kilwa Kivinje. On 18 April a sharp action between British and German forces had taken place within a few miles of Rumbo. Our attack on the German positions had been beaten off with considerable losses. Von Lettow himself was in command of this area, and continued to strengthen his forces there and also at Lindi. By 20 May Mpotora had been completely evacuated by the enemy.

The regiment was vaguely aware of this general movement, but much more consciously so of the processes by which it was carried out. During the month of April they gradually worked their way, chiefly in odd companies and detachments, from Kibata to Chemera, where they remained until 4 July, when they marched with No. 2 Column on a new offensive. Outwardly their movements during April are mere chaotic jerkings, though actually this is not so. What the effective numbers were is not recorded, as the Diary becomes less and less a source of information. Even the name of the Adjutant is not recorded, while one is left to presume that Captain J. C. T. Gaskell is acting as Commanding Officer. But as there are only three British officers with the regiment at the beginning of the month it is hardly to be wondered at that the records are not so detailed as might be desired. All three officers were constantly on the march with detached companies and patrols, so that only one British officer could have been with Headquarters at any given time. This great dearth of British officers among the Indian regiments—and the African—was a very serious matter and greatly reduced their fighting efficiency. It is deeply deplored by the successive G.O.C.s in their despatches throughout the East African campaign, yet it was entirely due to their own lack of vision and common sense. The Germans never suffered in this way although they were in the country throughout the duration of the war, the reason being that they deliberately nursed their white personnel knowing that white men cannot stand the hardships and diseases of a tropical country unless carefully looked after. Von Lettow in his *Reminiscences*, when discussing the drastic changes which he introduced in order to economise his porter transport, writes: 'Among other things it was laid down that henceforward no European should have more than five native attendants. That sounds a generous allowance to European ears, but under African conditions native attendance is really indispensable to the European. He requires at least one man or boy to cook for him and attend to his personal needs, and, in addition, it must be remembered that all baggage, kit, rations, blankets and tent material, has to be carried whenever he moves'. He goes on to defend this decision and almost writes an apology for it. When one knows how severe von Lettow was and how he never spared himself or his subordinates, such an apology is staggering to those British officers who were allowed two attendants and 40 lbs. of kit. The ordinary white soldier or non-commissioned officer was allowed nothing, but expected to carry on as usual. Von Lettow's scale applied to all white combatants. The result was that the German white personnel did not suffer unduly from sickness, and so were always available with their experience and moral stiffening, while the British went sick in masses and few officers could stand more than a year of the country. It is the difference between a scientific attitude to war and the time-honoured method of muddling through, between regarding fighting as a business and as a sport.

During all this time the usual small patrols were sent out and the usual posts and picquets maintained. Only the more important movements will be recorded. On 3 April Captain Gover with 150 rifles left Kibata for Kitambi. On the 5th the remainder of the regiment was ordered to relieve the 40th at Mtumbei Chini, while on the 6th Captain Gover's detachment was ordered to relieve the 2/2nd K.A.R. at Namatewa, Kitambi being taken over by a small detachment under an Indian officer. Both movements were delayed, one by a rumour that an enemy party was reported to be in the Kibata neighbourhood, the other because the rains had rendered a temporary and hitherto unnoticed river impassable. Headquarters reached Kitambi on the 9th, while Captain Gover got away to Namatewa, after the river had been bridged, on the evening of the same day. He arrived late the following afternoon 'after a very trying march'. The Diary entry is brief, besides 'trying times' were only too common, but for the reader's sake it may be well to give some idea of what this may mean. 'After working till late the night before to get things ready, we set out for a post about 12 miles away at daybreak. Half a mile from the starting-point we came to a flooded river; it proved to be out of a man's depth, and although we might have got the men across one by one, it was quite impossible to get the baggage over. Baggage I may say all has to be carried on coolies' heads: there are no animals or carts in this district. There was nothing for it but to go back, dump the baggage, and return to try and make a bridge. Making a bridge sounds all right in the abstract, but remember that here were streams running through impenetrable jungle, and as the country on either side is often swampy at the best of times, it is difficult to find out where the bank on the near side is, and still more difficult to find the further bank. Then there are none of the usual materials, rope, wire, nails, or planks, available; and although one is surrounded by millions of trees, one has to cut one's way through the undergrowth to get at the trunks, and when one has felled them they fall on the undergrowth and take a lot of getting out; lastly, there is no open space to collect one's material and put things together. The men, who had never done such a thing before, were simply bored with the whole business. At last I got them to get a move on and they spread out into the jungle to cut wood, but without any hope in their minds that it would be the slightest use if they did cut it; in the meantime I had other men on pulling down creepers and twisting them into ropes.

'The first pier I built almost entirely with my own hands, when suddenly a hawk-faced Afridi Indian officer realised that there was something in it after all and plunged into the water at my side to help; then the men began to get interested; at first they had all denied that they could swim, now several of them remembered that they could. It was a perilous time as the material was of necessity very light, and they would crowd round and get in each other's way and nearly bring the whole thing down into the 10 feet deep torrent below; however, by nightfall we were half-way across, and next day we finished it and took the baggage over at four in the afternoon. Plodding through the swamps we marched till dark, halted till the moon was up, and then plodded on again. At 4 a.m. we came to another stream where there was an old German bridge, but the water was 3 feet above the level of the road, and the bridge itself had a gap at the crown. Once one had discovered where the gap was it was fairly all right, and we established a line of men and passed the baggage from hand to hand; everything went well for about an hour and then the remnants of the old bridge collapsed. I decided on a raft. We cut down several trees and dragged the logs to the water's edge only to find that the wood was heavier than water and sank! Oh what a country! Then we made ropes of creepers and at last dragged everything across; 4 a.m. to 9 a.m. and mostly by moonlight! For the rest of the way there was no serious obstacle, but going was very slow through the floods and mud. We arrived at our destination at 3.30 p.m. after marching for $23\frac{1}{2}$ hours, six of which were spent in the water, and this was on the top of two days building the bridge. Just at the very end we ran into an enemy patrol which after firing a few rounds withdrew, and that was just as well for us as the men were absolutely done up and could hardly put one foot in front of another.'

The Indian officer referred to above was Subedar Sarbiland, who soon afterwards became Subedar-Major. He was a tower of strength throughout all this very trying period and throughout the whole of the year, whether in camp, on patrol or fighting.

On 11 April the 57th Rifles arrived from Nkulu and took over the following day. On the 13th half the remaining strength of the regiment marched from Namatewa under Lieut. Goldsmith, who with Lieut. MacIvor had reported for duty on the 11th, and Lieuts. Edelstone and Guy of the 57th who were attached temporarily. The remainder, together with Headquarters, left two days later, so that on the 16th the regiment found itself once more in Namatewa doing very much the same things and living pretty much in the same way as on its first visit. Only the floods were slightly greater and malaria was if anything more rampant. There were the usual meeting patrols towards Nambanji and Ngarambi which met almost daily, though what they said when they met is not recorded. There is a mystic entry on the 16th which says: 'Nambanji patrol sends out patrols to look for Nambanji: are shown road which crosses river 5½ feet deep and deep swamp'. It rather looks as if the Adjutant was very tired and was writing up a nightmare. All the time, long-distance patrols were sent out under British and Indian officers. Subedar Sahib Dad patrolled in the direction of Nanguiwe. He had great difficulty in crossing the river which was in flood. In a small fight he lost one man, killed. On the 26th Captain Gover with a detachment marched for Kitambe *en route* to Chemera, and was followed two days later by Headquarters. By 3 May, when Subedar-Major Sarbiland and Subedar Sahib Dad brought in their detachments, they were all assembled.

Chemera maintained its evil reputation. Major Gover records: 'This spot seems to be peculiar for the thickness of the water and the swarms of lice. The water is so thick that it clogs a filter at once, and we are trying to catch some rain-water in our waterproof sheets. As for the aforesaid fauna, well, one scratches and scratches till one's arms ache and then one begins to scratch again! Eugh!!...'

The regiment, or what was left of it, remained in Chemera until 2 June, but by this time they were so reduced with sickness and the hardships and privations of the past four months that only a handful of men were really fit for and capable of work. Such as were fit were engaged in the usual camp duties, as Chemera was defended by a ring of trenches. From time to time larger patrols were sent out to capture German patrols reported by natives to be somewhere in the Chemera region. But it was always a case of hunting a shadow. Various meeting patrols were also sent out as a routine matter to keep in touch with the other units of the Brigade.

On 8 May Lieut. Robert, Subedar Sherbat Khan, Jemadar Nur Khan II, Jemadar Rajwali Khan and 26 other ranks rejoined, chiefly from leave, though some from hospital. On the 15th the regiment was ordered to send out a patrol of 50 men under a British officer to proceed to Libangani and to patrol not further than a two days' march from that place. There were other instructions also as to sketch-maps and descriptions of the country. Rations were to be taken for eight days. The patrol returned on the 23rd having carried out its orders. Only once did it encounter an enemy patrol, which retreated after a short exchange of shots during which a sepoy was wounded. But the interest of the patrol lies in the fact that when the 50 men were detailed for duty there was not a single fit sepoy left with the regiment. Nor were these 50 really fit, for one by one they dropped out and returned as best they could to Chemera. Captain Gover on his return had with him 11 men only. These on 23 May represented the effective fighting strength of the regiment. The rest were all more or less ill. Captain Gover estimated that there must have been about 1000 porters engaged between Kilwa and Chemera bringing up food-supplies for the regiment, that is, 1000 porters to maintain 11 effectives! On the 24th Lieut. Palin with 7 other ranks arrived from the signalling school in Morogoro, but before the month was out Lieuts. Brilliant and MacIvor were evacuated, the former with malaria, the latter with black-water fever. Lieut. Robert also went sick with malaria about this time and had to be evacuated.

June saw the beginning of better things. The rains began to abate and the country to dry up, so that mechanical transport again became possible. With more and better food and with the better weather the health of the men began to improve, while towards the end of the month came news of large new drafts. On the 1st the regiment marched for Kirongo(ware), which had been made the depôt and assembling-point for No. 2 Column, halting for the night at Mahonga and arriving at their destination early next morning. They remained at Kirongo until 19 July, when once more they were on the march and fighting.

At Kirongo the men were entirely refitted with clothes and equipment. They needed to be, for if not naked they were not far from being so. Their clothes had by this time become nothing more than collections of dirty rags, while only the uppers of their boots remained. They were also adequately and regularly fed for the first time in nine months. One officer writing home says: 'Yesterday we got some potatoes, the first that I have had in this country, and they might have been the choicest fruit by the way we fell on them...'. He was only voicing the sentiments of all the regiment, whether officers or men.

The better conditions soon made a very marked difference in the physique and in the health of all ranks, but it took time to get the men fit for the toils of long marches and fighting, so they were left in reserve when the column marched on 4 July. The month of June was quite uneventful as far as the regiment was concerned, and the Diary merely records the usual escorts, small patrols and parades. On the 22nd they took over the defence of the northern perimeter of the camp from the 2/3rd K.A.R. On the 30th Captain Gaskell left for Kilwa to take over the new drafts which had arrived at Dar-es-Salaam on the 26th and which were on their way to Kilwa.

The column marched out for the new offensive on the 4th as already mentioned, but the regiment did not reach the firing line until 20 July. The first ten days were passed in the usual monotony of patrols and parades. On the 10th Captain H. P. Steel of the 129th, Lieut. Mackinnon, I.A.R.O., 3 Indian officers, with 504 other ranks from the 129th and 130th depôts, arrived at Ssingino just outside of Kilwa Kivinje. Major Lewis, who had just returned from Morogoro, and Captain Gaskell were awaiting them. They marched at once for Kiwatama via Matola and reached their destination on the 12th. The next day Lieut. Palin, 7 Indian officers and Headquarters joined them. Two days later Lieut.-Colonel Hulseberg also arrived from

Ssingino. Most of the regiment was now at Kiwatama, but there were still detachments at Kirongo and Mnasi under Captain Gover and Captain Gaskell.

Immediately on arrival at Kiwatama they relieved the 8th South African Infantry picquets. On the 15th Subedar-Major Sarbiland with 50 men took over Minindi Post. On the 17th Subedar Karam Dad with 50 men escorted the Hull Howitzer Battery to Mtshakama on the Mawudji River. On the 18th Lieut. W. Christopher, R.A.M.C., reported for duty. The next day they marched out as Divisional Reserve, leaving Lieut. Mackinnon with an Indian officer and 122 other ranks as garrison, and arrived at Narungombe on the last day of the battle which was being fought at that place. They were too late to take any part in it.

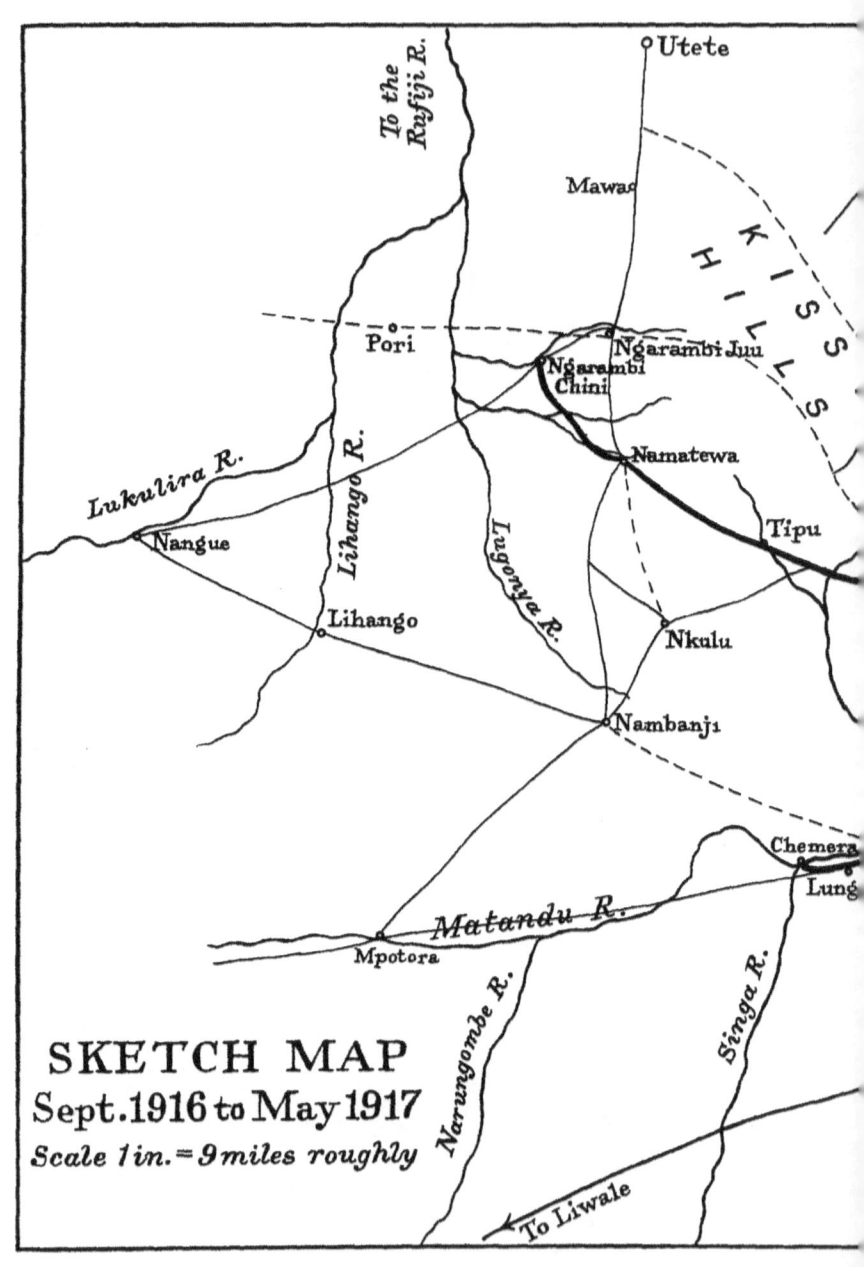

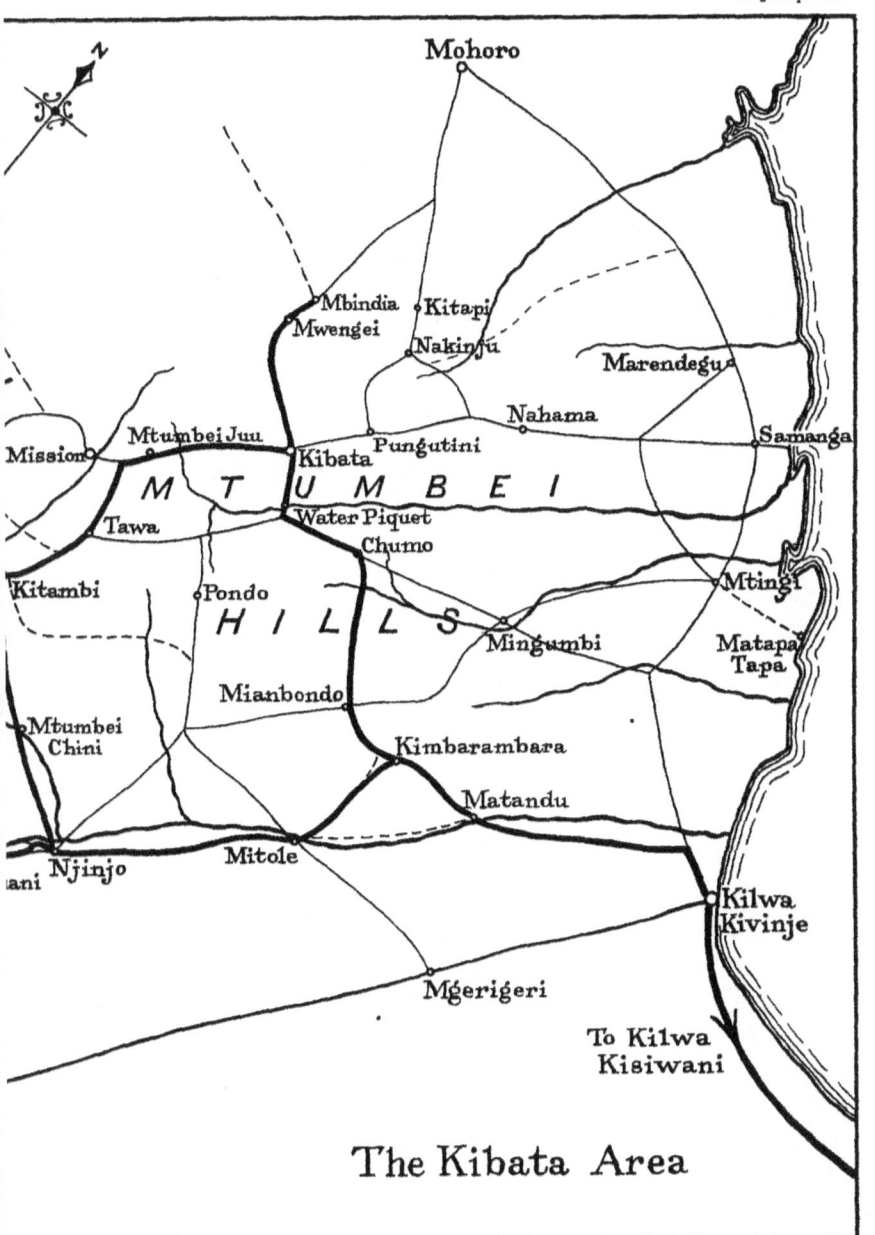

# CHAPTER XV

18 July–18 Sept. 1917: General situation; Nanyati affair; At Mssindy; Preparations for marching out

THE fighting in 1917 was the most bitter of the whole East African campaign. The enemy was now in a territory where 'there were no strategical objectives such as had been offered by the Moschi area, the Tanga and Central Railways, Tabora or Dar-es-Salaam. The country now held by the enemy was, for the most part, wild and inhospitable; means of communication were practically non-existent; and even the better-known places, such as Liwale and Massassi, were, from a military point of view, mere geographical expressions'. The new Commander-in-Chief had come to the conclusion that the only hope of a successful issue lay in a war of attrition. It was to be pawn for pawn, or if necessary two pawns and more for one of the enemy, as the British pawns could be replaced while the German ones could not. 'It therefore became obvious to me, at a very early stage, that our true objective in the coming campaign must be the enemy forces in the field, and that the completion of the conquest of German East Africa could only be brought about by hard hitting, and plenty of it.'[1]

At the opening of the new campaign the enemy forces were divided into two main bodies. The smaller of the two, consisting of some 3000 men, was based in Mahenge and held the country west, north and east of that place to a radius of some 70 miles.

The larger force, commanded by von Lettow-Vorbeck himself, with a strength of about 5000, occupied the Kiturika Hills in the coastal area facing Kilwa and Lindi. These were the pick of the German forces. In addition to

[1] Despatch, dated 21. i. 18, p. 172.

these bodies there were two important detachments, one of four or five companies under von Stuemer in Portuguese East Africa, the other under Naumann north of the Central Railway. These demanded attention, and so drew away a considerable number of troops from the main objective, the enemy forces in the Kiturika Hills.

Facing the main German force there was a Brigade at Lindi under Brigadier-General O'Grady, while between Kilwa and Mohoro, 'and holding the country for thirty-forty miles inland', were two columns under General Hannyngton. With the disposition of the remainder of the British forces we are not concerned here, except to note that the Nigerian Brigade, less one battalion, was at Kimbambawe on the Rufiji.

The long and excessively wet rainy season had greatly weakened all the British forces both in numbers and physique. Battalions were mere shadows of their real strength, and most of the so-called effective troops were weak through long months of semi-starvation and bad living. Such conditions were bad in every way, for in addition to the evils already mentioned, they lowered the morale of the men, and when the strengths were built up again it was with troops which were inexperienced in bush fighting and the ways of the country. The enemy, on the other hand, were in good health and well fed. They had passed the rains mostly in the hills away from the swamps and near their food-supplies, so that when the dry season returned they were fit and rested, while their morale was high and they were all experienced troops who knew the country intimately. It is one of the paradoxes of this war that the enemy were nearly always better fed than we, certainly until the end of 1917. The explanation lay partly in the nature of the campaigns, but largely in faults committed by the Higher Command.

Van Deventer had come to the conclusion that the back of the enemy opposition must be broken before the next rainy season. This is seen when he writes: 'It was evident that the enemy's chief objective was to play for time; to keep the net from closing on him, and to hold out in German East Africa, if possible, till the next wet season, hoping that the rains would then prevent our maintaining the long lines of communication that would be necessary before one brought him to bay. His hopes were doubtless raised by the abnormal rainy season that had just come to an end, for much of the country was still waterlogged and could not be fit for mechanical transport for some time, and thus the period available for active operations was considerably reduced'. It was not so much the enemy's hopes as the fears of the Higher Command, based upon the disastrous experiences of the past five months, which dictated the new policy of hard hitting. After all, if there were to be casualties and overflowing hospitals it were better from fighting than sickness, as given moderate generalship but good troops the enemy would have casualties too. It was to be, as it always was, much more a soldier's war than anything else.

The main advance was to be from Kilwa and Lindi, while operations were also undertaken against the enemy forces at and around Mahenge. Von Stuemer and Naumann were also to receive attention. It was hoped to begin the real advance about the end of June, when 'the state of reinforcements and transport at Kilwa would probably permit one to begin operations in that area against the enemy's main force'.

The forces in the Kilwa area were divided into two columns, No. 1 under Colonel Rose[1] consisting of the 33rd Punjabis, the Gold Coast Regiment, 2/2nd K.A.R., and the 22nd (Derajat) Mountain Battery, to which were added later the 8th South African Infantry. No. 2 Column under Colonel Grant[2] in which were the 57th Rifles, 129th Baluchis, 1/3rd K.A.R., 2/3rd K.A.R., 11th Hull Heavy

[1] Afterwards Colonel Orr.  [2] Afterwards Colonel Ridgeway.

Battery and the 27th Mountain Battery. To these were added the 7th South African Infantry and a company from the 3/3rd K.A.R.

A third and smaller column consisting of the 3/3rd K.A.R., less one company, and 200 rifles of the 40th Pathans was formed under Colonel Taylor.

No. 1 Column was concentrated at Rumbo with a strong detachment opposite Kimamba Hill and a smaller detachment between. No. 2 Column was at Kirongo with detachments at Namatewa, Chemera and Mnasi.

At the beginning of June 'the enemy was holding a general line running from Kimamba Hill, adjoining Kisiwani Harbour, up the right bank of the Ngaura River to Makangaga, and thence across to Kilaganeli, 8 miles south of Kirongo, and to Nahende, on the Liwale road. Kimamba Hill, the rising ground opposite Rumbo, Kilaganeli, and Nahende were held by strong detachments. A total of 18 companies was known to be on this front, of which 11 were between Kimamba Hill and Makangaga. There were also two or three enemy companies to the north-east of Madaba, which sent constant patrols eastward'.

The position was a very strong one, as the enemy had had plenty of time to choose and prepare his defences; moreover should he fall back it was always on carefully selected positions where his supplies would be awaiting him. The immediate British objective, apart from that of inflicting losses in accordance with the new strategy, was to drive the enemy south of the Kiturika Hills and to make him show his intentions as to the line of his retirement, whether towards Liwale or Massassi.

The advance was slightly delayed but began on 4 July as already mentioned, and followed the usual plan of converging columns. Nos. 1 and 2 Columns moved out against the enemy positions round Mnindi, on the Mtshakama road, while No. 3 Column, leaving Wungwi, made for Nambanditi. There was almost constant fighting from the

5th until the 20th, on which date the enemy evacuated Narungombe. Two of the engagements were particularly severe, and the losses at Narungombe were heavy on both sides, though much more so to the British, as they were the attackers, and also as a large number of the wounded were burnt to death owing to the bush being set on fire. The enemy withdrew towards Mihambia, and eventually established a line from that place to Ndessa with a strong outpost on his left flank at Nanyati. The British forces held the line of the Mawudji River. Here until about 19 September the front stabilised itself, as the British forces could not advance any further till their transport was ready and until the Nigerians and fresh Indian troops were brought up. Meantime the offensive had been transferred to the Lindi sector where the fighting was even more severe. As a result of the fighting in the Kilwa region the Kiturika Hills had been cleared, so that things were more comfortable in Kilwa, but apart from the casualties inflicted on the enemy little else had been effected.

The 129th saw none of this heavy fighting, as they only joined No. 2 Column the evening before Narungombe was evacuated. They were still very split up, but on the evening of the 21st were at last concentrated, except for Lieut. Mackinnon's detachment, at Rumbo, when Captains Gaskell and Gover brought in their men from Mnasi and Kirongo respectively. The regiment remained at Rumbo for a week, during which time it was reorganised. Here much work was done in training bombers and instructing machine gunners. The Diary records the arrival of Stokes guns and Lewis guns, two new weapons for this part of East Africa. There were also the inevitable patrols and numerous camp duties. The day before they marched out Captain H. V. Lewis went sick with malaria and was admitted to hospital. His illness was a great loss to the regiment, especially at this time.

On the 28th the regiment, consisting of 6 British officers

including the Medical Officer, 16 Indian officers, 450 men with 7 machine guns, marched at the head of the column to Nangagchi via Mtandawala. Thence they marched alone, late the following evening, to Mssindy to reinforce the 1/3rd K.A.R., where they remained until the evening of 4 August, engaged on the usual routine duties.

At 5 p.m. on the 4th they marched out as part of a small column with orders to attack the enemy at Nanyati. This place had been reconnoitred on the 3rd by an officer's patrol which had drawn fire. It was estimated that there were about 40 enemy rifles. A porter deserter stated that there were 30 German whites, 150 askaris and 3 machine guns, but he was thought to be exaggerating. It was further reported that there were no entrenchments. It was not realised that Nanyati was really held in considerable force and covered the enemy line stretching through Mihambia-Ndessa, though it ought to have been guessed that it would be entrenched. Actually it was a very carefully prepared position with an excellent field of fire.

The column consisted of some 300 rifles, of which 200 were Baluchis and the rest 1/3rd K.A.R., 1 section 22nd (Derajat) Mountain Battery, 1 Stokes gun and 1 Sub-section Field Ambulance and was under the command of Lieut.-Colonel Hulseberg. The 129th were commanded by Captain Gaskell with Captain Steel as his Adjutant.

The country between Mssindy and Nanyati is covered by dense bush with very narrow native paths winding through it, so that progress was exceedingly slow. At 7 p.m. Nasuras Shamba was reached. By this time it was too dark to see, so a perimeter camp was formed and the column slept till 3 a.m., when the moon gave sufficient light to make marching possible. The country now began to be more open, so that one could see some 200–300 yards. About 5 a.m. the guide informed them that they were in the vicinity of Nanyati, and the scouts began to feel out cautiously. Gradually the dawn came but still no enemy, 'and someone says "another blank day...". Then about fifteen shots in quick succession and the day has begun'. It was now about 5.40 a.m. The advance-guard under Lieut. Palin, with Jemadars Nek Mahomed and Murtaza, pushed forward steadily, while the two guns swung into action, shelling in the direction of the enemy's anticipated retreat. The distance from the enemy entrenchments at this point was probably 2500 yards, though their existence at the time was unsuspected. The firing came from some huts, situated on a slight rise, held by an enemy picquet. After the first few shots came another long silence, broken by occasional shots, as the men pushed forward across a stretch of cultivated land and into more bush which was fairly dense. Gradually the distance lengthened until a mile or more had been covered, and again expectations had died down, as it seemed to be a case of the usual patrol firing a few shots and retreating. A nullah was reached and occupied. Beyond this the ground opened up again into 'park land' sloping gently up and with a visibility of some 200 yards. The advance-guard began to push rapidly up the slope, and for a moment the day seemed over. 'Well, thank goodness this show is over without any casualties', says Gaskell. 'Send up and tell the advance-guard commander that we shall be having breakfast soon.' But there was to be no breakfast that morning for anyone, and Headquarters would require no more breakfasts. As so often happened the serious fighting came when it was least expected.

No sooner had the main body reached the nullah than heavy machine-gun and rifle fire was opened on the advance-guard, who were already well up the slope and within range of the enemy main position, which had been carefully sited and prepared. In view of the volume of fire and the unknown strength of the enemy great caution was necessary in any further advance. Neither Captain Gaskell nor Captain Steel had actually seen any fighting of this nature, while many of the sepoys were young recruits. The result was that Captain Gaskell, who was in command of the regiment, threw his men into action too quickly, and having committed himself against an enemy of at least equal numbers in a prepared position was compelled to take the great risk of reinforcing the firing line by sending up all his reserves, even to the extent of leaving Headquarters almost unguarded.

Lieut. Palin was immediately reinforced by the remaining two platoons of 'D' Company and gradually advanced to within 170 yards of the enemy trenches. Here further advance was impossible for the moment, as all cover had been cleared away and any advance had to be in the open. The general position about this time was as follows: Column H.Q. were some 1500 yards north of the nullah, close to the path, with two platoons of the 1/3rd K.A.R. in general reserve. Close by were the two guns of the 22nd Mountain Battery with the other two platoons as a protection. There were two machine guns guarding the left flank of the guns and Headquarters. Regimental H.Q. were just south of the nullah with Captain Gover's company still in hand. With the 129th H.Q. was Major G. V. Dreyer, R.A., who had accompanied his section 'as it looked as if it might be a tricky show'. Major Dreyer was connected by telephone with his guns, while Captain Gaskell was also connected in the same way to Column H.Q.

Between 7.30 and 7.45 a.m., very soon after the advance-guard had pushed up the slope and had been reinforced, the firing became increasingly severe. Captain Gaskell then ordered Captain Gover forward with two platoons of 'A' Company. No. 3 platoon under Subedar Nur Khan, and No. 4 platoon under Jemadar Mahomed Bakhsh thereupon advanced on the right and left of the path. No. 3 bore away too much to the right, but were brought back in the right direction by Captain Gover. This platoon eventually came in on the left flank of the enemy's position and got within 30 yards of it, but were unable to charge home because of our own fire from the company on the enemy's front. Almost immediately after Captain Gover had advanced, the remaining two platoons were thrown in, so that Headquarters had now no reserve or protection save for a picquet of seven men with a Lewis gun.

What happened behind the firing line will never be known exactly. Major Dreyer, who had gone forward to watch the effect of his gun fire, became uneasy about the left flank. 'After a time I came to the conclusion that the enemy were working round our left.... I reported this to Column H.Q, by telephone.' A platoon of the 1/3rd K.A.R. were sent up, while Major Dreyer ordered his guns to shell the threatened flank. He also ordered Lieut. Boshoff to fire a few shells from the Stokes gun in the same direction, but the gun very soon went out of action, as it had used up its ammunition. Shortly after 8 a.m. Major Dreyer met Lieut. Palin and discussed the situation, which was far from being altogether satisfactory. While they were talking they heard firing in their rear and this increased in intensity. Soon after this they also came under fire from the rear, and came to the conclusion that it was from the K.A.R. platoon. Lieut. Palin had sent back runners a little previously to this, but nothing had happened. He now went back himself to see what was happening and if possible to direct the K.A.R. From that time he was not seen again. What happened to him will be told shortly.

The situation in the firing line was now thoroughly unsatisfactory. Captain Gover with his company could get no further owing to our own fire. He repeatedly sent back runners to Headquarters giving the situation, but neither runner nor message returned, which was not surprising as Headquarters had ceased to exist. On the enemy's front 'D' Company was also awaiting instructions from Headquarters, or failing that from its Company Commander, though no one knew of his whereabouts. And so the morning wore on. 'It nears midday, the sun becomes unendurable, we have had no food since yesterday evening. Many of my men and three of the machine guns are out of action. The psychological moment has passed, there are not enough of us left to do much good now.... A man comes creeping up through the grass, and says the Colonel commanding the column wants to see me. Is he sure? Yes. Where is the officer commanding the 129th? He does not know.'

Major Dreyer's fear for the left flank had not been without foundation. The risk had been taken and the price paid. Probably just about the time Major Dreyer met Lieut. Palin, a German patrol, estimated in the report submitted to Column H.Q. at Mssindy at some 50 men, had made its way through the bush on the 129th's left flank. It had first encountered the K.A.R. platoon on its way up to Major Dreyer and had retreated into the bush, though only after inflicting severe casualties on the K.A.R., of whom but seven survived. Instead of retreating, the patrol had worked its way along the edge of the bush, and coming upon Headquarters had charged out and annihilated them. Captain Gaskell was shot through the head, Captain Steel through the heart, Captain Newton, who was attending to the wounded close by, had his arm severed, the Havildar-Major and two or three sepoys were also shot dead. A few men escaped into the bush.

After wiping out Headquarters the patrol worked its way up the line of communication towards the rear of 'D' Company, and it was only some 60 or 70 yards away when Lieut. Palin ran into it. Palin, seeing askaris, very naturally mistook them for the 1/3rd K.A.R. platoon, which he knew was coming up and so walked straight up to them. To his astonishment he saw Captain Newton being hustled along 'in a dazed condition and pumping out blood by the quart from the stump of his arm'. No one was offering to give him first aid, so Palin rushed up to him. An askari fired

BRIGADIER-GENERAL J. A. HANNYNGTON
C.B., C.M.G., D.S.O.

at him twice at only a few yards range but missed, and Palin, realising by now that they were German askaris, went up to the doctor and tried to stop the haemorrhage. This he had almost done when the German officer in command of the patrol, shouting that there was no time for bandages, tore them off. Captain Newton very soon bled to death and was left where he fell. Lieut. Palin remained a prisoner until he was released by the 2nd Nigerians on the Makonde Plateau some four months later. He rejoined the regiment at Dar-es-Salaam.

Major Dreyer waited for some time, but as Lieut. Palin did not return, and as he could not get into communication with any British officer, 'decided that if the position was to be taken before the arrival of German reinforcements, it must be done at once'. He, therefore, ordered the Subedar-Major to move the regimental reserve to within 400 yards of the firing line, and was about to issue orders for the assault 'when he (the Subedar-Major) informed me that the reserve had been thrown in at the beginning of the fight'. At this moment the six survivors of the K.A.R. platoon arrived. Major Dreyer was forced to the conclusion that, 'with no reserve and with no knowledge of what lay in front of us, it was out of the question to attack'. A patrol sent to the left front was 'quickly destroyed'. He made his way back, therefore, to Column H.Q., which were now at the nullah, and was there informed that the Regimental H.Q. had been annihilated. Going forward once more he passed Headquarters, lying about as they had been shot, and at 10 a.m. again reported the situation, this time by telephone. He was informed that reinforcements had been despatched from Mssindy, and urged that when they arrived they should be employed in helping to capture the enemy position. This request was refused, as Column H.Q. at Mssindy did not wish to become involved in heavy fighting. At 11.15 a.m., under orders from Lieut.-Colonel Hulseberg, he began to withdraw the 129th. This was done very slowly at first, as it was necessary to collect the killed and wounded, for whom there were no stretchers. These were carried back while the firing line fell back very slowly, 'taking three-quarters of an hour to do the first 600 yards'. Captain Gover's two platoons on the right also withdrew. A halt was made by the gun position where they entrenched and also buried the dead. Casualties had been heavy—25 per cent of those engaged—but were particularly so among the officers. Of the British officers all were casualties except Captain Gover. Four of the nine Indian officers were killed or wounded. Of these Subedar Sherbat Khan and Jemadar Nek Mahomed were killed, both in the firing line. Subedar Sherbat Khan was one of the few original Indian officers and had served with the regiment in Flanders. He had seen much fighting and had always set a fine example. Curiously enough he had gone into this action quite sure that he would not be killed, having said so to Captain Gover when moving forward. Subedar Saif Ali Khan and Jemadar Ghulam Kadar were wounded.

The column marched back to Mssindy that day, arriving there about midnight. A strong K.A.R. patrol was left behind which reconnoitred the Nanyati positions and found them abandoned. Evidently the enemy had withdrawn about the same time as the column was falling back and were in a hurry to do so, as the K.A.R. found a complete machine gun with spare parts, a tripod of a second gun, and 5000 rounds of small-arms ammunition. A diary captured some weeks later contained the following entry: 'Yesterday at Nanyati our troops had a smart encounter with the enemy. As so often happens in this country, both sides finally retired simultaneously'. It would also appear that the enemy patrol which did so much damage arrived on the spot by accident and was not a deliberately planned counter-attack.

The total 129th casualties were 43, of which half were

killed. Major Dreyer in his report 'drew particular attention to the steadiness of the 129th in spite of the large number of young soldiers in the ranks'. He especially mentioned Subedar-Major Sarbiland, 'whose coolness and contempt for danger were most noticeable'.

Nanyati is a very typical example of the East African bush fighting, with its surprises and difficulties. In itself it was only one of many unpleasant 'incidents' which might and did happen from time to time. It in no way affected the morale of the regiment, which regarded it and its losses as part of the day's work. Nor was it entirely fruitless. The enemy never occupied the place again, and so the way was made clearer for the advance against Ndessa some weeks later. The rest of the month passed without anything of interest happening. There were picquets on Mtumba Hill, patrols along the Mssindy-Nangagchi road, garrisons at Lungo and endless practice and training, especially with the machine guns and Lewis guns. There is an echo of former days in a short Brigade entry dated the 11th. 'Enemy's camp at Ndessa sniped by party of Baluchis.' This was the work of Havildar Reshmin with a party of five Mahsuds.

September is also uneventful until the 18th. Between the 12th and that date a number of junior officers are attached for duty, namely Lieut. T. S. Uberoi, I.M.S., Lieuts. Piper and Leese of the 57th and the 29th respectively, and Lieuts. Guy, Fox, Pratt, and Mitchell, I.A.R.O. Also Lieut. Pilkington and one Stokes gun, though in this case the officer's attachment was incidental to that of the gun.

# CHAPTER XVI

18 Sept.–29 Nov. 1917: Attack on Ndessa-Mihambia line; Offensive continues along valley of Mbemkuru; Action at Namehi; Advance on Ruponda; Fighting to Lukuledi; Back to Ruponda resting; The final drive; Von Lettow crosses into Portuguese territory; Operations against Tafel; Final fight of regiment at Mwiti Water

BY the middle of September van Deventer was ready for the second stage of his offensive in the Kilwa area. There was now sufficient transport for the whole force, which had been considerably strengthened by the arrival of the bulk of the Nigerian Brigade, the 25th Indian Cavalry, the 55th Rifles and the 127th Baluchis.

The general plan was 'to make a combined movement southwards from the Kilwa area and south-westwards from Lindi, engaging the enemy wherever met with'. It was hoped 'thus to be able to deal with the enemy main force, whatever course it might take. If it went westwards towards the Liwale-Mahenge area, the Kilwa force could be diverted in that direction, while the Lindi force occupied Massassi and cut off retreat to the south. If it stood to fight against the Kilwa force, the Lindi force would come in against its flank and rear. If it were divided against the Kilwa and Lindi forces, or opposed mainly to the latter, then the Kilwa force was strong enough to press back anything that might oppose it, and attack the flank or rear of the portion opposing the Lindi troops. Meantime the western forces were to press on vigorously and keep all enemy troops in the Mahenge area fully contained'.

The forward move began on the 19th against the enemy position between Ndessa and Mihambia. This was held by some six companies under Captain Koehl but was not so strongly garrisoned as it had been, as von Lettow, thinking the main advance was coming from the Lindi front, had marched with four companies and two guns to reinforce

General Wahle. His arrival had been well timed, and if he did not achieve what he wanted, he at least prevented the British from achieving their objective.

The enemy positions were well prepared, so that a direct attack was impossible. It was decided, therefore, that No. 1 Column from Narungombe should attack Mihambia while No. 2 Column, in which were the 129th, should turn the Ndessa flank. At the same time the Nigerians were to move out from Mssindy by a more circuitous route against Mawarenye and try to cut off the enemy's retreat. The 25th Cavalry 'were despatched on a special mission to destroy the enemy food depôts at Nangano and on the Mbemkuru between there and Nahungu'.

The movement against the Ndessa flank was particularly difficult. Its success depended largely upon its secrecy, so that it needed to be executed quickly, but the bush in this region was exceptionally dense while the tracks were unknown. The column had to march for two days on a compass bearing, no easy matter. This bearing had been obtained by sending out an aeroplane which dropped smoke bombs on the Ndessa trenches, while two observers, one on Mtumba Hill near Mssindy, the other on high ground near Mbindia, took bearings on the smoke column. From these bearings a sketch was plotted giving the magnetic bearings and the lengths of each section.

On the 18th No. 2 Column left Mssindy and marched to a point one mile west of Mtumba Hill and bivouacked. Next day the march was continued due south until 7 p.m. 'No. 2 Column, led by an officer with a compass, and carefully pacing the distance, marched through the forest to a point "A" where they bivouacked at nightfall; at dawn they proceeded to point "B" where the direction was again changed; as each unit arrived at points "C", "D" and "E", they wheeled left, advanced a certain distance and then deployed right and left, bringing them into line in the rear of the German position. Immediately on reaching their positions they made a boma along their front....' The 129th were on the extreme right of the British line.

The whole movement was a very fine piece of work, and the enemy were completely surprised as their attention had been engaged by a skeleton frontal attack. Throughout that day and the next they made repeated efforts to break through the British positions, but were beaten off. The 129th had 'A', 'C', and 'D' Companies in the firing line. Put in this way it sounds as if they were in some strength, but actually they mustered about 250 rifles all told.

By the evening of the 21st patrols reported that Ndessa Chini had been evacuated. As usual the enemy had withdrawn successfully, round the column's right flank, though they had lost considerably during the two days' fighting. Next day the regiment marched to Kitandi. In their retreat the enemy bumped into the Nigerians, who lay across their line of retreat at Bweho. Here also there was severe fighting, but again they managed to get away south to the Mbemkuru River, while the column followed after them.

The four days of marching and fighting had imposed a great strain on the men as there was a desperate shortage of water. 'We had no water from noon on the 20th till the morning of the 24th, except what each man carried. The water that we found on the morning of the 24th had been defiled.' The Diary makes no record of this, nor of the magnificent spirit shown by the men of the 129th and the 127th in helping the 22nd Battery. Major Dreyer records on the 22nd: 'Our horses and mules had had no water for 67 hours. To-day they got half a gallon....We marched till 15.30 hours. At 17.00 hours ordered on to help the Nigerian Brigade heavily engaged at Bweho Chini. I gave them all the water we had in our pakhals and then went to beg from the infantry. Everyone was desperately hard up for water, yet the 129th gave us one pakhal, which equalled 25 per cent of what they had, and the 2/3rd K.A.R.

two gallons'. On the 23rd he records: 'the 127th Baluchis offered to help us to carry or drag our guns as the mules were all in. However, water was reached at 14.30 hours so it was not necessary to accept this fine offer, made by men who were themselves worn out by thirst'.

On the 23rd they reached Mawarenye, but left again on the evening of the 24th, after such diversions as laying an ambush which did not come off, cutting a road through the scrub, and doing the usual patrolling and picqueting. On the 25th Nkiu was occupied without opposition. The regiment, which was advance-guard to the column, pushed across the Mbemkuru and bivouacked on the south bank. Here they remained until the afternoon of the 28th patrolling and cutting roads for the motor transport which was to follow. A new arrival about this time wrote: '51 miles of the most fearful road. Just a track driven straight through the jungle. We went over the scene of last week's fighting, and now the troops in front line are being supplied by motor-car! It is really wonderful how the motors get along'. It was still more wonderful how infantry got through, chopping their way mile after mile through the scrub.

On the 28th they marched to Beka and the next afternoon to Narungu. Here Lieut.-Colonel W. N. Hay took over command of the regiment from Lieut.-Colonel Hulseberg, D.S.O., who had been transferred to the 127th, his own regiment. Colonel Hulseberg had been with the regiment almost continuously since it landed in January 1916. With him went Lieuts. Fox, Pratt and Mitchell, their places being taken by Lieut. Hawkes, 54th Sikhs, and Lieuts. Woodward and Bannerman, 52nd Sikhs, who had arrived with Colonel Hay. On the 30th the regiment was transferred to No. 1 Column at '8 miles camp'.

On 1 October the strength of the regiment was 10 British officers, including the Medical Officer, 16 Indian officers and 462 other ranks. Of the British officers all were very junior save for the Commanding Officer and Major Gover. The transfer to No. 1 Column marks the beginning of a fresh period of fighting. The next two months saw much heavy and exhausting marching and a series of large and small attacks, all of which formed part of a much larger programme of operations and which greatly reduced the fighting strength of the enemy.

Until 7 October the column followed the valley of the Mbemkuru and then turned south making its way via Ruponda to the Lukuledi River, following the enemy as they withdrew towards the Massassi area.

The Mbemkuru at this time 'was a small stream flowing through a shallow valley with low well-wooded hills enclosing it. The country was as usual eminently suited for rear-guard actions, so that the advance was necessarily slow. On the 1st the 129th were at the tail of the column, swallowing everybody's dust, but soon contact was made with the enemy near Mitoneno, where they had taken up a position on some low hills south of the river. The 2/2nd K.A.R. and the Gold Coast Regiment were soon engaged, while the Baluchis were in reserve with some 200 rifles—the remainder having been detailed for escort and picquet duty. In a short time they were ordered to reinforce the firing line and were gradually fed forward by Colonel Hay. It was the usual blind fighting: 'The firing was heavy but no enemy was seen'. About 6.30 the enemy retired. Lieut. Bannerman and Jemadar Mewa Khan were wounded, though not seriously, while 4 men were killed and 10 wounded. After dark they sorted themselves out. Fortunately the moon came up to help them; rations did not, so they made the best of it.

The column advanced once more on the 4th along the Namehi road on the south bank of the river with the 129th at the head of the main body. Very much the same scene was re-enacted. About 8 a.m. the advance-guard came up against the enemy at Ruangwa Chini, and after the usual preliminaries the 129th were ordered off to the left against the enemy's right flank. The bush was very thick, so that progress was slow. After advancing some 2000 yards they drove in an enemy picquet on a ridge. Then turning northwards towards the road they cleared another knoll and halted a little way beyond to await the advance of the other troops which were attacking along the road. Finding they had advanced too far they fell back to the knoll while the 1/3rd and 2/2nd K.A.R. came up on their flanks. The new line had hardly been established before the enemy counter-attacked with considerable vigour. The brunt of the attack fell on the centre held by the 129th: the critical point being a knoll of bare rock on the regiment's left. Had this been taken the enemy could have enfiladed the whole of the British line. The knoll 'was solid rock and one could not dig in on it at all; "sangars" that were made did more harm than good as the rock was of a very splinterable variety'. Captain Mackinnon was mortally wounded and a machine gun knocked out at the end of the ridge which they were defending. The machine-gun porters then added to the confusion by bolting. The Adjutant, Lieut. Piper, immediately rallied a few men and stopped the enemy attack, while Colonel Hay sent up another machine gun to replace the first. Once more the attack developed, when, just at the critical moment, the second gun was knocked out and its crew killed and wounded by a misdirected shell from one of the Gold Coast Regiment's guns. The situation was saved this time 'by the steadiness of an Indian officer with a few men and of Lieut. Foster, 27th Mountain Battery, who held up the enemy: and the 2/2nd K.A.R. drove them off'. The Indian officer was Subedar-Major Sarbiland, who as usual was always equal to any emergency. Major Gover also helped very materially. Lieut. Woodward, who had been sent up to reinforce the position, found Major Gover already there, 'standing up on the top of the knoll scorning to take the slightest cover as usual'. The casualties were 3 killed and 9 wounded in addition to Captain Mackinnon.

But the enemy had not retired, as was discovered almost immediately the column advanced next morning. The 129th formed the advance-guard but had proceeded barely a quarter of a mile when firing began from a small hill held by a party of the enemy. This was cleared in about half an hour with the loss of a few men, and the regiment, 'having re-formed, advanced astride the road' for some 300 yards, when they came again under fire, this time from the enemy's main position. As at Nanyati the bush had been cleared so that the assault would have to be delivered well in the open. Three companies were soon in the firing line, but no progress could be made. 'Several efforts were made throughout the day, but the enemy had every point marked down and our men were hit directly they showed at all.' Fortunately there were a good number of large ant-hills which gave cover and even permitted some slight observation. Two other battalions on the left were also held up. About 4 p.m. the column retired to the camp of the previous night, while Major Gover with 'D' Company remained on the captured hill. Jemadar Karam Dad was wounded, 5 other ranks killed and 22 wounded.

Next morning the column marched at 6 o'clock, and made a wide detour to the south with the intention of coming in on the enemy's rear. At the same time the Force Reserve Column went on along the road but found the enemy positions had already been abandoned. They also found a gun which had been knocked out the previous day. The column made a few prisoners, and learned that the enemy casualties had been more or less equal to their own. They also 'captured a telephone and then got an askari taking a chit asking why no answer was coming along it'.

The march now continued in a south-easterly direction towards Ruponda along the valley of the Ngandi River, a tributary of the Mbemkuru. Progress was at the usual slow pace, about 10 to 12 miles a day, as every yard had to be felt and searched lest the enemy should be in waiting. On the 9th the Mnero Mission was reached after 'a long march with no water *en route*, and we expected to have to fight for our next drink'. Fortunately the enemy had withdrawn, but 'in case of a trap two companies were pushed rapidly through to occupy a ridge beyond and guard against counter-attack'.

The following day Ruponda was occupied after very slight opposition. 'This place had been occupied by the enemy for a long time and they had a hospital there.' This was occupied by the 129th, who also found 'some welcome stores of food, maize and flour'. Unhappily Lieut. Piper was sniped as they approached Ruponda and died next morning. This was the only casualty, but left that semi-resentful feeling which such casualties do.

They remained in the vicinity of Ruponda with No. 2 Column until the 16th, when they rejoined No. 1 Column at Mnero Mission. The week was occupied in the usual way with picqueting and patrolling and also with marching and counter-marching. On the 12th they hunted for a German patrol with the usual success. Next day they marched to '11-mile post on Ruponda-Mnero road in accordance with orders received from Hanforce'. On the following day they marched to Mbemba for similar reasons. There they became part of the Force Reserve, but only for a day, when they marched back to Mnero Mission to join No. 1 Column as already mentioned. By this time a considerable number of men had gone sick, 'principally from exhaustion'. On the 17th they were back in Ruponda and took over the post from the 1/3rd K.A.R. Between that date and the 24th No. 1 Column of the Kilwa force 'successfully raided' Lukuledi Mission. The despatch informs us that 'Colonel Orr, with No. 1 Column, leaving Ruponda on the 17th, reached Lukuledi next day, and had a sharp fight with two or three enemy companies.... On the 21st the column was attacked at Lukuledi by the force which it had previously fought, reinforced by at least three other companies. The enemy were repulsed with loss.... The column then withdrew, reaching Ruponda on the 24th. Valuable information about the country, roads, water, etc., had been obtained, which proved of great use to us later on'. This is rather euphemistically put. The truth was that the raid only became such when the enemy was found to be too strong, and the general situation was such as did not warrant any further stretching of an already too extended line of communication. The same despatch informs us: 'The line from Kilwa had now been stretched so far that maintenance of the forces fed from it was becoming a serious problem...'. Also there was considerable fear that the enemy might cut it altogether, with disastrous results.

The raid on Lukuledi involved very considerable strain and fatigue on the already tired and weary men, as rations were running out as usual and even water had to be dug for. But they did not come in for any fighting as they were acting as escort to the Ammunition Column and Field Ambulances. At the Lukuledi Mission they found good water, but Colonel Hay records in his diary: 'However, it is a very depleted regiment now. The men are tired out and want a rest. The coughing at night is dreadful. If we could get a month's rest I think we should be a regiment again'. Instead of a rest they had a skirmish next day, which was much more important than the regiment's slight casualties would indicate. Major Gover, who was wounded in this action, writes of it: 'It is true that the 129th had only three casualties but this was probably due to their digging in. Von Lettow, after suffering 33 per cent casualties on the Lindi front, came across by forced march to Lukuledi and joining with his companies already in that vicinity attacked No. 1 Column. The attack was executed so skilfully that it was a complete surprise; he wiped out the camp and transport of the 25th Cavalry (situated about a mile north of the column camp), and captured a large quantity of ammunition, thereby immobilising that regiment; at the same time he attacked No. 1 Column itself south of the camp and inflicted quite severe casualties on them. During the afternoon one of his companies approached within about 100 yards of the north side of the camp, and had they known that it was only held by myself and a few other wounded men they could have rushed it and destroyed a lot of baggage and probably the Hull howitzers also, as they do not seem to have had any escort at that moment; fortunately they assumed that the perimeter was occupied, and desisted; von Lettow himself records, "an attack on the camp without the advantage of surprise had little hope of success"'.

The Diary dismisses this affair tersely: 'The regiment was to have proceeded to Domundo with the column, but as the column started the 1/3rd K.A.R., who were occupying the Lukuledi Mission, were heavily attacked and the regiment was sent up to take a position on their left. After great difficulty, owing to not being able at first to get into touch with the 1/3rd K.A.R., the regiment entrenched itself on the K.A.R. left. Major Gover and two men were wounded'. Major Gover's loss to the regiment was a very real one 'as he was the only pre-war officer with the regiment. No one else of more than two years' service'. But the loss was more than that of an experienced officer. A junior officer wrote of him that he was 'absolutely devoid of fear and absolutely imperturbable', and that he 'inspired both the men and junior officers with untold confidence'.

As usual the enemy counter-attacked, 'but the Stokes section spoilt the show through excess of zeal. Half-a-dozen shells were in the air before you could say "knife", and this choked the enemy off before he had properly come under fire'. It was an exhausting day.

They remained at the Mission until the evening of the

next day when they marched to rejoin the column, and having done so marched all night as advance-guard to Chingwea, which was reached at 3 a.m. They 'bivouacked in column of route on the roadside. Actually they dropped with exhaustion in their tracks and slept where they lay, but were away again by 2.30 on the same day, the 23rd, and got into camp after 7 p.m. very tired after 25 miles in 24 hours'. To help them on a porter 'threw down a box of bombs and two exploded, killing two and wounding twelve porters'.

They remained at Ruponda until 6 November, as the Higher Command had 'decided to spend the next fortnight in active patrolling and in refitting and resting the troops before beginning what promised to be the final phase of operations in German East Africa. Until 6 November no further movement of importance took place on the eastern front'.

There is no doubt that the comparative rest at Ruponda was not only welcome but necessary, though the 'refitting' was not very obvious. Water was not too plentiful, though enough for drinking purposes. Rations were still short: 'we are supposed to make two days' rations last for three days, but have not got the full two days' allowance'. On the day following this entry they 'got an ox and distributed it', but against this the 'small allowance of rum has run out'. By the 31st the regiment was 'more or less washed and cleaned now, but there are so many duties that it is hard to fit in washing time'. There were daily parades and instruction in musketry and some long patrol work. They were also reinforced by a draft made up of a few men from India and the rest from hospital under Lieut. L. W. Guiton of the 67th Punjabis.

By 6 November everything was ready for the final drive. The German force under Tafel, some 1800 strong, had been driven away from the Mahenge-Liwale area and was moving southwards to the Rovuma, while the main enemy forces under von Lettow were now concentrated in a relatively small area between Mahiwa, Nangoo and Lukuledi, with minor forces at Manacho and Newala. Once more it was hoped to drive him into a corner and come to a final decision. Had there been some real troops along the Rovuma instead of the Portuguese, expectations might have been realised. As it was he extricated himself, though not without severe losses, and retreating into Portuguese territory carried on hostilities with diminishing vigour until the Armistice.

The general idea of the new offensive was for the Lindi force to advance against Mahiwa while the Kilwa force pushed south, threatening the enemy flank and rear. Accordingly No. 2 Column pushed on to Lukuledi Mission while No. 1 Column reached a point a few miles to the east.

The first day's march was over the well-known track to Chingwea, on which occasion the regiment acted as advance-guard. It was evidently an evil place even for East Africa, for it is recorded: 'Water very scarce and filthy too. Horrid camp and I never want to see it again'. Next day they formed the rear-guard and marched to Igumi, a long march of nearly 18 miles. The column had to cut its way most of the time as the bush was so dense, and having arrived had to dig for water. On the 9th the march was to Chigugu on the Massassi-Lindi road and then the next day to the Ndanda Mission, which was occupied after very slight opposition. Sixty-four Germans and 129 askaris, mostly sick, were captured. On the 11th they had a little fight. This developed as the result of a patrol, under Subedar Nur Khan, being sent to drive in an enemy picquet which was still in position some 1000 yards away on the ridge occupied by the regiment. The picquet fell back and Nur Khan's patrol bumped the enemy's main position. He held on until the remainder of the regiment, less 100 rifles, was brought up to assault the position, which seems to have been somewhat similar to that at Mwengei. In spite of the smallness of their numbers, about 130, they eventually turned the enemy out of his position with the loss of Jemadar Fakhar Din wounded, 1 other rank killed and 7 wounded. The Stokes gun materially assisted in preparing the way. Leaving a picquet they then returned to camp. On the 12th the column returned to Chigugu leaving the 129th behind to await the arrival of the Nigerian Brigade, which marched in during the afternoon. They then rejoined the column. Meantime the enemy had been driven, after hard fighting, out of Mahiwa and Nangoo and was falling back on Chiwata, which was reported to be a strong natural position on the edge of the Makonde Plateau. It was expected that he would put up a fight in this place.

Chiwata was to be attacked from the north with the Lindi force and from the west with the bulk of the Kilwa forces, while the mounted troops operated towards Kitengari against the line of retirement. No. 1 Column was directed therefore to march to Mwiti, which was occupied on the 14th after some slight opposition. The regiment was not engaged in this action as, having been advance-guard the day before when marching to Namakongwa, it was now in reserve.

On 15 November the column rested from its labours, but the 129th were ordered to proceed to a village some 7 miles away where a small German force was reported to be. Having arrived, the village headman informed them that two Germans and ten askaris had been captured there the day before by a cavalry patrol. Further search found nothing except a deserted camping-place, and so they marched back to Mwiti. There they rested until 2 p.m. the next day, while the column moved out to Miwale Hill where there was some slight opposition.

Early on the 15th it became evident that the enemy did not intend to defend Chiwata seriously and were withdrawing to Lutshemi some miles further south-east. Chiwata was occupied that morning by the Nigerian Brigade and No. 2 Column after slight opposition. Ninety-eight Germans and 425 askaris surrendered, while a considerable number of British prisoners were released.

The various forces were now directed against Lutshemi. No. 1 Column marched via Miwale, the Nigerians from Chiwata and No. 3 Column from its position on the plateau. No. 2 Column was in reserve at Mwiti, 'while the Mounted Column moved east with the object of cutting communication between Kitengari and Newala'. On the 18th Lutshemi was occupied after two days' fighting. Some 300 Germans and 700 askaris were taken prisoner and a certain number of British prisoners released, amongst whom was Lieut. Palin, captured at Nanyati. The main enemy force slipped away once more to the south-east towards Simba's followed by No. 3 Column. No. 1 Column had taken little part in the heavy fighting or in the capture of Lutshemi. They had marched on Lutshemi from Miwale which they entered on the evening of the 18th, and found it 'littered with rifles, ammunition, kit and food, showing that the enemy's departure had been a hurried one'.

Tafel's force was now demanding attention. It was known to be moving south with the object of effecting a junction with von Lettow, but up till the 20th its exact position was unknown. On the 20th came definite information that it was on the upper reaches of and moving down the Bangalla River, while it was reported that von Lettow was making for the Rovuma with the intention of moving westwards to meet Tafel.

No. 1 Column was ordered at once to Newala, No. 2 Column to Massassi on the 22nd and thence on the 23rd to the Bangalla, while the Nigerian Brigade concentrated at Massassi. No. 3 Column, having returned from the pursuit of von Lettow, was directed to Mwiti.

The hope of capturing von Lettow's force had not been realised, but the next few days were made exciting in trying to round up Tafel. This excitement was, of course, largely confined to G.H.Q, and the Headquarters of the various columns. The smaller units knew little, save that they were being shuffled about even more rapidly than usual, while rations were rather more scanty than before. They were, however, buoyed up by the knowledge of large captures of prisoners and the release of many British comrades.

Tafel was unaware that von Lettow had abandoned the Makonde Plateau and so was moving in that direction. On the night of the 22/23rd he passed through Mtimbo, and on the 25th his advanced troops had engaged a British post at Tschirimba Hill. By this time he had discovered his mistake and was trying to break away and was reported to be making for Luatala. A cavalry patrol backed by the 129th Baluchis was immediately sent in that direction, with what results will be seen shortly. On the 27th a small party of 37 Germans, 178 askaris and 1100 porters surrendered at Luatala, while on the 28th Tafel with all his force laid down their arms. This included 111 Germans, over 1200 askaris and 2200 porters.

To return to No. 1 Column. On 19 November it was ordered to Lulindi, marching via Manyamba's with the 129th as advance-guard. The official Diary merely records 'No opposition'. A private diary records how the regiment met a chaplain so heavily burdened with this world's goods in the form of comforts for the body that he could not move them all. They therefore lent him two porters and also assigned to him a shady mango tree under which to sit. In return he gave them 'two dozen tins of milk and me a shaving brush and pipe'. No mention is made of spiritual comforts. The Commanding Officer records: 'Another B.O. gone sick. My second in command has just two years' service and I have three officers still younger'. There were only five British officers including the commanding officer. On the 20th the column was ordered to occupy Newala and marched to Kiwambo. Thence the next day they advanced to Newala. As opposition was expected and there was no water to be had *en route* the 129th were left behind at Kiwambo to guard the kit and also to arrange for water to be sent to the column, should it fail to occupy Newala that night. The precaution was found to be unnecessary, as the place was abandoned, save for some sick and wounded. Next day the column returned to Kiwambo and marched on the 23rd for Luatala, which was reached after a hot and dusty march. Having arrived they had to dig for water, 'which was bad when we got it'. The following day they were ordered to the Rovuma River at the junction of the Bangalla on the Portuguese border. As it was very hot they marched from 5 p.m. till midnight. Orders had been issued to leave behind any men who were not really fit, so that the total strength of the regiment was 3 British officers, 9 Indian officers and 250 men with machine guns and Lewis guns. This was as well, for they were to have a trying time. At 5 a.m. next day the column was *en route* once more and reached the Rovuma about 10 a.m., having covered some 25 miles. They arrived too late to do any good, but Tafel's movements, as already mentioned, caused the immediate return of the 129th. That same evening they were ordered to draw rations, cook and eat them, and to return as soon as possible to Luatala. Rations were drawn by 1 a.m. on the 26th, and by 4 a.m. the regiment was on the march, having had five hours' sleep the previous night. They marched all night. At 10.30 they met a cavalry patrol which had only recently passed Mwiti Water. These reported all clear, so they pushed on for another hour in a very exhausted condition hoping to get water and find rest, when 'suddenly a few shots were heard on our left flank'. Immediately the advance-guard, under Lieut. Woodward, came under heavy machine-gun and rifle fire. They pushed forward to take up a good defensive position. As they neared the crest of a low slope Subedar Karam Bakhsh, who was leading his men, was shot through the head. A little later Subedar Malasin, who had only very recently rejoined, was hit in the arm by a soft-nosed bullet, and the arm practically severed. He died that evening, having lost too much blood. In the hospital they tried to induce him to take brandy, but he refused.

The enemy pressure was now very great: they were not only pressing on in front but were coming in on both flanks. It was impossible to hold the line, which was pressed back steadily. The confusion was made worse as the porters stampeded, *en masse*, throwing down their loads. So also did the machine-gun porters, so that the machine guns ran out of ammunition. Very gradually, under the command and example of their officers, the almost completely exhausted sepoys rallied, and with the help of the cavalry patrol managed to shake off the enemy after about 2 miles. Finally a counter-attack, organised and led by Lieut. Hawkes in the later stages of the fight, permitted the withdrawal to be completed. They got back to camp about 5 p.m., having lost most of their baggage, but having brought away the machine guns. They lost 2 Indian officers, 12 men killed, 2 Indian officers and 27 men wounded and 7 men missing—a total of 50 out of 250. The names of the wounded Indian officers are unfortunately not recorded, as at this time the Diary was very scantily kept. Colonel Hay was fortunate in not being among the casualties, as at one point the enemy got very close up. The man next to him was killed, while a bullet grazed his hand.

They were fortunate to get away at all, as they had bumped into one of Tafel's columns, the news of whose presence had only become known on the night of the 25/26th. General Hannyngton had sent an urgent message for the whole of No. 1 Column to move back, 'but the Brigade Major did not decipher the message till the morning, when it was too late'. Lieuts. R. G. Woodward and G. E. Hawkes were recommended for the M.C., while four of the men were recommended for the D.S.M.

They reached the camp of the main column on the Miesse River about 5 p.m., absolutely exhausted and with no food. The column marched back to the Rovuma the next day, but the regiment remained at the Miesse camp until the morning of the 29th when they again marched to Mwiti Water, but this time to prepare a camp for the prisoners of war who had surrendered the day before to No. 1 Column on the Rovuma. These arrived in the afternoon under the escort of the 55th Rifles and were part of the force which had handled them so roughly on the 26th. The same day they were detailed as a permanent escort to the prisoners of war column which was to march to Lindi.

And so abruptly, and almost unexpectedly, their fighting in East Africa came to an end. Mwiti Water was their last action in the Great War though none of them realised it. Their withdrawal had been decided upon on 17 November, the month when G.H.Q. had agreed to the withdrawal of all Indian troops from East Africa before the next wet season should begin. It was made possible by the heavy losses which had been inflicted upon the enemy in the last few months. Though von Lettow was still in the field he had now only some 2000 men and could never hope to be a real source of danger. But van Deventer was right when he wrote: 'An equally arduous campaign, though on a very much smaller scale, will, however, probably still be necessary before the German force in Portuguese East Africa is finally brought to book, for the country is vast and communications are difficult'. This was to be left to the K.A.R., which had by now been expanded into a very considerable force.

In the same despatch van Deventer wrote: 'The last six months of the German East African campaign have been of a most exacting nature.... As the area of operations diminished, so the potential advantages of these interior lines increased and the fiercer became the fighting. The morale of the enemy never wavered, and nothing but the determined gallantry and endurance of the troops finally crushed him'. The fighting had indeed been severe, but the demands made on the troops in other ways were more so. What they endured will never be realised by those who have not fought in such a country. It was in truth pawn for pawn, and both pawns and knights had sacrificed themselves willingly and loyally. So also had those of the enemy, for whom it was a war of annihilation. Led by a magnificent leader they had fought magnificently and were still to do so.

SKETCH MAP
Period
May to Dec. 1917

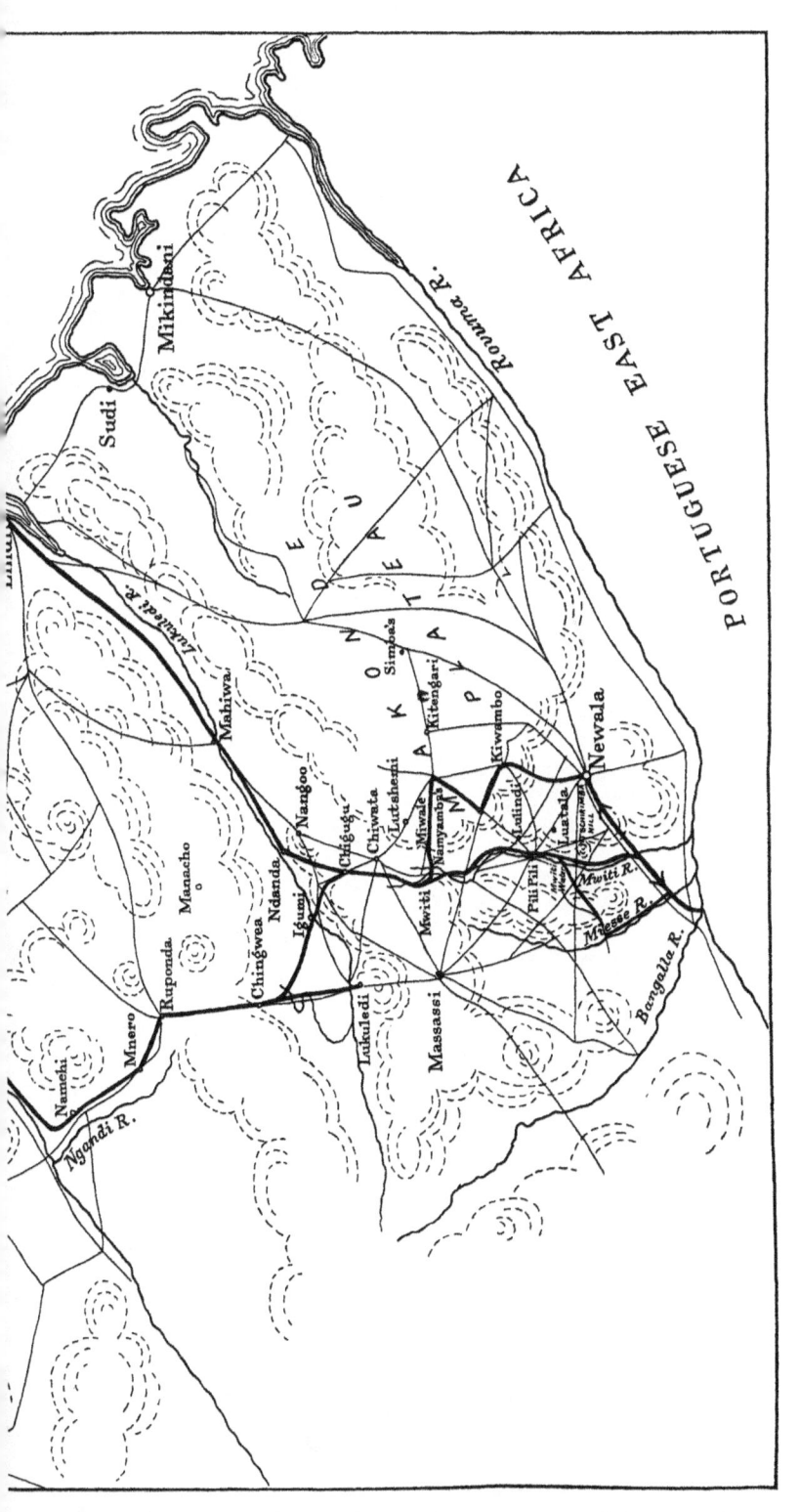

# CHAPTER XVII

1 DEC. 1917–11 Nov. 1918: March to Lindi; Arrival at Dar-es-Salaam; Sail for Karachi; Arrival in India; Reorganisation; Armistice

THE War History of the regiment ends with the fight at Mwiti Water. It only remains to record their return to Karachi, where the regiment was reorganised and built up again preparatory to despatch either to Mesopotamia or Palestine. The Armistice, however, came just about the time when they were fit and ready for fresh adventures.

On 30 November the regiment made an early start for home and marched to Pili Pili, where Captain N. G. Guy and Lieut. C. F. W. Leese rejoined. Here the prisoners' kit was inspected and much of the 2nd-line transport, lost on the 26th, was recovered. On 1 December Lieut. H. D. A. Bannerman rejoined and Major McCormick reported for duty.

Already the rains were beginning, but their advent could be regarded with a more philosophical eye now that there were only ten more marches before Lindi was reached. On the 3rd they were inspected at Namakongwa by General Hannyngton, who came to bid them farewell. There were '250 on parade, and only 11 men were present who went to France with Hannyngton in September 1914'. 'Of these only one man has been with us all along.' Alas! the name of this stalwart has not been recorded. The following day they 'got on to an old German main road and away from the tracks we had cut through the bush'. Rations were still scarce, but they were marching in the right direction. On the 7th they reached Mahiwa. Two officers were sent on to the railhead in a car to get 'hospital comforts, and they brought back a case of champagne and a case of Oxo. Two pints of "bubbly" apiece and soup enough for a month!' It is also recorded: 'Heavy fighting here six weeks ago and graves have not been dug deep enough. Bodies must still be lying about in the bush. Smell very bad'. On the 8th they reached the railhead at Mtama. 'Rail is only two-foot gauge. Ford car engines are mounted to draw trucks.' But the regiment had to march and was away by 5.30 a.m. The Commanding Officer came on by train as he was not fit, but found his men already in camp and settled down, when he arrived at 1.30 p.m. They pushed on again and eventually reached Lindi on the morning of the 11th. Here the prisoners were handed over, and on the 13th they embarked once more on H.M.T. *Barjola* for Dar-es-Salaam, where they arrived next day and where they remained until the end of the month. Here they found a new draft on its way to reinforce them under Major H. W. F. Clive, and here too they collected all their sick and wounded from the various hospitals, so that by the time they were ready to sail their strength exceeded 1000. Lieut. Palin also rejoined.

Before sailing they were completely reclothed and re-equipped, and finally on 4 January, 1918, marched down to the wharf accompanied by the pipers of the 40th Pathans, who piped them on their way and on board ship, the *Princess*, an ex-enemy Atlantic liner.

The first few days were uneventful and the sea smooth, but on the 10th came a 'nasty head wind' and also news of an enemy raider. The latter did not inconvenience them so much as the former. Then once again smooth seas and finally Karachi at 11 a.m. on the 17th. A few men landed that day, but the main body were disembarked on the 18th and marched to the Rest Camp.

On the 19th the regiment was given a public reception by the Municipality in the grounds of Frere Hall. In addition to the officials of the Municipality there were present the Commissioner in Sind, the General Officer Commanding the Karachi Brigade, the garrison and a large number of guests. The regiment, through its Commanding Officer, was thanked for its services and congratulated on its fine war record. The address, which was read by the President of the Municipality, was then presented to Lieut.-Colonel Hay in a silver casket. Colonel Hay made an appropriate reply, and after the usual formalities the regiment marched back to camp where they spent the evening feasting. The evening's entertainment was also provided by the Municipality but chiefly organised by old members of the regiment.

The next day all those who had returned from East Africa went off to their homes on three months' leave, while British officers attached from other regiments returned to their own units. Almost immediately orders were received to form a second battalion to the regiment. Colonel Walton was appointed to command it with Lieut. V. G. Robert, M.C., as Adjutant.

Until the men returned from leave the regiment was merely a depôt, but there was much to be done. After the necessary arrangements had been made for the transfer of Indian officers and men to the 2nd Battalion—and this in an Indian regiment is not the simple process it is in a British unit—Lieut.-Colonel Hay conducted a long recruiting tour throughout the Punjab in order to obtain the recruits necessary to build up the battalion once more. Here, too, there were considerable difficulties, as by this time the Punjab was beginning to feel the drain of men.

Once the men had returned, or rather such as had not been discharged on account of sickness, wounds and general unfitness, came long months of training and efforts to build up a fresh and efficient battalion. How difficult this was can hardly be realised by those who are only cognisant with the present-day organisation with its 'training battalion'. It was more than making bricks without straw. There was a complete paucity of all ranks who were really fit to train the recruits. The young British officers who were posted knew not a word of the men's language, so that the first thing to be done when they arrived was to establish a class in Hindustani.

Early in April the battalion moved up to Quetta, and when inspected later in the month 'was still in the embryo stage engaged in squad drill and musketry'. The constant change of officers, owing to the numerous courses to be attended and also to the demands for reinforcements in Mesopotamia and Palestine, made training even more difficult than it need have been, but in spite of all difficulties steady progress was made. On one occasion 'a musketry return of the Mahsud and Afridi platoon was so good that the Brigadier suspected treachery and collusion, and ordered the practices to be performed again under his own eagle eye. There was a very distinct grin of triumph on the faces of the Mahsuds when the Staff Officer in the butts signalled a result even better than the previous performances, and the Brigadier went away more favourably inclined to Mahsuds than he had been before'. But then he had never seen the Mahsuds in East Africa, where they used less ammunition than anyone else and produced more corpses.

In August the battalion went into training camp in the Hanna valley, and in September into Brigade training camp at Bostan. At the end of this period a Brigade attack was carried out on a position with ball cartridge at full service strength. The Divisional Commander expressed his satisfaction with the training of the battalion and Brigadier-General Christian congratulated the battalion on the marked progress that had been made since his last inspection. The 1/129th was once more fit for service.

On 22 August came news that Brevet-Colonel (Temporary Brigadier-General) J. A. Hannyngton had died in hospital at Ismailia of pneumonia. His death was very deeply regretted by the regiment with whom he had served so long and whom he had commanded in Flanders and

East Africa. Only a little time before he had received the C.B., on which occasion Lieut.-Colonel Hay, C.I.E., had been awarded the D.S.O. for services in East Africa.

In September and October came the influenza epidemic which caused the death of 50 men, their last casualties, and which raged throughout the whole army. Hospitals were wholly inadequate for such an epidemic which swept away some 12,000,000 in India alone: more than all the dead in the Great War. As if Nature in scornful contempt were demonstrating how much more efficient she still was in destruction as compared with the human race.

On 12 November came news of the Armistice.

To face p. 220.

Nairobi
Magadi L
Kajiado
Magad L.
LONGIDO
KILIMANJARO
BRITISH EAST AFRICA
MERU
Moschi
Taveta
Voi
Arusha
Mombasa
Kilindini
GERMAN EAST AFRICA
Pangani R.
USAMBARA
Vanga
Korogwe
Tanga
Pemba
Kondoa-Irangi
MASSAI STEPPE
Handeni
NGURU

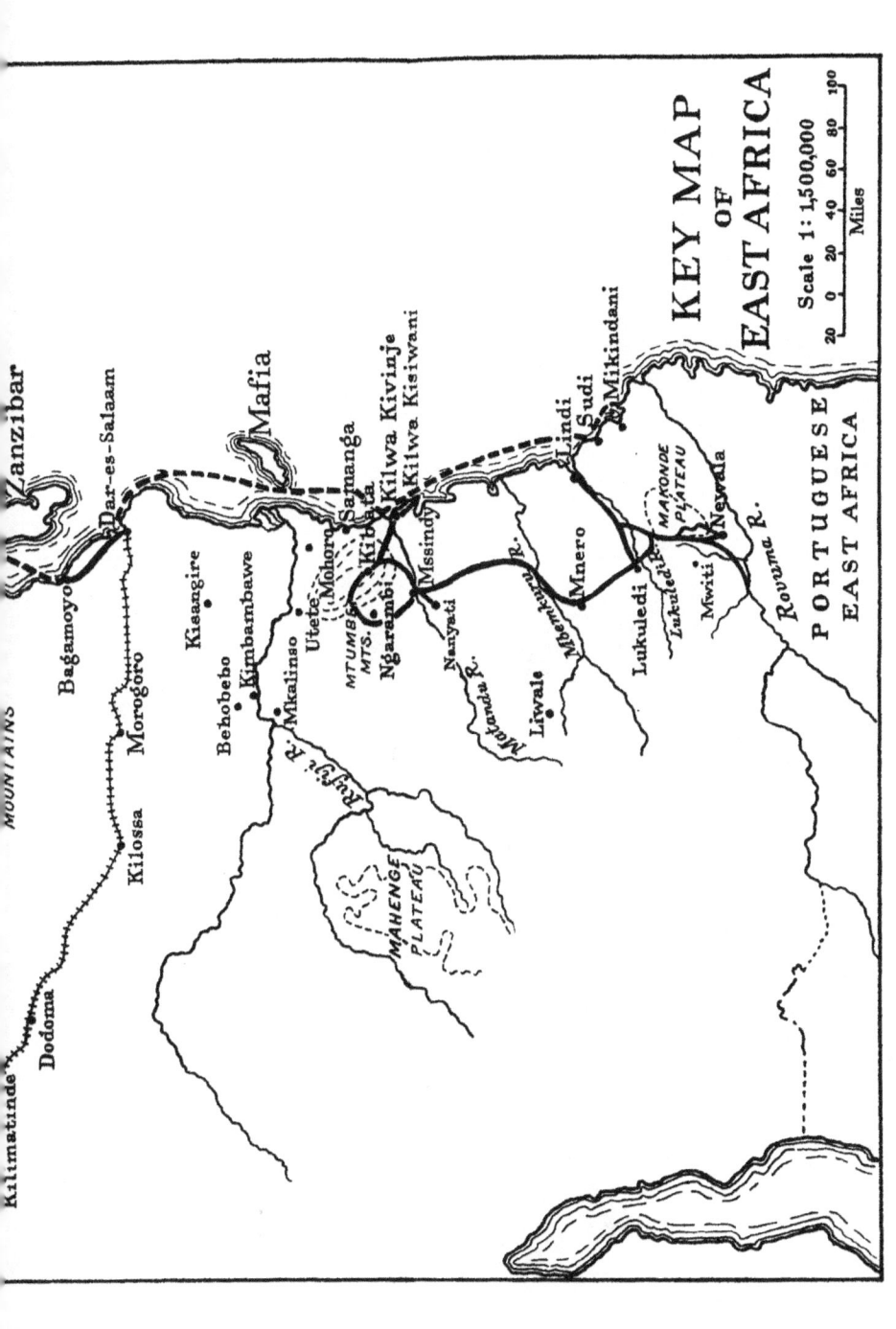

# APPENDIX I

List of officers serving with the regiment at the outbreak of war:

Southey, Lieut.-Colonel W. M.

Hannyngton, Major J. A., C.M.G.,[1,4] 2nd in Command.
Hay, Major W. N.,[4] Zhob Militia.
Potter, Major H. W. R.[1,4]
Adair, Captain W. F.[1,4]

Hamer, Captain M. A.,[2] Staff Capt., Bareilly Bde.
Lindesay, Captain F. S.,[2] Cantt., Magistrate's Dept.
Maclean, Captain F. A.
Borton, Captain C. E.,[1,2] Malay States Guides.
Hill, Captain H. A.[2]
Hampe-Vincent, Captain P. C.[1]
Ussher, Captain S.[1]
Dill, Captain R. F.[1]
Clive, Captain H. W. F.,[3] Burma Military Police.
Steel, Lieut. H. P.[1]
Griffith-Griffin, Lieut. F. M., Adjutant.
Lewis, Lieut. H. V., Q.M.
Browning, Lieut. C. S.[1]

Atal, Major P. P. L.,[1] M.O.

Mala Khan, Afridi, Subedar-Major.
Amir Khan, P.M., Subedar.
Ahmed Din,[1] Mohmand, Subedar.
Zaman Khan, P.M., Subedar.
Makhmad Azam, Mahsud, Subedar.
Turkestan, Mahsud, Subedar.
Baloch Khan,[2] Mahsud, Subedar.
Azad Gul,[1] Afridi, Subedar.
Azam Khan, Afridi, Subedar.
Saiffullah,[2] Mahsud, Jemadar.

[1] Killed or died on service.
[2] Did not serve with the regiment during the war.
[3] Joined with a draft at Dar-es-Salaam, 14 December, 1917, too late for service.
[4] Double-Company Commanders.

Nawab Khan, P.M., Jemadar.
Dadin Khan, Mahsud, Jemadar.
Mir Bad Shah, Mahsud, Jemadar.
Abdullah Khan, P.M., Jemadar, Ind. Adj.
Ghulam Muhammad,[1] P.M., Jemadar.
Lal Sher,[1] Afridi, Jemadar.
Kadar Khan, Jemadar.
Saidan Shah, Afridi, Jemadar.
Muhammed Bakhsh, P.M., Jemadar.
Zar Baz, Afridi, Jemadar.
Jafar Ali,[1] P.M., Jemadar.
Masaod Khan, Afridi, Jemadar.
Ghulam Mohamed, P.M., Jemadar.

[1] Killed or died on service.

# APPENDIX II

## BRITISH OFFICERS WITH THE REGIMENT IN FRANCE AND EAST AFRICA

D. = Died; K. = Killed; P.W. = Prisoner of War; R. = Rejoined; S. = Sick; T. = Transferred; W. = Wounded.

| Name | Regiment | Date of arrival | Remarks |
|---|---|---|---|
| Lieut.-Colonel W. M. Southey | 129th | | Brig.-Gen. Bareilly Bde 2. i. 15; Major-Gen. ?. v. 19 |
| Major J. A. Hannyngton, C.M.G. | ,, | | Brig.-Gen. 2nd E.A. Bde 21. iii. 16; D. 21. viii. 18 |
| Major H. W. R. Potter | ,, | | K. 20. xii. 14 |
| Major G. G. P. Humphreys | 127th B.L.I. | 22. viii. 14 | K. 30. x. 14 |
| Captain W. F. Adair | 129th | | K. 30. x. 14 |
| Captain F. A. Maclean | ,, | | W. 30. x. 14; T. R.A.F. H.Q. on recovery |
| Captain P. C. Hampe-Vincent | ,, | | K. 26. x. 14 |
| Captain R. F. Dill | ,, | | W. 30. x. 14; K. 11. iv. 15 |
| Lieut. F. M. Griffith-Griffin | ,, | | W. 26. iv. 15; T. 26. ix. 16 as Bde Major 3rd E.A. Bde |
| Lieut. H. V. Lewis | ,, | | W. 30. x. 14; accidentally wounded 25. i. 15; S. 27. vii. 17; T. to India |
| Lieut. C. S. Browning | ,, | 12. ix. 14 | W. 16. xii. 14; K. 9. xii. 15 |
| Major P. P. L. Atal | I.M.S. | | K. 23. xi. 14 |
| Captain S. Ussher | 129th | 26. ix. 14 | K. 16. xii. 14 |
| 2nd Lieut. A. G. Boulton | Interpreter | 27. ix. 14 | T. 10. xii. 15 when regt. left Europe; died later |
| Major A. H. Buist | Guides | 16. xi. 14 | Leave 7. i. 15; did not rejoin |
| Captain C. A. G. Money | 130th K.G.O. | 16. xi. 14 | W. 16. xii. 14, 26. iv. 15; K. 13. xii. 15 |
| Lieut. C. M. Thornhill | 24th Punjabis | 16. xi. 14 | T. to Corps H.Q. as G.S.O. 3, 14. vi. 15 |
| Captain H. C. Rome | 20th ,, | 17. xi. 14 | K. 18. xii. 14 |
| Captain D. G. Robinson | 46th ,, | 8. xii. 14 | T. to 58th Rifles 11. xii. 14 |
| Captain R. D. Davies[1] | 127th B.L.I. | 8. xii. 14 | W. and P.W. 20. xii. 14 |

[1] Now commanding the battalion, June 1932.

| Name | Regiment | Date of arrival | Remarks |
|---|---|---|---|
| Lieut. J. G. O. Moses | I.M.S. | 23. xi. 14 | T. 13. xii. 14 |
| Lieut. W. C. Paton | ,, | 13. xii. 14 | T. 17. xii. 14 |
| Major W. J. Mitchell | 124th D.C.O. | 31. xii. 14 | T. 26. iii. 15 to 40th Pathans |
| Captain A. Delmé Radcliffe | 105th M.L.I. | 8. i. 15 | W. 9. iv. 15 |
| Major K. V. Kukday | I.M.S. | 17. i. 15 | T. 30. vi. 15 |
| Captain G. D. R. MacMahon | 124th B.L.I. | 17. i. 15 | W. 26. iv. 15 |
| Lieut. H. J. D. O'Neill | 127th ,, | 19. i. 15 | W. 21. iii. 16 |
| Lieut. F. C. G. Campbell | 40th Pathans | 21. i. 15 | T. 26. iii. 15 to 59th Rifles |
| Major A. G. Crawford | 84th Punjabis | 26. ii. 15 | T. 17. v. 16 to rejoin own regiment |
| Major B. F. R. Holbrooke | 124th B.L.I. | 26. ii. 15 | W. 26. iv. 15 |
| Major H. Hulseberg | 127th ,, | 30. iii. 15 | S. 28. iv. 15 (gassed 26. iv. 15); T. 29. ix. 17 to 127th |
| Major A. G. Kemball | 31st Punjabis | 28. iii. 15 | T. 13. iv. 15 |
| Major C. A. James | 126th B.I. | 24. iv. 15 | W. 26. iv. 15 |
| Lieut. J. S. Culverwell | I.A.R.O. | 26. iii. 15 | W. 26. iv. 15 |
| Lieut. M. H. Bickford | 38th Dogras | 13. vi. 15 | T. 15. vi. 15 to own regiment |
| Captain G. A. Phillips | I.A.R.O. | 15. vi. 15 | S. 19. i. 17 |
| Captain A. N. Dickson | I.M.S. | 29. vi. 15 | S. 23. xii. 16 |
| Major C. G. Woodhouse | 126th B.I. | 22. vii. 15 | T. 1. i. 16 to own regiment |
| 2nd Lieut. W. S. Thatcher | 93rd Burma I. | 22. vii. 15 | W. 25. ix. 15, 13. i. 17 |
| Captain E. P. Burd | 124th (D.C.O.) B.I. | 4. viii. 15 | W. 25. ix. 15 |
| Captain A. E. Stewart | 84th Punjabis | 11. viii. 15 | S. 30. viii. 15; R. 1. i. 16; T. 14. ii. 26 |
| Major G. M. Morris | 7th Dorsets | 11. viii. 15 | T. 17. ii. 16 to rejoin own regiment |
| Lieut. R. B. Wilson | I.A.R.O. | 12. viii. 15 | S. 4. xii. 16 |
| 2nd Lieut. A. P. Stone |  | 11. viii. 15 | S. ?. vi. 16 |
| 2nd Lieut. M. I. L. Smith | 13th K.R.R. | 5. x. 15 | W. 7. xii. 16 |
| Lieut. V. G. Robert | 129th | 1. xii. 15 | S. 21. vi. 17 |
| Lieut. R. S. P. MacIvor | I.A.R.O. | 7. v. 16 | S. 28. v. 17 |
| 2nd Lieut. E. M. Graham | 15th Liverpool Regt. | 27. iii. 16 | S. 10. ix. 16 |
| 2nd Lieut. N. W. W. Johnstone |  | 20. iii. 16 | S. 11. xii. 16 |
| 2nd Lieut. J. D. Jenkins | I.A.R.O. | 27. iii. 16 | T. 29. xii. 16 |

225

| Name | Regiment | Date of arrival | Remarks |
|---|---|---|---|
| 2nd Lieut. L. Brilliant | 129th | 7. v. 16 | S. 26. v. 17 |
| 2nd Lieut. W. S. Goldsmith | I.A.R.O. | 7. v. 16 | S. 23. iv. 17 |
| Lieut. G. A. T. Cox | ,, | 20. v. 16 | S. 18. xii. 16 |
| 2nd Lieut. C. W. Palin | 129th | 20. ix. 16 | P.W. 5. viii. 17 |
| Captain B. de L. Brock | 126th[1] | 11. xii. 16 | W. 15, xii. 16; T. 16. iii. 17; S. July 1917; Staff Capt. 2nd Bde |
| Lieut. A. H. Brown | I.M.S. | 22. xii. 16 | T. 23. i. 17 |
| Captain J. C. T. Gaskell | 69th Punjabis | 27. ii. 17 | K. 5. viii. 17 |
| Captain E. Newton | I.M.S. | 23. i. 17 | T. 16. iii. 17; R. 26. vii. 17; K. 5. viii. 17 |
| Lieut. J. W. G. Steell | S.A. R.A.M.C. | 16. iii. 17 | T. 17. vii. 17 |
| Captain A. C. Gover | 121st Pioneers | 5. iii. 17 | W. 21. ix. 17 |
| Lieut. E. Edelstone | I.A.R.O. | 12. iv. 17 | T. 2. v. 17 to 57th Rifles |
| Lieut. N. G. Guy | ,, | 12. iv. 17 | Returned to India with regiment |
| Captain H. P. Steel | 129th | 10. vii. 17 | K. 5. viii. 17 |
| Lieut. F. D. Mackinnon | I.A.R.O. | 10. vii. 17 | K. 4. x. 17 |
| Lieut. W. Christopher | R.A.M.C. | 18. vii. 17 | T. 26. vii. 17 |
| Lieut. T. S. Uberoi | I.M.S. | ?. ix. 17 | T. ?. x. 17 |
| Lieut. R. L. Piper | 57th Rifles | 14. ix. 17 | K. 10. x. 17 |
| Lieut. H. V. Fox | I.A.R.O. | 17. ix. 17 | T. 29. ix. 17 to original regiment, 127th |
| Lieut. A. R. Pratt | ,, | 17. ix. 17 | T. 29. ix. 17 to original regiment, 127th |
| Lieut. F. M. Mitchell | ,, | 17. ix. 17 | T. 29. ix. 17 to original regiment, 126th |
| Lieut.-Colonel W. N. Hay, C.I.E. | 129th | 29. ix. 17 | Returned to India with regiment |
| Lieut. G. E. Hawkes | 54th Sikhs | 29. ix. 17 | ,, |
| 2nd Lieut. R. G. Woodward | 52nd ,, | 29. ix. 17 | ,, |
| 2nd Lieut. H. D. A. Bannerman | 52nd ,, | 29. ix. 17 | ,, |
| Lieut. C. F. W. Leese | 29th Punjabis | 15. ix. 17 | W. 1. x. 17 |
| 2nd Lieut. L. W. Guiton | 67th ,, | 31. ix. 17 | Returned to India with regiment |
| Major G. McCormick | 72nd ,, | 1. xii. 17 | ,, |
| Major H. W. F. Clive | 129th ,, | 15. xii. 17 | ,, |

[1] Transferred permanently to 129th in November 1921.

# APPENDIX III

## INDIAN OFFICERS WHO SERVED WITH THE REGIMENT DURING THE WAR

D. = Died; K. = Killed; P. = Promoted; P.W. = Prisoner of War; R. = Rejoined; S. = Sick; T. = Transferred; W. = Wounded.

| Name | Regiment | Date of arrival | Remarks |
|---|---|---|---|
| Subedar Mala Khan | 129th | | P.W. 20. xii. 14; P. Subedar-Major |
| Subedar Makhmad Azam | ,, | | W. 1914 |
| Subedar Amir Khan | ,, | | W. and P.W. 20. xii. 14 |
| Subedar Ahmed Din | ,, | | K. 20. xii. 14 |
| Subedar Zaman Khan | ,, | | W. 30. xi. 14 |
| Subedar Turkestan | ,, | | W. 26. iv. 15, 22. vi. 15; S. ?. x. 16 |
| Jemadar Azad Gul | ,, | | K. 30. xi. 14; P. Subedar |
| Jemadar Azam Khan | ,, | | W. ?. iii. 15, 8. ix. 15; P. Subedar |
| Jemadar Nawab Khan | ,, | | W. 16. xii. 14 |
| Jemadar Dadin Khan | ,, | | W. 28. iv. 15; R. 7. v. 16; S. ?. viii. 16 |
| Jemadar Mir Bad Shah | ,, | | W. 30. xi. 14; S. ?. iv. 17; P. Subedar |
| Jemadar Abdullah Khan | ,, | | W. 30. vii 15, 6. ix. 15; P. Subedar 23. vii. 15; T. ?. vii. 17 |
| Subedar Ghulam Mohd. | 127th | | K. 30. xi. 14 |
| Jemadar Mir Bad Shah | ,, | | W. 30. xi. 14 |
| Jemadar Jafar Ali | ,, | | K. 16. xii. 14 |
| Subedar Adam Khan | ,, | | K. 16. xii. 14 |
| Jemadar Imandar | ,, | | W. 16. xii. 14 |
| Jemadar Kadir Khan | 129th | | W. 19. xii. 14; P. 8. viii. 14 |
| Jemadar Karim Khan | ,, | | K. 20. xii. 14; P. Jemadar 9. x. 14 |
| Jemadar Lal Sher | ,, | | W. 20. xii. 14; P. Jemadar 9. x. 14; P. Subedar 10. viii. 15 |
| Jemadar Masaod Khan | ,, | | W. 20. xii. 14 |
| Jemadar Id Mohamed | ,, | | W. and P.W. 20. xii. 14; P. Subedar 31. x. 14 |
| Subedar Shah Nawaz | 84th | | W. 18. iii. 15 |
| Subedar Zerghun Shah | 127th | 26. ii. 15 | W. 26. iv. 15, 4. ix. 15 |
| Jemadar Rustam Khan | 129th | | W. and P.W. 19. xii. 14 |
| Subedar Mohd. Ali | 84th | | W. 1915 |
| Subedar Karam Dad | ,, | | K. 26. iv. 15 |

| Name | Regiment | Date of arrival | Remarks |
|---|---|---|---|
| Jemadar Dittoo Khan | 84th | | W. 14. vi. 15 |
| Jemadar Gama Khan | 129th | | S. ? |
| Jemadar Rahim Ali | ,, | | W. 26. iv. 15; P. 16. xii. 14; Subedar 23. xii. 16; T. ?. vii. 17 |
| Jemadar Rahim Dad | ,, | | W. 26. iv. 15 |
| Jemadar Sher Jang | ,, | | W. 26. iv. 15 |
| Jemadar Didan Khan | ,, | | W. 26. iv. 15 |
| Jemadar Ghafar Khan | ,, | | W. 28. iv. 15; P. 30. x. 14 |
| Jemadar Saidan Shah | ,, | | W. 1915; D. 6. ii. 16 |
| Jemadar Sikandar Khan | ,, | | W. 27. iv. 15; P. 20. xii. 14; Subedar 17. xii. 16; T. ?. vii. 17 |
| Jemadar Sobhat Khan | ,, | | W. 19. v. 15; P. 21. xii. 14; returned to India with regiment |
| Jemadar Shah Zada | ,, | | W. 3. vi. 15; P. 27. iv. 15 |
| Jemadar Wali Dad | 124th | 11. viii. 15 | K. 28. viii. 15 |
| Jemadar Ayub Khan | ,, | | W. 16. xii. 16; P. 6. vii. 15 |
| Subedar Umar Khan | ,, | | W. 1915 |
| Subedar Muhd. Aslam | 126th | 22. vii. 15 | T. 1. i. 16 |
| Jemadar Id Muhamed | ,, | 22. vii. 15 | T. 1. i. 16 |
| Jemadar Lal Shah Gul | ,, | 22. vii. 15 | T. 1. i. 16 |
| Jemadar Sher Baz | 124th | 22. vii. 15 | W. 8. ix. 15 (died) |
| Jemadar Sundar Ali | 129th | | W. 11. ix. 15; P. 27. iv. 15 |
| Subedar Mehdi Khan | 124th | | W. 25. ix. 15; T. 14. ii. 16 |
| Subedar Mir Kambir Khan | 127th | 5. x. 15 | S. 18. xii. 16; P. Subedar-Major 14. ii. 16 |
| Jemadar Sherbat Khan | 129th | | K. 5. viii. 17; P. 21. xii. 14; Subedar |
| Jemadar Ghulam Jilani | 108th | | S. 30. vii. 17; P. 22. xii. 14; Jemadar-Adj.; P. Subedar |
| Subedar Bahadur Khan | 124th | | S. or T. ?. x. 16 |
| Subedar Sher Dil | 108th | | T. 14. ii. 16 |
| Jemadar Sarfraz | B.M. Police | | ?. |
| Jemadar Ahmad Khan | 108th | ?. xi. 15 | S. ?. x. 17 |
| Jemadar Sahib Dad | 127th | ?. xii. 15 | D. 29. viii. 17; P. Subedar 18. xi. 16 |
| Jemadar Zarif Khan | 124th | | W. 11. iv. 15; P. 16. xii. 14 |
| Jemadar Malasin | | ?. iii. 15 | K. 26. xi. 17; P. ?. v. 15 |

| Name | Regiment | Date of arrival | Remarks |
|---|---|---|---|
| Jemadar Nur Khan I | 129th | | W. 13. i. 17; P. 2. i. 16 |
| Jemadar Fateh Haider | ,, | | K. 13. xii. 16; P. 14. ii. 16 |
| Jemadar Nur Khan II | ,, | | P. 14. ii. 16; Subedar 4. iv. 17; returned with regiment to India |
| Jemadar Karam Bakhsh | ,, | ?. iii. 17 | W. 26. xi. 17; P. 14. ii. 16; Subedar 6. iv. 17 |
| Subedar Sarbiland | 127th | | P. Subedar 3. iv. 17; returned with regiment to India; P. Subedar-Major |
| Jemadar Durani | ,, | ?. iii. 17 | P. Subedar 3. iv. 17 |
| Jemadar Dasin Khan | 129th | | S. ?. v. 16 |
| Jemadar Sirdah Shah | ,, | | Subedar 2. i. 17; T. to detail camp Mohoro 17. iii. 17 |
| Jemadar Mohamed Sadiq | ,, | | K. 14. xii. 16; P. on death-bed |
| Subedar Muhammad Afzal | 124th | | W. 16. xii. 16; R. ?. xi. 17 |
| Jemadar Rajwali Khan | 129th | | S. ?. 6. 17; P. 14. xii. 16; Subedar 8. iv. 17 |
| Jemadar Hasham Din | 108th | | P. 23. xii. 16; Subedar 6. viii. 17 |
| Jemadar Mahomed Jan | 129th | | S. ?. iii. 17; P. 17. xii. 16 |
| Jemadar Nek Mahomed | ,, | | K. 5. viii. 17; P. 21. xii. 16 |
| Jemadar Bagh Khan | B.M. Police | | S. ?. v. 17; P. 30. xii. 16 |
| Jemadar Karam Dad | 129th | | W. 5. x. 17; P. 21. i. 17 |
| Jemadar Reshmin | 127th | | S. ?. viii. 17; P. 3. iv. 17 |
| Jemadar Fakhar Din | 108th | | W. 11. xi. 17; P. 4. iv. 17 |
| Jemadar Ghulam Kadar | 129th | | W. 5. viii. 17; P. 6. iv. 17 |
| Jemadar Fazal Dad | 124th | | P. 8. iv. 17; returned with regiment to India |
| Jemadar Murtaza | | | P. 10. iv. 17; Subedar 30. viii. 17; returned with regiment to India |
| Subedar Saif Ali | 130th | 10. vii. 17 | W. 5. viii. 17; also again |
| Jemadar Muhammed Bakhsh | 129th | 10. vii. 17 | P. Subedar 16. vi. 17; returned with regiment to India |
| Jemadar Allah Dad Khan | 130th | 10. vii. 17 | S. ?. x. 17; P. Subedar 6. viii. 17 |
| Jemadar Hayat Ali | 129th | | W. 1915; S. ?. x. 17; P. 16. vi. 17 |
| Jemadar Ghufran Khan | ,, | | P. 6. viii. 17; returned with regiment to India |
| Jemadar Pehlwan Khan | 127th | ?. xi. 17 | W. 1914; S. 11. xi. 17; P. 6. viii. 17 |
| Jemadar Mewa Khan | 130th | | W. 1. x. 17; P. 30. viii. 17 |
| Jemadar Nek Mahomed | 129th | | Returned with regiment to India |
| Jemadar Naim Khan | 130th | | W. 1915; P. 6. viii. 17; returned with regiment to India |
| Jemadar Mohsen | | | K. 26. xi. 17 |

# APPENDIX IV

## COMPOSITION OF THE INDIAN ARMY CORPS IN FLANDERS

### LAHORE DIVISION
Commander: Lieut.-General H. B. B. Watkis, C.B.

#### Ferozepore Brigade
Commander: Brigadier-General R. M. Egerton, C.B.
1st Battalion Connaught Rangers.
129th Duke of Connaught's Own Baluchis.
57th Wilde's Rifles (Frontier Force).
9th Bhopal Infantry.

#### Jullundur Brigade
Commander: Major-General P. M. Carnegy, C.B.
1st Battalion Manchester Regiment.
15th Ludhiana Sikhs.
47th Sikhs.
59th Scinde Rifles (Frontier Force).

#### Sirhind Brigade
Commander: Major-General J. M. S. Brunker
1st Battalion Highland Light Infantry.
1st Battalion 1st King George's Own Gurkha Rifles.
1st Battalion 4th Gurkha Rifles.
125th Napier's Rifles.

#### Divisional Troops
15th Lancers (Cureton's Multanis).
Headquarters Divisional Engineers.
No. 20 Company Sappers and Miners.
No. 21 Company Sappers and Miners.
Signal Company.
34th Sikh Pioneers.

#### Artillery Units
Headquarters Divisional Artillery.
5th Brigade R.F.A. and Ammunition Column.
11th Brigade R.F.A. and Ammunition Column.
18th Brigade R.F.A. and Ammunition Column.
109th Heavy Battery.

## MEERUT DIVISION
Commander: Lieut.-General C. A. Anderson, C.B.

### Dehra Dun Brigade
Commander: Brigadier-General C. E. Johnson.
1st Battalion Seaforth Highlanders.
1st Battalion 9th Gurkha Rifles.
2nd Battalion 2nd King Edward's Own Gurkha Rifles.
6th Jat Light Infantry.

### Garhwal Brigade
Commander: Major-General H. D'U. Keary, C.B., D.S.O.
2nd Battalion Leicestershire Regiment.
2nd Battalion 3rd Queen Alexandra's Own Gurkha Rifles.
1st Battalion 39th Garhwal Rifles.
2nd Battalion 39th Garhwal Rifles.

### Bareilly Brigade
Commander: Major-General F. Macbean, C.V.O., C.B.
2nd Battalion Black Watch.
41st Dogras.
58th Vaughan's Rifles (Frontier Force).
2nd Battalion 8th Gurkha Rifles.

### Divisional Troops
4th Cavalry.
No. 3 Company Sappers and Miners.
No. 4 Company Sappers and Miners.
Signal Company.
107th Pioneers.
Headquarters Divisional Engineers.

### Artillery Units
Headquarters Divisional Artillery.
4th Brigade R.F.A. and Ammunition Column.
9th Brigade R.F.A. and Ammunition Column.
13th Brigade R.F.A. and Ammunition Column.
110th Heavy Battery.

# APPENDIX V

## ORGANISATION OF THE BRITISH FORCES IN EAST AFRICA

In East Africa the British forces were reorganised and regrouped several times. On its arrival the 129th became part of the 2nd East African Brigade in the 1st East African Division which was commanded by Major-General J. M. Stewart, C.B. The 2nd East African Brigade was commanded by Brigadier-General S. H. Sheppard, D.S.O. It consisted of the following units:
    25th Royal Fusiliers,
    29th Punjabis,
    129th Baluchis.

But the 1st East African Division was such only in name. Actually it consisted of one Brigade—the 2nd East African—with certain Divisional troops.

After the arrival of the South African troops there was a general reorganisation at the beginning of April 1916. The 1st Division contained all the British, Indian and African units, while the 2nd and 3rd Divisions were entirely South African. The 129th remained with the 2nd East African Infantry Brigade, which was commanded by Brigadier-General J. A. Hannyngton, C.M.G., D.S.O. The composition of the Brigade was somewhat changed, so that it now consisted of the
    25th Royal Fusiliers,
    129th Baluchis,
    40th Pathans,
    3rd K.A.R.

In the Kilwa area the regiment formed part of the 3rd East African Brigade commanded by Brigadier-General Hannyngton. This consisted of the
    2nd Loyal North Lancashires,
    129th Baluchis,
    40th Pathans,
    1/2nd K.A.R.,
    2/2nd K.A.R.

The Loyal North Lancashires were so infected with malaria that they never took the field as a battalion though they provided some machine-gun crews.

As the situation developed the rest of the 1st Division was transferred to this area. It consisted of the 2nd and 3rd East African Brigades with Divisional troops.

When General Smuts left East Africa Lieut.-General Hoskins again reorganised the forces into columns, as it was found that the old Divisional organisation was unsuitable to the new conditions which had developed in 1917. The composition of the Kilwa forces, or the 'Hanforce' as it was styled, was as follows:

No. 1 Column (Colonel Rose; afterwards Colonel Orr):
33rd Punjabis,
Gold Coast Regiment,
2/2nd K.A.R.,
22nd Mountain Battery.

No. 2 Column (Colonel Grant):
57th Rifles,
129th Baluchis,
1/3rd K.A.R.,
2/3rd K.A.R.,
11th Hull Heavy Battery,
27th Mountain Battery.

No. 3 Column (Colonel Taylor):
3/3rd K.A.R. less one company,
40th Pathans, a detachment of some 200 rifles.

There was a certain amount of reshuffling from time to time as circumstances necessitated. Thus on 18 July, 1917, the columns were composed as follows:

No. 1 Column (Colonel Orr):
8th South African Infantry (less two companies),
Gold Coast Regiment,
33rd Punjabis,
2/2nd K.A.R.,
27th Mountain Battery.

No. 2 Column (Colonel Ridgeway):
7th South African Infantry,
1/3rd K.A.R.,
2/2nd K.A.R.,
22nd Mountain Battery.

No. 3 Column (Colonel Taylor):
   8th South African Infantry (two companies),
   3/3rd K.A.R. (less one company),
   40th Pathans (detachment).

The 129th at this time was almost non-existent through sickness, but was reinforced shortly afterwards.

In August 'Hanforce' consisted of the Nigerian Brigade, some 2164 rifles; Hanforce Column No. 1, 1005 rifles (129th, 260 rifles); Hanforce Column No. 2, 1133 rifles.

No. 1 Column (Colonel Orr):
   Gold Coast Regiment,
   2/2nd K.A.R.,
   ½ Stokes Battery (3 mortars),
   27th Mountain Battery (2 guns).

No. 2 Column (Colonel Ridgeway):
   1/3rd K.A.R.
   2/3rd K.A.R. } less detachments,
   3/3rd K.A.R.
   129th Baluchis.

Force Reserve:
   7th South African Infantry,
   The Kilwa Battery.

In November the 129th was with No. 1 Column, which was composed of
   1/3rd K.A.R.,
   2/2nd K.A.R.,
   129th Baluchis,
   55th Rifles,
   Gold Coast Regiment.
      Total some 2300 rifles.

No. 2 Column:
   127th Baluchis,
   2/2nd K.A.R.
      Total some 700 rifles.

# APPENDIX VI

## NOTE ON THE COMPOSITION OF THE REGIMENT

By LIEUT.-COLONEL H. V. LEWIS, D.S.O., M.C.

It is invidious to draw distinctions between the various classes of men who composed the 129th Baluchis, for all worthily upheld their reputation. At the beginning of the war the composition was 2 Coys. Punjabi Mohammedans, and 6 Coys. of Pathans, of whom 3 were Mahsuds, 1 Mohmand and 2 Afridis of the Kohat Pass. Nearly all of the Pathans enlisted in the battalion had homes across the Administrative Border of India, in territory which is virtually independent. Small wonder then if amongst people so situated, disloyalty had come when disloyalty could not be punished and the propaganda of German and Turkish agents could not be checked, and if cases of desertion had occurred as the long lists of casualties at the front became known.

This in fact happened in some units both in India and overseas, and the authorities were reluctantly compelled to close down transborder recruiting for all.

The result was a gradual increase in the proportion of Punjabis and decrease in Pathans in the 129th, a change which though understandable was quite unnecessary, since, with the exception of the five Mahsud deserters mentioned on p. 68, the conduct of all Pathans, Mahsuds, Afridis and Mohmands alike was exemplary. Whatever transborder men may have done to stain their reputation elsewhere, it should be recorded emphatically that far from staining the lustre of the 129th they took their full share in adding to it.

The Mahsuds had never before taken the field on the side of His Majesty's forces—as enemies they had often proved their worth: they now proved their metal as friends. Nearly every Mahsud who went overseas served in the 129th: double or treble their number would have been welcome, for whether in the cold and mud of Flanders or in the sticky heat of the Rufiji they proved themselves to be soldiers of the very highest order. The cessation of their enlistment was the very greatest loss to the battalion overseas.

Thus the battalion became more and more composed of

APPENDIX VI 235

Punjabis, who must therefore be considered to have been the backbone of the 129th in the Great War, and who by their steady courage and unquestionable loyalty not only upheld their own high reputation as soldiers but earned the fullest thanks of the 129th. [This substitution of P.M.s took place slowly until after January 1917. Thus in October 1916 there were 300 P.M.s out of a total of 518. Few reinforcements arrived before January, and of these some were certainly Mahsuds, though only a very small number. The last to arrive came with Captain Brock.]

The perusal of the History and of the Appendices enumerating the British and Indian officers who served with the 129th during the Great War shows that many different units were called on to provide reinforcements for us, especially during the stay of the regiment in France. Amongst the larger drafts were Orakzais from the 127th; Mahsuds and Wazirs from the 124th and 126th; Baluchis from the 127th [and 126th; a few Brahuis from the 126th]. These, coming from sister units, easily merged into the battalion and quickly became indistinguishable. The same applied to their officers.

Reinforcements from other units than Baluchis were mostly Punjabis, though we got some Afridis. In the case of large drafts, like that which came from the 84th Punjabis, officers accompanied them. These did their full share of good work and also became in due course merged into the 129th. It seems almost impertinence for me to express gratitude to these units for their assistance to the battalion, but I do.

Smaller drafts were not so easy to absorb. Possibly their British and Indian officers quickly became casualties. The other ranks tended to become sheep without shepherds, and, as time went on, the battalion became composed of men of a collection of units making a conglomeration which it is difficult to describe as the 129th. If my memory serves me right, some 13 units were included in the battalion before it left France, and, of these units, two were actually more strongly represented than the 129th itself. This state of affairs did not lead to efficiency, but with the depôt system of pre-war days it was inevitable. The sorting out which occurred after reaching East Africa was very beneficial, and thereafter the depôt was more capable of supplying the needs of the battalion.

The task of Captain Steel, who was left behind when the 129th went to France, was no enviable one. To him and other officers, clerks and N.C.O.s credit is due for the gradual building of order out of the chaos which existed when the depôt was first formed. Their superhuman tasks will, it is hoped, never need to be repeated, for in the Training Battalion organisation there exists in peace the organisation which Depôt Commanders of 1914 had to build up in war.

I should like to avail myself of the Appendix to record some of the incidents of the war which live most vividly in my memory.

This history has mentioned many instances of gallantry performed by men of all classes, and I will not repeat those here except to emphasise them. Foremost amongst them stand the exploits of the Punjab sepoy, Khudadad, V.C., and his equally gallant comrades in his Machine-Gun Section. All classes in the 129th went to compose this section, of which, alas, only one survived the storm of lead and steel which fell on that isolated salient of the battalion's sector at Hollebeke. I suppose that I am one of the few serving survivors of that salient, though I was not at its apex where the bulk of the bombardment raged. I saw the farm-building there, in which machine-gun belts were refilled, collapse and burst into flames which must have consumed many gallant men, and just in front of this, in the shattered fragments of but waist-high trenches, and isolated from the rest of the battalion, these sepoys earned for the 129th the proud distinction of the first Indian V.C. I cherish the reflected glory of having been in their vicinity.

I can speak personally, too, of the amazing exploits of the Mahsud Naik Ayub Khan which are recounted on pp. 57–61 of the history. Ayub Khan came to France from the 124th Baluchistan Infantry as a stretcher-bearer. A task so humdrum did not suit his temperament, and at his insistence he was transferred to a section. A reconnaissance of great merit, but which pales before his later exploit, earned him promotion to Naik. The frequent appeals from Corps for enemy identifications caused him to patrol 'No man's land' nightly and, meeting no success, he actually suggested a temporary desertion, stating that he was confident of his ability to escape. Captain O'Neill forbade him, but when he disappeared one night and all efforts failed to find him dead or alive, I was able to meet various (perhaps natural) insinuations of treachery by confident assurances that Ayub Khan could do no such thing. The I.O.M. and the promotion to Jemadar that he earned were hardly sufficient reward for his unique services. Jemadar Ayub Khan distinguished himself again on patrol work in East Africa when, after surprising a German patrol, he ran alone after them and set out to capture the officer. The latter halted, fired point blank at Ayub and missed. It took no time for him to close, and seizing the officer by the scruff of the neck and seat of the trousers he bore him to Lieut. Palin and dumped him down, saying, 'Here is a Hun'. Ayub was shot right through the face during the night attack on the 'Lodgement' at Kibata while, in company with an astonishingly brave youth called Naik Sahib Jan, leading the foremost wave of the assault. He survived his wound and still lives in his home near Piazha Rajhza in Waziristan.

Perhaps the conduct of a certain Mohmand sepoy, whose name even I have forgotten, is as brave as any I can recall. It occurred at Givenchy on 16 December after Major Potter and his gallant men had captured the left of the two German saps which formed our objective. Surprise enabled the first wave to cross; a belt of machine-gun bullets barred the way to all support. The bodies of those who tried to cross that narrow strip of 25 yards lay in a solid wall. Major Potter's advance had to be stayed till a trench could be dug through. To advance unsupported meant annihilation. 'Are there any volunteers to take a message across?' Two Mohmands step forward and one climbs the parapet. He pauses one moment and then rushes forward and dies. His comrade sees this. 'Now', he says, 'it is my turn.' I can only thank God that I was at hand to prevent him.

Dozens of incidents rise in my mind as I write. The anger of an Afridi sepoy, Sattar Khan, when the last remnants of the battalion were falling back from Givenchy, stands out vividly. 'Why should we go?' he demanded. 'We have no ammunition, but there are twenty of us and we have bayonets.' And as we doubled across the glacis between Givenchy and 'Pont Fixe' on the Canal, he clutched my arm: 'Let us go back', he urged.

Again, the Mahsud boy at Soko Nasai near Moschi, who during the German night attacks picked up two bullets in his left arm while the company lay as force-reserve in the midst of the camp. Orders came to reinforce the firing line and I ordered the company to rise. The Mahsud boy appeared, bleeding profusely. I told him to report in hospital. 'No,' he said, 'you have two arms; take my rifle. I have one arm and will take your revolver. We will both go to the perimeter.'

I feel that I cannot omit from this story of gallant men of the 129th the exploits of Hakim Khan. He was a Mahsud and like some others of that tribe he was, to say the least of it, eccentric, and at the same time like most of them did not know what fear was. The first time he made himself prominent was on the ship bearing I.E.F. 'A' from India to France. The Captain with the O.C. troops was doing his rounds with his usual following behind him. Among the sea-sick was Hakim Khan, who was just strong enough to stand up when rounds approached. When I, somewhere at the tail of the procession, came up to where he was standing I heard him loudly calling for onions from each officer as he passed. He had great faith in onions as an antidote for sea-sickness. This incident earned for him the nickname of 'Piyaz Khan'. Piyaz is the Hindustani for onion.

He next distinguished himself by falling out of the train in the excitement of acknowledging the cheers of the French at some station between Marseilles and Orleans. He was luckily only bruised and followed on in the next troop train.

He soon had an opportunity of showing what he was made of in action. In October 1914 the regiment was pushed back from its trenches in front of Hollebeke with very heavy losses. I came across Hakim Khan about a mile behind our original line. He was standing by the side of a dying British officer, whom he had carried out of action for nearly a mile, under extremely heavy gun and machine-gun fire. As a mark of gratitude the officer had given him his field glasses before he died. That is an example of his bravery, now comes the eccentricity.

Hakim Khan told me briefly what had occurred, and then without a word started off alone across an open field towards the advancing enemy. I ordered him to come back, but I might as well have saved my breath. He said he was going to avenge the sahib's death—the sahib was a complete stranger to him before this incident—and he disappeared alone over the crest line, which was temporarily giving us some shelter from bullets. I never knew what revenge he succeeded in getting, though I bet he got some. He turned up again some time during the night and rejoined his company in the new line which it had occupied.

The next two incidents both occurred at Festubert in December 1914. Men were frequently being hit on leaving the communication trench which led back to Festubert. Snipers were suspected in the ruined houses of the village. The Colonel told me to take some men to find out their hiding-place and to shoot them down. My scheme was to send Hakim Khan as a bait down the usual communication trench. He was to draw the fire, while the rest of us went round behind to locate the snipers by the sound of their shots. It was necessary to send him alone, as only single men were shot at. I told Hakim Khan to walk down the trench right to the end as if he suspected nothing, but he suggested that he should walk outside so as to make quite certain that the enemy should spot him and fire. I told him to obey orders and he reluctantly agreed. Then we went off and took up our position. We waited in silence for a shot for about a quarter of an hour but heard nothing. Then some distance off we heard the sound of heavy footfalls. This turned out to be Hakim doing 'knees up' down the metalled road. He had obeyed his orders as far as the end of the trench where he emerged into the road: then, annoyed at his want of success in drawing fire, he decided to make a last effort to attract the attention of the snipers by making as much noise as possible.

Nobody but Hakim Khan could possibly have survived the other Festubert incident. The German trenches were from 60 to 100 yards away from ours, but their saps often ran up to within 30 yards of us. Only the Germans had bombs in those days; we had not yet even got our jam tins returned to us. This was a particularly active bit of the front, and both sides were fully alert. You can imagine my surprise when a sentry told me that Hakim had left our trench with a rifle and was going over in broad daylight to a German sap. I ran to a loophole—a head was not safe over the top—and saw Hakim Khan walking across 'No man's land'. He went right over to a German sap-head, looked down into it for a few seconds and then walked back to our trench. Not a shot was fired at him! I asked him what the devil he meant by such stupidity. He calmly answered, standing strictly to attention, that he wanted to get a German rifle. When I asked him what he saw in the sap he said that there were three Germans in the sap-head, who ran away. When I asked him why he did not shoot them, he replied that the Germans were digging and had no rifles. Since my own eyes saw him looking into the sap I can readily believe the part of his story about the three Germans.

Next time I saw Hakim Khan was in the trenches at Givenchy, shortly afterwards. He was hit in the stomach and the arm, and I persuaded him with great difficulty to take some morphia, which was against his religious principles. The trenches were blocked with wounded, and it was some time before we could get him back. He was in great pain but he never made a complaint. He got over the stomach wound but lost an arm. He was returned to the depôt in India, and there spent his time pestering the Depôt Commander to be allowed to return to the regiment in the field.

I saw him once more in Quetta in 1920. One evening I was in my bungalow after dinner when a tattered man entered the door and stared wildly at me. It was Hakim Khan. He just had time to cry out 'Thank God I have got home', and then fell on the floor. I took him to hospital, where for some time he hung between life and death. Eventually he recovered and I took him into my service as a perfectly useless choukidar. I parted with him, with difficulty, some months later when I came home. I have since heard that a blood feud in his country has ended his extraordinary life. A blood feud and one arm do not go well together in Waziristan!

Space prevents me from expanding on the steadfast courage and devotion to duty of Punjabis like Havildar Abdullah Khan, I.O.M., who rose by sheer merit from Clerk to Subedar-Major, or of Sepoy Fateh Khan who earned promotion and a decoration by keeping his machine gun in action in his sap at Givenchy until the masses of Germans not only reached his parapet but entered his own trenches behind him. I cannot recount in detail the gallantry of the Mahsud remnants who captured the right sap at Givenchy and who, when bombed back into the extremity of the captured sap, maintained themselves alive till dusk by bayonet charges down the trench and by returning to the enemy his own bombs before they had time to explode. Havildar Wasim Khan and Sepoy Sahib Jan, I.O.M., I.D.S.M., stand out in my memory of those events. Neither can I tell the story of Sepoy Nambot, my own Mahsud orderly, who miraculously survived the war, was brought in to me blindfolded by Gurkha troops in Waziristan in the Mahsud campaign of 1919, and was eventually killed, carrying my revolver, in a blood feud in his own country. God rest his soul.

I cannot, however, resist one last story. It concerns a Mahsud, Havildar Zerdad, called by his intimates, amongst whom I numbered myself, Qalaband. The story is included in the history, but is so remarkable that it deserves treating in greater detail. Our outposts east of Moschi lay on the River Ruwù, which was crossed by a road and a railway. These converged some 8 miles eastward on a station where the German forces lay. Qalaband led a gang of Mahsud lads who called themselves 'jangian' (warriors), and he occasionally took

## APPENDIX VI

them out on exploits. One morning I sent him with his jangian to reconnoitre down the railway towards the German position. At dusk he returned with the following report:

'I moved down the railway till I reached a ridge covering the station where I judged the enemy would have a picquet, and on scouting forward I saw one. I placed the jangian in the grass alongside the railway with orders to open fire if I was fired on, and I proceeded down the railway alone towards the picquet in order to capture it. As I got near a black sentry saw me and brought his rifle to the present, covering me. He shouted out "Kwenda", which means "Go away". I replied "Hapana piga", that is "Don't shoot". But as I got quite close he shot and missed. So I fired and the jangian behind fired and the picquet ran away. From the picquet position we saw many Germans leave their huts and occupy such and such positions. I could do no more, so I returned'.

Qalaband saw a look of incredulity on my face. Why had he advanced alone? What hope had he of capturing the German picquet single-handed? I was frankly sceptical and he knew it. Qalaband demanded to be allowed to go down the road next morning. I consented and he left at dawn. At dusk he returned and made his report.

'As I approached that same ridge covering the station I knew there would be a Hun picquet there, so I placed my jangian as before in the grass by the road. This time I did not advance in the open on the road, but moved stealthily through the grass. As I expected there was a picquet on the ridge. A white officer was inspecting it. So I crept up quite close behind a big tree. First I shot the officer, then the sentry, then the Lance-Naik and then a bugler.'

Qalaband paused for a moment and then he said, 'Here is the officer's revolver, the sentry's rifle, the Lance-Naik's stripe and the bugler's bugle. And now, Sahib, do you believe my first story?' I did, and I said so emphatically.

I have said enough. What more is needed? I trust that what I have written in this short story of gallant men of the 129th Baluchis will, together with the history itself, serve to set an example worthy of emulation to those who to-day serve, or to-morrow will serve, in the 4th Battalion of the 10th Baluch Regiment.

FORT SANDEMAN,
16. xii. 31.

[The square brackets indicate additions by me. W. S. T.]

# APPENDIX VII

## CASUALTIES

It is not easy to give the exact casualties suffered by the regiment, though theoretically it ought to be. All that can be given are estimates. These are more accurate for France than for East Africa, as the Diary is more detailed for the former.

I have endeavoured to estimate the casualties both directly and indirectly. The Diary for France actually records 146 killed, 944 wounded, 166 sick and 119 missing. A different estimate made at an earlier date than mine by the compiler of the Diary précis is 124 killed and 163 missing. In the précis estimate the number of killed is certainly inaccurate. On the other hand the missing are higher than my figures. My total for killed and missing is 265 against the précis figure 287. A difference of 22 (see below). Only 166 men are recorded as going sick. There must have been very many more. This can be shown by indirect calculation as follows:

| | |
|---|---:|
| Original strength of regiment | 790[1] |
| Add drafts as recorded | 1757 |
| | 2547 |
| Deduct strength in December 1915 | 794 |
| | 1753 |
| Deduct 49 men transferred to 57th | 49 |
| Therefore total casualties must be | 1704 |
| Deduct recorded K., W., M. and S. | 1375 |
| Unaccounted for | 329 |
| Deduct the extra 22 missing | 22 |
| Unaccounted for | 307 |

[1] Men only.

The majority of these were without doubt sick; but I think that a certain small number might quite safely be included in the other casualties.

That there should have been so many sick is not surprising. To plunge suddenly Indian troops into a damp country such as Flanders at the beginning of the autumn would have been a strain in peace time. To do so in time of war was to make a demand which could only be warranted by the urgency of

APPENDIX VII 243

the times. The first winter came too soon for proper organisation, and the troops suffered terribly from exposure. The base camp at Marseilles was overflowing with the wrecks of the first winter—men who had been ill with pneumonia, pleurisy, rheumatic fever, etc. The British troops from India suffered equally badly.

How many of the wounded and sick died in hospital is unrecorded, and I have been unable to find out anything. But out of 944 wounded and 473 sick (166 and 307) a certain number must have died.

There is no record of the 119 missing. Whether any returned after the Armistice from Germany I do not know, but I think very few did. Practically all were killed: a certain number were burned, some died.

In East Africa the battle casualties were considerably smaller than in France, while the sick casualties were proportionately larger.

The figures given in the Diary précis are 88 killed and 214 wounded. My figures taken direct from the Diary are 80 killed, 222 wounded, 4 missing. The sick casualties are not given. These two sets of figures agree very closely, especially if one adds the missing to the killed. Certainly some of the wounded must have died. It is unbelievable that only 4 died.

The only references to sickness are verbal and there are practically no figures. We must make an estimate in the same way as we did for France. But here there is an additional difficulty. Not all the draft strengths are recorded. Thus the Diary for 25 February, 1916, gives no figures for the newly arrived draft. Lieut. Palin's draft of 300 recorded as arriving at Dar-es-Salaam is certainly inaccurate. I was at the depôt in Karachi when he sailed and certainly he did not take 300 men. It must have been much less, though I cannot now remember. He may have picked up some sick cases discharged from hospital in East Africa and gathered in some of the details left behind for various reasons during the march to Dar-es-Salaam, but even then I cannot accept the figure of 300. Lieut. Guiton's draft is not recorded at all, and I only found it out through an entry in the private diary of Lieut.-Colonel Hay. I think that many of Guiton's draft, which was over 100 men, must have been sick cases discharged from hospital.

Taking all things together and allowing for double counting (as in the case of men who went sick, recovered and rejoined) about 1900 men passed through the regiment. Many of these men came and went several times, so that the actual number of fresh details was probably less. Sickness, as I have already said, was only reported very occasionally, but I have arrived at a provisional figure of about 1575. This corresponds roughly with the figures ascertained by other methods. This is arrived at as follows:

| | |
|---|---:|
| Original strength of regiment | 576 |
| Add drafts as recorded | 1900 |
| | 2476 |
| Deduct strength on 1 December, 1917 | 317 |
| | 2159 |
| Deduct men transferred, say ... | 278[1] |
| | 1881 |
| Deduct recorded K., W. and M. | 306 |
| Unaccounted for | 1575 |

[1] This may be an over-estimate.

I have corresponded with officers who were with the regiment during the rainy seasons and they all stress the excessively high sick rate during those periods. It was not inconsiderable when I was with the regiment. This can be exemplified by the complete collapse of the regiment through malaria when it reached Handeni. In this case the malaria had been contracted in the Ruwu swamps a few months earlier. The following rainy season, numbers were even more reduced. Major Gover told me that on one occasion there were only 11 men who were fit for duty in the whole regiment. Captain Palin confirms this. Lieut.-Colonel Hay also emphasised the very heavy sick list due chiefly to malaria, but also to systematic under-feeding and bad feeding combined with excessive marching and fatigues.

That a considerable number of men must have died of malaria, dysentery, black-water fever, etc., is certain. We all knew of cases so dying, and I, myself, knew of many deaths at the base.

In nearly every case the regimental strengths at the beginning of the month, when they are given, include a considerable number of men who were sick and who would have been in hospital in peace time. One had to be pretty bad before it was noticed in East Africa.

There is no doubt that the sick rate was higher than it need have been, but that is a subject which need not be discussed here.

APPENDIX VII 245

The total casualties would be roughly as follows:
Killed and missing   349 (+ 22 probably)
Wounded              1166
Sick                 2084

A certain number of the wounded and sick certainly died, so that it is not unreasonable to place the total dead at about 500. This figure does not include officer casualties.

The relation between total casualties and the total strength of the regiment is shown in the following calculation:

*Estimate of total number of men present with the regiment throughout the whole of the war.*

| | |
|---|---:|
| Original strength ... ... ... ... ... | 790 |
| Add drafts as recorded ... ... ... ... | 1757 |
| | 2547 |
| Deduct difference between December strength in Flanders and January strength as sailing for East Africa, i.e. transferred troops ... ... | 218 |
| | 2329 |
| Deduct transfers 49 + 278 ... ... ... ... | 327 |
| | 2002 |
| Add drafts received in East Africa ... ... | 1900 |
| | 3902 |
| Of these K., W., M. and S. were ... ... ... | 3621 |
| Not casualties[1] ... ... ... ... ... | 281 |

[1] Actual strength on 1 December, 1917, was 317, that is, 36 in excess.

Actual battle casualties were 1537 out of 3902, i.e. 40 per cent roughly.

Total casualties were (3621 − 36) = 3585 out of 3902, i.e. 92 per cent roughly.

It might be argued that the transferred men should be included in the total strength. If so these figures would be as follows:

Actual battle casualties were 1537 out of 4447, i.e. 34·5 per cent.

Total casualties were (3621 − 36) = 3585 out of 4447, i.e. 80 per cent.

But these men were only transferred to other war areas and did not remain in their home depôts.

It is not without interest to study the regimental strengths given at the beginning of each month. The wastage due to all causes can then be seen. These figures include officers and men.

|           | 1914   | 1915 | 1916   | 1917   |
|-----------|--------|------|--------|--------|
| January   | —      | —    | 580    | 484    |
| February  | —      | 393  | 744    | 497    |
| March     | —      | 725  | —      | 397    |
| April     | —      | 653  | 732    | —      |
| May       | —      | 234  | —      | —      |
| June      | —      | 261  | 657    | 144    |
| July      | —      | 203  | 250[4] | 651[7] |
| August    | —      | 481  | 440[5] | —      |
| September | 809    | 705  | —      | 441    |
| October   | 753[1] | 663  | 491[6] | 477    |
| November  | 534[2] | 749  | —      | 327    |
| December  | 214[3] | 822  | —      | 332    |

[1] 17 October. On 23 October it was 659.
[2] 17 November. As recorded by the Brigade.
[3] 20 December.
[4] On 4 July only 158.
[5] On 25 August 341.
[6] 18 October.
[7] 20 July 764; 28 July 466.

*Note.* Since going to Press Lieut.-Colonel H. V. Lewis has supplied me with the detailed list of casualties of 'pucka' 129th sepoys. These are as follows:

*France.*

|                    | British officers | Indian officers | Other ranks (Indian) | Fol- lowers |
|--------------------|------------------|-----------------|----------------------|-------------|
| Killed             | 6                | 7               | 73                   | —           |
| Death accepted     | 1                | —               | 33                   | —           |
| Died prisoner of war | —              | —               | 49                   | —           |
| Wounded            | 14               | 29              | 467                  | 1           |
|                    | 21               | 36              | 622                  | 1           |

No sick are included in these lists: nor any deaths from disease except in cases of prisoners of war.

*East Africa.*

|  | British officers | Indian officers | Other ranks (Indian) | Followers |
|---|---|---|---|---|
| Killed | 3 | 4 | 37 | — |
| Died of wounds | 2 | 1 | 8 | — |
| Died of disease | — | 2 | 46 | 1 |
| Wounded | 5 | 8 | 114 | — |
|  | 10 | 15 | 205 | 1 |

Again no sick are included.

The total dead are given at 246 (excluding officers). In view of the fact that the regiment was heavily reinforced from other units, especially in France, my estimate of about 500 dead seems eminently reasonable.

# APPENDIX VIII

## *Part I*

### RECOMMENDATIONS IN FRANCE

*These recommendations are quoted exactly as in the originals.*

#### OFFICERS

MAJOR J. A. HANNYNGTON, C.M.G.

On the 30th October (1914) when his Company, which had been left in command of Captain Maclean, had broken to a great extent, Major Hannyngton succeeded in rallying it and got it back into the trenches. The next day the Company was thoroughly steadied and Major Hannyngton led them with the greatest coolness in a counter-attack on a farm captured by the Germans. The farm was recaptured.

Recommended by Lieut.-Colonel W. M. SOUTHEY.
Honour or Reward—D.S.O.

MAJOR H. W. R. POTTER.

On the 30th October (1914) carried out a retirement covering the remainder of the battalion and Cavalry Brigade with the greatest coolness. On the night of the 31st October, when the Germans captured a farm in his position in the outpost line, constructed a trench 50 yards away from it and kept them shut up unable to move till reinforcements arrived.

Recommended by Lieut.-Colonel W. M. SOUTHEY.
Honour or Reward—D.S.O.

LIEUT. F. M. G.-GRIFFIN.

As Adjutant worked indefatigably. On several occasions I had to send him up to the firing line with messages, under heavy fire by day and night. Always cool and collected.

Recommended by Lieut.-Colonel W. M. SOUTHEY.
Honour or Reward—M.C.

LIEUT. H. V. LEWIS.

On the 30th October did excellent work in commanding Major Humphreys' Company when that officer was wounded, bringing them out of action in good order after a very heavy attack. On the night of the 31st October behaved with the

APPENDIX VIII 249

greatest courage, being one of the first into the farm. On several occasions carried messages to the firing line under heavy fire.

Recommended by Lieut.-Colonel W. M. SOUTHEY.
Honour or Reward—M.C.

MAJOR P. P. L. ATAL, I.M.S.

Did extremely well every day, attending wounded under fire. On the 30th he proceeded to Hollebeke village and dressed a man's wounds under heavy fire (shell and rifle). Always cool and courageous.

Recommended by Lieut.-Colonel W. M. SOUTHEY.
Honour or Reward—D.S.O.

SUBEDAR MAKHMAD AZAM.

Did very good work in the trenches and kept his Company well in hand. At night he hardly slept, going round all his firing-line trenches to encourage the men. Steadied his Company well on the 30th (October 1914) under a heavy attack.

Recommended by Lieut.-Colonel W. M. SOUTHEY.
Honour or Reward—2nd Class I.O.M.

JEMADAR MIR BAD SHAH.

A young officer who showed great coolness and judgment on the 30th October (1914). Kept his men well in hand and set them a good example during the retirement.

Recommended by Lieut.-Colonel W. M. SOUTHEY.
Honour or Reward—2nd Class I.O.M.

SUBEDAR-MAJOR MALA KHAN.

Has carried out his duties as Subedar-Major most satisfactorily. His Company has been well looked after and has always done good work. As I mentioned before, this Company did not bear the brunt of the attacks on the 26th or 30th October (1914), but they have always done quiet and useful work and the Subedar-Major has been well to the fore.

SUBEDAR AMIR KHAN.

Has done good honest work—as steady as a rock—a man well advanced in years, but with a stout heart. As above, his two platoons were not on the front attacks on the 26th and 30th (October 1914), but his Company has invariably set a good example of steadiness to the whole regiment, thanks to this Subedar's example.

LIEUT. H. V. LEWIS.

Who commanded the machine-gun section and continued to work his gun until the enemy had got right into the trenches. He then collected what men he could and conducted a steady retirement causing considerable loss to the enemy. (2nd mention.)

JEMADAR MIR BAD SHAH.

Commanded the party which seized the right sap on the 19th December. This party was attacked pretty well for the whole twenty-four hours they were in the sap. This officer behaved splendidly. Had he failed to do so, the whole party would have been lost. Lieut. Drew, R.E., who was in the sap, mentioned his behaviour in the highest terms.

MAJOR J. A. HANNYNGTON, C.M.G.

Gave the greatest assistance in the attack made by the 59th Rifles and was indefatigable in his efforts to make the attack a success. On every occasion this officer has shown himself to be full of resource and energy, and I would like to bring his excellent services to notice. (2nd mention.)

LIEUT. F. M. G.-GRIFFIN.

As Adjutant has not had opportunities of distinguishing himself in the firing line, but his work throughout some very trying days has been admirable. He never spares himself, and I can confidently recommend him as a first-class officer. (2nd mention.)

LIEUT. H. J. D. O'NEILL, 127th Q.M.O., B.L.I., attached to 129th D.C.O. Baluchis.

Action for which commended—Reconnaissance work carried out on night of 17/18 March.

Vide Lahore Division wire I.G. 926, dated 19th March. The reconnaissance report carried out by Lieut. O'Neill and party 129th Baluchis was forwarded to Indian Corps and has been returned with the following remarks by the Corps Commander: 'A very good bit of work. Please tell Lieut. O'Neill I have noted his name and asked the Brigadier-General to include him in his list for mentions'.

The proper form in duplicate, recommending Lieut. O'Neill for the Military Cross, was duly submitted. The same form contained the name of

LIEUT. F. M. G.-GRIFFIN, 129th Baluchis.

Action for which commended—For continuous good work in the field as Adjutant of the Regiment since October. Continually exposing himself in getting orders and instructions conveyed to Company Commanders. (3rd mention.)

Recommended by Major J. A. HANNYNGTON, Commandant.

Honour or Reward for which recommended—D.S.O.

From the Ferozepore Brigade, No. S.C. 208, dated 10.10 a.m., 23 September, 1915:

LIEUT. GRIFFIN's excellent work with search party is fully recognised and the attention of the Division has been called to it.

LIEUT. H. J. D. O'NEILL, 127th Q.M.O. Baluchis. Ypres, April 26th.

As machine-gun officer he performed brilliant work in covering both the advance and subsequent retirement from a very advanced position. His guns were most ably handled and rendered great service. (2nd mention.)

Recommended for M.C.

LIEUT. C. M. THORNHILL, 24th Punjabis. Ypres, April 26th–30th.

During operations this officer performed splendid work in rationing and supplying the regiment at great personal risk. Also, in connection with the Transport, when it was being shelled and confusion setting in. Stalking and shooting a German sniper in Ypres while it was being shelled.

Note by Divisional Commander: 'Lieut. Thornhill's name should be brought to notice when recommendations are called for in connection with Ypres'.

Recommended for D.S.O.

MAJOR H. HULSEBERG, attached from the 127th Q.M.O. Baluchis.

Gallant behaviour at Ypres on April 26th in leading and holding on to the furthest point reached. Though suffering from the effects of gas, he hung on until ordered back at night. The Officer Commanding Connaught Rangers reported to me regarding his behaviour.

Recommended for D.S.O.

JEMADAR MALASIN. Ypres, April 26th.

For particularly brave leading. He pushed on with very few men to the furthest point reached and hung on until given orders to retire at night.

Recommended for the I.O.M., 2nd Class.

JEMADAR AYUB KHAN. Ypres, April 26th.

In command of a party sent out at night to recover wounded. Reported by the officer in charge of search parties as 'the moving spirit of the lot and full of pluck'.

Brilliant reconnaissance work from trenches near Neuve Chapelle on June 23rd. Running great risks to obtain the required information. He is always to the fore in scouting work, repeatedly bringing in useful information. (2nd mention.)

Recommended for the I.O.M., 2nd Class.

MAJOR ARTHUR GOSSET CRAWFORD, attached from 84th Punjabis.

For gallant leading in the attacks at Ypres on 26th and 27th April, 1915. He was in command of the leading Company and held on to the furthest point reached. In all subsequent work he has always been most cool and set an excellent example to all ranks.

Recommended for the D.S.O.

LIEUT. CHARLES STUART BROWNING.

For conspicuously good work during the campaign. Was wounded when leading the attack on enemy's sap at Givenchy in December 1914. Since his return he has performed continuously good work, conveying orders under fire and setting a splendid example to the men.

Recommended for the M.C.

SUBEDAR ZERGHUN SHAH, attached from the 127th.

For gallant conduct and good service in the field. He was wounded at Ypres on 26th April, 1915, whilst gallantly leading his men after the British officers had been wounded; and again wounded at Neuve Chapelle on 4th September, 1915, whilst carrying out a very dangerous reconnaissance.

Recommended for the I.O.M., 2nd Class.

JEMADAR SUNDAR ALI, attached from the 84th Punjabis.

For gallant conduct on 14th August, 1915, in going out under shell fire and carrying in men who were severely

APPENDIX VIII 253

wounded. He made two separate journeys to do this of some 60 yards.

Again, on 16th April, 1915, he did the same, going again to bring in another man who was badly wounded by shell fire. (2 mentions.)

Recommended for the I.O.M., 2nd Class.

JEMADAR GHULAM JILANI.

For conspicuously good work since arrival of regiment in France. He has given the greatest assistance throughout in working rations and 1st-line Transport and all work behind the line. During the Ypres fighting of October 1914 and April 1915, when the regimental transport got badly shelled, he acted most coolly in getting it out of danger. His work has been invaluable throughout the whole year in France.

Recommended for the I.O.M., 2nd Class.

*MEN*

No. 4050 SEPOY KHUDADAD, 129th D.C.O. Baluchis.

On 31st October, 1914, at Hollebeke, Belgium, the British Officer in charge of the detachment having been wounded, and the other gun put out of action by a shell, Sepoy Khudadad, though himself wounded, remained working his gun until all the other five men of the gun detachment had been killed.

Recommended by Lieut.-Colonel W. M. SOUTHEY.

Awarded V.C.

No. 118 LANCE-NAIK NEK AMAL.

On the 26th October (1914) when Captain Vincent was wounded, with great coolness went out from a trench and attended to him within 100 yards of the enemy. Unable to bring him in alone, went back to the trench and brought out another man with him and took Captain Vincent under cover.

Recommended by Lieut.-Colonel W. M. SOUTHEY.

Honour or Reward—V.C.

No. 4355 HAVILDAR WASIM KHAN.
No. 307 SEPOY ABDUL RAHMAN.
No. 36 SEPOY GHAZAN SHAH.
No. 455 SEPOY HAKIM KHAN.
No. 3750 LANCE-NAIK AMIRULLA.

These men all did good work on night patrols, moving right up to the enemy's saps and throwing bombs in, thereby causing a good deal of consternation and stopping any further attempt of the enemy to continue their saps towards our line.

SEPOY HAKIM KHAN went out in broad daylight on one occasion right up to one of the saps where he saw a German. He would not shoot him as the man had no rifle with him. He came away, as a naik in the trenches ordered him to do so; otherwise he would have gone on down the trench.

No. 233 SEPOY HAZRAT MUHAMMAD.

Employed as bicycle orderly. Has done excellent work in bringing messages from Brigade Headquarters. Every night when in the trenches, there was continuous heavy firing and bullets were flying about Festubert and the road over which the orderlies came. This sepoy never waited for the firing to slacken, but came and went with the greatest regularity.

No. 3151 SEPOY MIRZA KHAN.

A reservist employed as bicycle orderly. The same remarks apply to him, as he worked alternately with Hazrat Muhammad.

No. 3833 SEPOY JALAL KHAN.

Was specially mentioned to me by Lieut.-Colonel Nicholson, Commanding East Lancashire Regiment, for having on the night of 15/16th November (1914) done him invaluable service in guiding parties of his men, who had lost themselves, to the firing trenches on his own initiative.

No. 2985 HAVILDAR RAHIM ALI.

Collected as many men as he could find and assisted Lieut. Lewis in conducting a steady retirement.

No. 3836 LANCE-NAIK FATEH HAIDER.

Exposed himself repeatedly to the enemy's fire at 50 yards range while repairing the parapet, so as to enable the machine gun to have a clear field of fire. Showed great coolness during the retirement.

No. 3985 SEPOY SATAR KHAN.

Showed conspicuous coolness during the retirement.

No. 453 SEPOY SAHIB JAN.

Showed conspicuous bravery on the 19th. On one occasion when pushed by the enemy he charged three Germans, confronting them in the trench, and drove them right back.

APPENDIX VIII 255

No. 3271 NAIK NEK MUHAMMAD.
No. 231 SEPOY MIHA JAN.
No. 322 SEPOY GUL SHER.
No. 100 SEPOY MISKIN.

All did good work in the sap on the 19th.

No. 2268 HAVILDAR NUR KHAN.
No. 2012 SEPOY AULYIA KHAN.
No. 4367 SEPOY MEHRAB GUL.

These men are regimental signallers and stand out as having done particularly good work. They have had to repair continuously lines cut by fire and have exposed themselves fearlessly and frequently.

Recommended by Major HANNYNGTON, Commandant.
Honour or Reward for which recommended—I.D.S.M.

No. 2046 COLOUR-HAVILDAR MALASIN, 124th Q.M.O., Bal. L.I., attached to 129th D.C.O. Baluchis. Ypres.

For pushing on, leading and encouraging men most gallantly to the furthest point reached in the attack of the 26th April. Held on until ordered to withdraw at night.

Recommended for I.O.M.

No. 471 SEPOY RAJI KHAN, 129th D.C.O. Baluchis. Ypres.

Conspicuous gallantry when carrying a message under heavy shell and rifle fire. He was hit by a fragment of a shell which exploded 3 yards away from him. Though wounded, he carried on and delivered the message, which was an urgent one.

Recommended for I.O.M.

No. 3640 NAIK AYUB KHAN, 124th D.C.O. Bal. I., attached to 129th D.C.O. Baluchis. Ypres.

In command of a party sent out at night to recover wounded. Reported by the officer in charge as 'the moving spirit of the party and full of pluck'. Frequently fired on, he coolly proceeded with his duty.

Recommended for I.D.S.M.

S.C. 526: 30. vi. 15: The Corps Commander has promoted Naik Ayub Khan to be Jemadar and has also asked for a money award for him.

No. 4446 NAIK MEHR GUL, 129th D.C.O. Baluchis.
No. 86 SEPOY JELA KHAN, 129th D.C.O. Baluchis.
For bold scouting work in the trenches opposite Neuve Chapelle. These two men went out several times although the German trenches were only 200 yards distant and obtained useful information.
Recommended for I.D.S.M.

No. 4321 SEPOY GHULAM HUSSEIN. Ypres.
For carrying Major Holbrooke, who was wounded, into safety under heavy fire; then assuming command of a number of shaken men and making them work at a trench to form a rallying point, and setting a splendid example to the others.
Recommended for I.D.S.M.

No. 3836 HAVILDAR FATEH HAIDER.
Continuous good work with the machine-gun sections since October last. His conduct has twice been specially brought to notice by the Machine-gun Officer in connection with the fighting at Givenchy in December 1914 and at Ypres in April 1915. (2nd mention.)
Recommended for the I.O.M., 2nd Class.

No. 1163 NAIK KARMA KHAN, attached from the 84th Punjabis.
Volunteering for and commanding a search party which proceeded in broad daylight to search for a N.C.O. in front of the enemy's trenches who was thought to be wounded. A dangerous bit of work, well carried out.
Recommended for the I.O.M., 2nd Class.

No. 4038 SEPOY JAHAN KHAN, 124th D.C.O. Bal. I., attached to 129th Baluchis. Ypres.
For gallantry in pushing forward in face of heavy fire to the furthest point reached by the attack. Specially recommended by his Double Company Commander for coolness and assistance.
Recommended for I.D.S.M.

No. 4305 SEPOY MISTAKIN.
No. 246 SEPOY DAD KHAN.
For despatch work since October 1914. These two men have stood out in carrying messages under fire where other communication has failed. They have never failed during their nine

months of work and continual risk. They were conspicuous at Ypres where messages had to be carried over 500 yards of open fire-swept ground.
Recommended for I.D.S.M.

No. 4565 SEPOY ABDULLA KHAN, attached from 124th.
No. 184 SEPOY SARWAR KHAN.

Volunteering to go out on patrol by day in order to bring in a comrade supposed to be lying in front of the German trenches. They went out in broad daylight quite close up to the enemy.
Recommended for the I.D.S.M.

No. 11 NAIK KAMIN KHAN, attached from 127th Baluch L.I.

For particularly bold reconnaissance on the night of August 28/29th, 1915, to obtain special information asked for. This man has always been to the fore in command of patrols, showing fearlessness combined with sound action. He is responsible for a great deal of the information supplied by this regiment.
Recommended for the I.O.M.

No. 22 LANCE-NAIK ALIM KHAN.

For continuously good work during the year. He has done most excellent work in scouting and reconnoitring. Has been already twice recommended for reward previously and his conduct has been repeatedly brought to notice by his Company Commander—conspicuously in helping to bring in the body of an officer where the other man concerned was granted an I.O.M.
Recommended for the I.O.M.

No. 3 NAIK BAGH MAHOMED.

At Ypres on 26th April, 1915, was badly wounded when serving his machine gun but refused to go to aid-post, and continued to work his gun as long as it was of any use to do so. He has been with the machine guns for the year and been frequently brought to notice for his fearlessness under fire and good work.
Recommended for I.O.M.

No. 1172 SEPOY BURHAN ALI.

On September 24/25th, 1915, he carried out a very bold and useful reconnaissance to find out the effect of our gun fire on the enemy wire. He crawled along the enemy's wire for some

distance and brought in a particularly good report. The fact that the enemy were very much on the *qui vive* made the work particularly dangerous.
Recommended for I.O.M.

No. 2637 HAVILDAR BODLA KHAN, attached from 127th.

For good reconnaissance work on the nights of August 26/27th and 27/28th. On the latter occasion the Subedar was killed and Havildar Bodla Khan again went out to bring in the body of the dead Subedar.
Recommended for I.D.S.M.

No. 260 SEPOY BADSHAH MIR.
No. 1197 LANCE-NAIK SHAH ZAMAN, attached from 84th Punjabis.

For continuously volunteering to accompany reconnoitring patrols on any dangerous work in front of the line. They have both done most excellent and useful work in obtaining information—particularly on the night of September 24/25th.
Recommended for I.D.S.M.

No. 4358 HAVILDAR ZER DAD.

For particularly good work in charge of picked men for scouting. A most cool, brave man, chosen to observe and report in any exposed or dangerous position when correct information was required. He has done most useful work—especially on September 25th.
Recommended for I.D.S.M.

The last roll of recommendations was submitted on 1 December, 1915. In it certain Followers were recommended for a gratuity or a special medal for 'continuous good service with the regiment since arrival. They came from India with the regiment and have often been under fire':

*Public Followers.*
   Sweepers: IMAM DIN and AMI LAL;
   Langris: WALI MAHOMED, HASHIM ALI and HUSSEIN;
   Drabis: 712 LANCE-NAIK VILAYET KHAN and 758 FAZL.

*Private Followers.*
   Syces: BODESI and TILAK;
   Servants: ABDUL KARIM and AHMED KHAN.

On 13 May, 1915, the Ferozepore Brigade called for recommendations for Russian decorations—the 3rd and 4th Classes of the Cross of St George and the 1st, 2nd, 3rd and 4th Classes of the Medal of St George.

1. *St George's Cross:*

This is equivalent to the Victoria Cross for N.C.O.s and men in Russia. A man must get the 4th Class before he is entitled to the 3rd Class, but in this instance the Russian Military Attaché thinks this regulation need not be adhered to. The distinction between the 3rd and 4th Class is one of valour and not of rank, and roughly speaking the 3rd Class may be taken to represent our V.C. and the 4th Class the D.C.M.

2. *St George's Medal:*

There are four classes. The 1st and 2nd Classes are in gold and should be given to N.C.O.s. The 3rd and 4th Classes are silver and are intended for private soldiers. In the case of these medals it is necessary to have the names of the men engraved on the rim of the medal. The Russian Military Attaché lays great stress on the importance of having the full name and particulars of each recipient of these orders and medals and, in the case of the 3rd and 4th Class St George's Cross, an account of the particular act of gallantry for which these orders are given.

No. 118 SEPOY NEK AMAL. Hollebeke.

On October 26th, when Captain Vincent was wounded, with great coolness went out from a trench and attended to him within 100 yards of the enemy. Unable to bring him in alone, he went back to the trench and brought out another man and so brought in Captain Vincent. (Was recommended for V.C. but was granted I.O.M., 2nd Class.)

Recommended for St George's Cross, 3rd Class.

(Was awarded on this recommendation St George's Cross, 4th Class.)

No. 3836 SEPOY FATEH HAIDER. Givenchy.

Owing to direction of advance of enemy the machine gun was unable to fire sufficiently to a flank. He exposed himself with great gallantry on the parapet to the enemy's fire at 50 yards range in inlaying the embrasure so that the gun might be brought to bear, in which he was successful.

Recommended for St George's Cross, 4th Class.

(Was awarded St George's Medal, 4th Class.)

No. 4355 HAVILDAR WASIM KHAN. Givenchy.

Commanding a patrol with great gallantry. Proceeded out in front of trench and attacked with bombs a sap-head where the enemy were working. He bombed the sap and prevented any further work.

Recommended for St George's Medal, 1st Class (and was afterwards awarded it).

No. 69 HAVILDAR SOHBAT KHAN. Hollebeke.

When in command of a section of trench, was the last to evacuate it when the Germans advanced on October 30th, 1914, being one of the few survivors. Since that he has on various occasions shown coolness and gallantry in action.

Recommended for St George's Medal, 2nd Class.

(Was afterwards recommended for a French decoration.)

No. 471 SEPOY RAJI KHAN. Neuve Chapelle.

Conspicuous gallantry in carrying an urgent message across open fire-swept ground. Was wounded in the arm during the execution of this duty, but carried on and delivered the message.

Recommended for St George's Medal, 3rd Class.

(Was afterwards awarded the I.O.M., 2nd Class.)

No. 4321 SEPOY GHULAM HUSSEIN. Ypres.

Carrying back Major Holbrooke, who was wounded, under heavy fire. Secondly, rallying demoralised men and putting a section of road ditch into a state of defence, which afterwards proved to be a useful rallying-point.

Recommended for St George's Medal, 4th Class.

(Was afterwards awarded the I.D.S.M.)

On 16 October, 1915, the following recommendations for French decorations were sent forward:

No. 69 HAVILDAR SOHBAT KHAN.

For conspicuous gallantry on 30th October, 1914, at Hollebeke, Belgium, when leading his men up to the firing line under a very heavy shell and rifle fire. He set a splendid example to his men, who were outnumbered, and was one of the few survivors. He has since shown coolness and gallantry in action and was wounded on 19th May, 1915, near Neuve Chapelle.

No. 2985 HAVILDAR RAHIM ALI.

For gallantry at Givenchy on 20th December, 1914, and great coolness in handling his men under heavy fire.

## Part II
### RECOMMENDATIONS IN EAST AFRICA
#### OFFICERS

MAJOR CHARLES ARTHUR GILBERT MONEY, 130th Baluchis, attached to 129th.

As Second-in-Command of the regiment, although no action took place, did most useful work during the period the regiment was employed in occupying the seaport town of Dar-es-Salaam and further south in German East Africa.
Recommended by Lieut.-Colonel HULSEBERG.
Recommended for 'Mention in Despatches'.

CAPTAIN HAROLD VICTOR LEWIS, 129th Baluchis.

Has done excellent work, often in very trying and difficult circumstances. Although no actions took place, he was present at the occupation of Dar-es-Salaam and the southern parts in German East Africa.
He already possesses the Military Cross, received in France, 1915.
Recommended by Lieut.-Colonel HULSEBERG.
Recommended for 'Mention in Despatches'.

LIEUT. (TEMPORARY CAPTAIN) HAROLD VICTOR LEWIS, M.C., Indian Army.

He carried out a valuable reconnaissance and drove off an enemy party of twice his strength. He set a fine example throughout. (Second mention in East Africa.)

CAPTAIN CHARLES STUART BROWNING, 129th Baluchis.

This officer has been invaluable. Was present during the occupation of the seaport towns from Dar-es-Salaam and south of that place. He has been already recommended for the Military Cross in France in 1915, for gallantry.
Recommended by Lieut.-Colonel HULSEBERG.
Recommended for the M.C.

LIEUT. ROBERT BARRON WILSON, Dorsetshire Regiment, attached to the 129th Baluchis.

As Quarter-Master of the regiment has done excellent work often during the most trying and difficult circumstances.
Recommended by Lieut.-Colonel HULSEBERG.
Recommended for 'Mention in Despatches'.

SUBEDAR MIR KHAMBIR KHAN, 127th Baluchis, attached to 129th.

Although no actions took place between 1st July and 15th September, 1915, this Indian officer has rendered valuable assistance during marches and trying and difficult circumstances. He was present at the occupation of Dar-es-Salaam and the other seaport towns.

Recommended by Lieut.-Colonel HULSEBERG.
Recommended for O.B.I.

SUBEDAR BAHADUR KHAN, 108th Indian Infantry, attached to 129th Baluchis.

Although no action has taken place, has done excellent work.
Recommended by Lieut.-Colonel HULSEBERG.
Recommended for 2nd Class, I.O.M.

CAPTAIN FORRESTER GRIFFITH-GRIFFIN, 129th Baluchis.

Date and place of action—4th June, 1916, at Ngoha River, German East Africa.

Showing great initiative, coolness and resource when enemy's rifle fire suddenly opened from the thick bush and during the fight that ensued.

Several previous mentions; possesses M.C.
Adjutant of the regiment.
Recommended for Brevet-Majority.

CAPTAIN ARTHUR NORMAN DICKSON, I.M.S., attached to 129th Baluchis.

Date and place of action—4th June, 1916, at Ngoha River, German East Africa.

Medical Officer of the regiment. Attended the wounded, coming at once up to the front under heavy rifle fire with coolness, thereby steadying the African stretcher-bearers, who were at first inclined to bolt.

No previous mention.
Recommended for the M.C.

JEMADAR KHAN AHMED, B.M.P., attached to 129th Baluchis.

Date and place of action—4th June, 1916, at Ngoha River, German East Africa.

Commanded a small patrol to locate enemy's position. In doing this drew a heavy rifle fire on his patrol but approached within a few yards of enemy's position, achieved his object,

and withdrew in safety without any casualties. Throughout he showed extraordinary firmness and determination.
Recommended for I.O.M.

2nd LIEUT. VIVIAN GODWIN ROBERT, 13th K.R.R., attached to 129th Baluchis.

Date and place of action—12th October, 1916, Nyambonde.

When in command of the Advance Guard of the Kibata Column on the advance on Kibata, was attacked heavily in the bush by the enemy who were holding the water-holes. He at once pushed through the bush with his Advance Guard thus getting out of range of the enemy's machine guns, and drove him out, killing two whites and one askari. He showed great initiative, I consider, for a young officer.
No previous mention.
Recommended for 'Mention'.

SUBEDAR SARBILAND, 127th B.L.I., attached to 129th Baluchis.

Date and place of action—9th December, 1916, Kibata.

For gallantry during the first night attack by us on the 'Lodgement'. After the death of the British officer (Captain Browning), maintained the attack for twenty minutes under the enemy's entanglements until casualties and want of ammunition compelled him to retire.
No previous mention.
Recommended for I.O.M., 2nd Class.

SUBEDAR ABDULLAH KHAN, 129th Baluchis.

Date and place of action—9th December, 1916, Kibata.

For gallantry in defence of the redoubt on Picquet Hill. By his gallantry and example undoubtedly contributed largely to the retention of the redoubt under intense artillery fire.
No previous mention.
Recommended for I.O.M., 2nd Class.

CAPTAIN ARTHUR NORMAN DICKSON, I.M.S., attached to 129th Baluchis.

Date and place of action—6th to 29th December, 1916, at Kibata.

During the whole of this period this Medical Officer showed great devotion to duty. Though unwell himself, he frequently had to operate during intense fire, on one occasion the hospital coming under enemy's machine-gun fire. When Major Money,

129th Baluchis, was hit on Picquet Hill, he at once moved out under rifle and machine-gun fire to the picquet to give what help he could. I have previously sent this Officer's name in for an honour. During most of the time he was Senior Medical Officer of the Post.

Recommended for M.C. (2nd mention.)

LIEUT. CHARLTON WALTER PALIN, 129th Baluchis.

Date and place of action—7th December, 1916, Kibata.

For gallantry in the defence of No. 2 Redoubt on Picquet Hill on 7th December, 1916. The Redoubt was badly shelled, parapets falling in causing a number of casualties, 70 shells, mostly H.E., falling in or near No. 2 Redoubt. This officer, who was commanding No. 2 Redoubt for a time, though three times buried by falling parapets, by his continuous coolness and zeal, under intense artillery fire, kept his men together and maintained his hold of the redoubt.

No previous mention.
Recommended for M.C.

TEMPORARY MAJOR HAROLD VICTOR LEWIS, 129th Baluchis.

Date and place of action—15th December, 1916, Kibata.

Arranged and commanded the bombing party on the night of 15/16th December, 1916, against the enemy, who had secured a lodgement on an important tactical point on our picquet position. The seizure of the latter would have endangered our security in rear. The action was successful, the position taken. It was greatly due to this officer that the achievement was a success. He already possesses M.C. and one bar. (3rd mention.)

Previous mentions—December 1915; August 1916.
Recommended for D.S.O.

2nd LIEUT. W. S. THATCHER, I.A.R.O., attached to 129th Baluchis.

Date and place of action—15th December, 1916, Kibata.

Led the bombing party on the night of 15/16th December, 1916, against the enemy with great gallantry, being slightly wounded, thus driving the enemy out of his position and securing an important point on our picquet line.

No previous mention.
Recommended for M.C.

## APPENDIX VIII

SUBEDAR MUHAMMED AFZAL, 124th Bal. Infy., attached to
129th Baluchis.

Date and place of action—15th December, 1916, Kibata.

Led his men with gallantry and greatly assisted 2nd Lieut.
W. S. Thatcher in a bomb attack. Slightly wounded.

No previous mention.

Recommended for the I.O.M., 2nd Class.

JEMADAR AYUB KHAN, 129th Baluchis.

Date and place of action—15th December, 1916, Kibata.

Acted with great gallantry in a bomb attack against an
enemy position on night of 15/16th December, 1916. Wounded.
Already possesses 2nd Class I.O.M.

Previous mention—August 1915.

Recommended for I.O.M., 1st Class.

SUBEDAR GHULAM JILANI, 129th Baluchis.

For consistent good work and devotion to duty under
adverse conditions throughout the campaign.

2nd LIEUT. VIVIAN GODWIN ROBERT, 13th K.R.R.,
attached to 129th Baluchis.

Date and place of action—13th January, 1917, Mbindia.

For gallantry during the attack on Mbindia Hill. When
2nd Lieut. W. S. Thatcher was wounded this officer carried
on the attack and pursuit, and by his fine example led on the
men against the enemy's hidden position in the bush, until all
our objectives had been gained and the enemy put to rout.
(2nd mention.)

Recommended for M.C.

CAPTAIN GEORGE ALEXANDER PHILLIPS, I.A.R.O.,
attached to 129th Baluchis.

Date and place of action—12th and 13th January, 1917,
Mwengei.

For coolness and bravery under fire during the attack, and
ability in conducting the operations of the 12th January, culminating in the occupation of the commanding position whence
the attack of the 13th January was launched.

(The above are the words used in a report on the action by
Major H. V. Lewis who was in charge of the attack in that area
on the 13th.)

No previous mention.

Recommended for 'Mention'.

LIEUT. ROBERT SANDEMAN PEISLEY MACIVOR, 129th Baluchis.

Date and place of action—15th September, 1916 to 5th May, 1917.

Arrived in East Africa on 14th January, 1916, appointed Officiating Adjutant 22nd March, 1916. Was in command of machine-gun detachment detached from regiment and employed with 2nd Brigade from June to September when, I understand, he did good work during the fighting on the Dunthumi. Served with the regiment all through the Kibata fighting and the attack on Mbindia. Is a good Adjutant and a very useful officer in every way.

No previous mention.

Recommended for 'Mention'.

JEMADAR SIKANDAR KHAN, 129th Baluchis.

Date and place of action—13th January, 1917, Mwengei.

For daring disregard of his own safety during the attack on the 13th January, 1917, while keeping the attack moving forward and from becoming disorganised.

No previous mention.

Recommended for 'Mention'.

SUBEDAR SHERBAT KHAN, 129th Baluchis.

Date and place of action—15th September, 1916 to 5th May, 1917.

For consistent good work and especially when commanding a Company in the Advance Guard from Kibata to Mwengei.

No previous mention.

Recommended for 'Mention'.

JEMADAR KARAM DAD, B.M.P., attached to 129th Baluchis.

Date and place of action—15th September, 1916 to 5th May, 1917.

For consistent gallantry and initiative on patrol work, good work in action and efficiency and cheerfulness under adverse conditions.

No previous mention.

Recommended for 'Mention'.

CAPTAIN ARNOLD CHARLES GOVER, 121st Pioneers, attached to 129th Baluchis.

Date and place of action—5th August, 1917, Nanyati.

Acted with great coolness and gallantry throughout the

action, inspiring his men with confidence, and established himself with his Company on the enemy's flank. When all the British officers were casualties and only the Indian officers were left, this officer took over command of the battalion and conducted the retirement with skill and coolness.

No previous mention.

Recommended for M.C.

ACTING SUBEDAR-MAJOR SARBILAND, 127th Bal. L. Infy., attached to 129th Baluchis.

Date and place of action—5th August, 1917, Nanyati.

Led his platoon in the most gallant manner, showing a fine example to his men under trying circumstances, with a complete indifference to personal danger. When all the British officers were missing or casualties, he continued to handle his men with judgment and coolness till the retirement was effected. (2nd mention.)

Previous mentions—I.O.M., 2nd Class; General van Deventer's Despatch, *London Gazette*, 4th June, 1917.

Recommended for I.O.M., 1st Class.

SUBEDAR NUR KHAN, 129th Baluchis.

Date and place of action—5th August, 1917, Nanyati.

Led his platoon with gallantry under heavy fire, setting a fine example to his men throughout the action.

No previous mention.

Recommended for I.O.M., 2nd Class.

LIEUT. R. G. WOODWARD, I.A.R.O., M.C.

Date and place of action—26th November, 1917, Mwiti Water.

For conspicuous gallantry and devotion to duty. He held his men together during a strong enemy attack. He encouraged them by his courageous example. His gallantry afforded a most inspiring example at a critical time.

Recommended by Lieut.-Colonel W. N. HAY for M.C.

LIEUT. (A/CAPT.) GORDON EDWARD HAWKES, Sikhs. I.A.

Date and place of action—26th November, 1917, Mwiti Water.

For conspicuous gallantry and devotion to duty. He rallied parties of men who were being forced back by the enemy's attack. He collected a small party, with which he formed a rear-guard, and held up the enemy's advance. His courageous example was of the greatest value at a critical time.

Recommended by Lieut.-Colonel W. N. HAY for M.C.

*MEN*

No. 3 HAVILDAR BALA KHAN, 129th Baluchis.

Has rendered excellent service during the period 1st July to 15th September, 1916.

Recommended by Lieut.-Colonel HULSEBERG for the I.O.M., 2nd Class.

No. 1296 NAIK MUHAMMAD JAIM, 129th Baluchis.

Has done good work during above period. Was present at occupation of southern ports in German East Africa.

Recommended by Lieut.-Colonel HULSEBERG for I.D.S.M.

No. 4479 LANCE-NAIK ROSHAN ALI SHAH, 129th Baluchis.

Has done good work during the above period.

Recommended by Lieut.-Colonel HULSEBERG for I.D.S.M.

No. 4284 HAVILDAR MEWA KHAN, 129th Baluchis.

Has been invaluable in trying and difficult circumstances at times, though no actions have taken place.

Recommended by Lieut.-Colonel HULSEBERG for I.D.S.M.

No. 625 SEPOY LAL BADSHAH, 129th Baluchis.

Date and place of action—9th December, 1916, Kibata.

For gallantry during the night attack on the 'Lodgement'. Was with the first line that reached within a few yards of the enemy trenches and helped to pull out stakes in the chevaux-de-frise. Forced then to retire with the rest of the first line owing to casualties and lack of ammunition.

No previous mention.

Recommended for the I.D.S.M.

No. 230 SEPOY KHALIFA KHAN, 127th Bal. L. Infy., attached to 129th Baluchis.

Date and place of action—4th December, 1916, Kibata.

For gallantry during the night attack on the 'Lodgement'. Was with the first line that reached within a few yards of the enemy trenches and helped to pull out the stakes in the chevaux-de-frise. Forced to retire with the rest of the first line owing to casualties and lack of ammunition.

Recommended for I.D.S.M.

## APPENDIX VIII

No. 398 NAIK HAJI KHAN, 129th Baluchis.
Date and place of action—7th December, 1916, Kibata.
For gallantry in the defence of No. 2 Redoubt under intense artillery fire. When the parapets were falling in, this N.C. officer kept a constant watch over the parapet.
No previous mention.
Recommended for I.D.S.M.

No. 44 LANCE-NAIK FATEH KHAN, 129th Baluchis.
Date and place of action—7th December, 1916, Kibata.
For gallantry on night patrol, when in command going close up to the enemy trenches and bringing back useful information in spite of the close-range fire he was subjected to. He was wounded next day.
No previous mention.
Recommended for I.D.S.M.

No. 596 SEPOY MUNSIB DAR, 129th Baluchis.
Date and place of action—7th December, 1916, Kibata.
Conspicuous gallantry as No. 1 of his machine gun. He was constantly at his gun under heavy artillery and machine-gun fire. He had no cover. His fire kept down the fire of two hostile machine guns being employed against the Redoubt on his left. Dangerously wounded next day, he died of wounds.
No previous mention.
Recommended for I.O.M., 2nd Class.

No. 4053 HAVILDAR FAZL DAD, 129th Baluchis.
Date and place of action—9th December, 1916, Kibata.
For gallantry during the night attack on the 'Lodgement'. Led his men within 10 yards of the German trenches where he maintained himself, pulling out the stakes of the chevaux-de-frise, until casualties and lack of ammunition compelled him to retire.
No previous mention.
Recommended for the I.O.M., 2nd Class.

No. 3485 HAVILDAR ASGHAR KHAN, 129th Baluchis.
Date and place of action—9th December, 1916, Kibata.
For gallantry during the night attack on the 'Lodgement'. Led his men within 10 yards of the German trenches where he maintained himself, pulling out the stakes of the chevaux-

de-frise until casualties and want of ammunition compelled him to retire. He was severely wounded on 10 December.
No previous mention.
Recommended for the I.O.M., 2nd Class.

No. 3151 HAVILDAR MIRZA KHAN, 127th Bal. L. Infy., attached to 129th Baluchis.

Date and place of action—15th December, 1916, Kibata.

Formed one of the party in a bomb attack on an enemy position on night of 15/16th December, 1916, leading his men with great gallantry. The attack was a success.
No previous mention.
Recommended for I.O.M., 2nd Class.

No. 66 HAVILDAR JABAR KHAN, 129th Baluchis.

Date and place of action—15th December, 1916, Kibata.

Led his men with great gallantry in a bomb attack on an enemy position on night 15/16th December, 1916. The attack was a success.
No previous mention.
Recommended for I.O.M., 2nd Class.

No. 453 NAIK SAHIB JAN, 129th Baluchis.

Date and place of action—15th December, 1916, Kibata.

Acted with great gallantry as one of a bombing party on the night 15/16th December, 1916. The attack was a success. He possesses I.O.M., 2nd Class.
Previous mention—December 1914.
Recommended for I.D.S.M.

No. 4469 LANCE-NAIK GUL JAN, 124th Bal. Infy., attached to 129th Baluchis.

Date and place of action—15th December, 1916, Kibata.

Acted with great gallantry as one of a bombing party on night of 15/16th December, 1916. The attack was a success.
No previous mention.
Recommended for I.O.M., 2nd Class.

No. 436 SEPOY MEHR JAN, 129th Baluchis.

Date and place of action—15th December, 1916, Kibata.

Acted with great gallantry as one of a bombing party on night of 15/16th December, 1916, against enemy position. The attack was a success.
No previous mention.
Recommended for I.O.M., 2nd Class.

No. 4565 SEPOY ABDULLAH KHAN, 124th Bal. Infy., attached to 129th Baluchis.

Date and place of action—15th December, 1916, Kibata.

Acted with great gallantry, forming part of a bombing party on night of 15/16th December, 1916, against enemy position. The attack was a success. (2nd mention.)

No previous mention.

Recommended for I.O.M., 2nd Class.

No. 4160 LANCE-NAIK BABRI KHAN, 124th Bal. Infy., attached to 129th Baluchis.

Date and place of action—15th September, 1916 to 5th May, 1917.

He has been frequently brought to notice for good work and keenness. On one occasion he insisted on rejoining his unit although he had not recovered from a wound in the leg.

No previous mention.

Recommended for 'Mention'.

No. 4328 LANCE-NAIK GHULAM HAIDAR, 124th Bal. Infy., attached to 129th Baluchis.

Date and place of action—15th September, 1916 to 5th May, 1917.

He has consistently behaved with gallantry and initiative above the average and always set an example to the men with him.

No previous mention.

Recommended for 'Mention'.

No. 4520 NAIK DOWD SHAH, 129th Baluchis.

Date and place of action—15th September, 1916 to 5th May, 1917.

As N.C.O. i/c machine gun has shown great judgment and efficiency in making the best use of his gun and in spotting and bringing fire to bear on fleeting targets irrespective of the enemy's fire.

No previous mention.

Recommended for 'Mention'.

No. 290 HAVILDAR SARDAR SHAH, B.M.P., attached to 129th Baluchis.

Date and place of action—13th January, 1917, Mbindia.

Coolness under very heavy fire and himself bringing his

Maxim into action and firing it when most of the gun team, whose commander he was, were wounded.

No previous mention.

Recommended for 'Mention'.

No. 3679 HAVILDAR IMAM DIN, 129th Baluchis.

No. 2630 COLOUR-HAVILDAR ALIM SHAH, 124th Bal. Infy., attached to 129th Baluchis.

No. 757 SEPOY MISRI KHAN, 129th Baluchis.

No. 225 NAIK MOHAMED RAHIM, 127th Bal. L. Infy., attached to 129th Baluchis.

Date and place of action—13th January, 1917, Mbindia.

All four commended for gallantry in the attack on successive enemy positions. That the attack was a success and the enemy put to rout was largely due to the efforts of these N.C.O.s and men.

No previous mention.

Recommended for 'Mention'.

No. 1436 HAVILDAR GHULAM KADAR, 108th Infy., attached to 129th Baluchis.

Date and place of action—13th January, 1917, Mwengei.

For gallantry in the attack at Mwengei. When running towards the machine-gun emplacement, one enemy machine gun opened fire. He shouted to his men to charge the gun and himself set the example.

No previous mention.

Recommended for 'Mention'.

No. 4493 HAVILDAR BAGH KHAN, 129th Baluchis.

Date and place of action—13th January, 1917, Mwengei.

For conspicuous gallantry in leading his men during the attack at Mwengei.

No previous mention.

Recommended for 'Mention'.

No. 4320 LANCE-NAIK TOR KHAN, 127th Bal. L. Infy., attached to 129th Baluchis.

Date and place of action—12th January, 1917, Mwengei.

He crawled out three times in front of our trenches under fire to light smoke bombs as signals to aeroplanes. The enemy were 100 yards distant and the bush was cut down.

No previous mention.

Recommended for 'Mention'.

APPENDIX VIII 273

No. 4053 HAVILDAR FAZL DAD.
No. 3485 HAVILDAR ASGHAR KHAN.
No. 625 SEPOY LAL BADSHAH.
No. 230 SEPOY KHALIFA.

All again commended for gallantry at Kibata on 9th December, 1916 (as above described) and recommended for 'Mention', provided awards submitted for approval on 5. i. 17 are not approved.

No. 398 NAIK HAJI KHAN, 129th Baluchis.

Date and place of action—7th December, 1916, Kibata.

For gallantry in the defence of No. 2 Redoubt under intense artillery fire. When the parapets were falling in this N.C. officer kept a constant watch over the parapet.

No previous mention.

Recommended for 'Mention', provided award submitted for approval on 5. i. 17 is not approved of.

No. 44 LANCE-NAIK FATEH KHAN, 129th Baluchis.

Date and place of action—7th December, 1916, Kibata.

For gallantry on night patrol, when in command, going close up to the enemy trenches and bringing back useful information in spite of the close-range fire he was subjected to. He was wounded next day.

No previous mention.

Recommended for 'Mention', provided award submitted for approval on 5. i. 17 is not approved of.

No. 653 NAIK SHAH NIWAZ, 21st Punjabis, attached to 129th Baluchis.

Date and place of action—5th August, 1917, Nanyati.

When all the rest of his machine-gun detachment had become casualties he worked his gun with perfect coolness for about two hours within 60 yards of the enemy.

No previous mention.

Recommended for I.O.M., 2nd Class.

No. 447 LANCE-NAIK TORSUM, 127th Bal. L. Infy., attached to 129th Baluchis.

When in command of a machine gun with the Advance Guard handled it with skill, and acted with coolness and gallantry throughout the action.

No previous mention.

Recommended for I.O.M., 2nd Class.

T

No. 1787 SEPOY YUSUF KHAN, 130th Baluchis, attached to 129th Baluchis.

Date and place of action—5th August, 1917, Nanyati.

As advance scout displayed great initiative and resource. He was wounded.

No previous mention.

Recommended for I.D.S.M.

No. 1357 SEPOY BASHKIR, 129th Baluchis.

Date and place of action—5th August, 1917, Nanyati.

As advance scout displayed great initiative and resource.

No previous mention.

Recommended for I.D.S.M.

The following forty names were submitted for the I.M.S.M., for 'Devotion to Duty in theatre of War'. None had received previous mention.

No. 192 HAVILDAR SHER BAHADUR, 129th Baluchis.

No. 261 HAVILDAR GUL AHMAD, 129th Baluchis.

No. 1671 HAVILDAR ALI BAHADUR, 129th Baluchis.

No. 3635 HAVILDAR FAZIL ILAHI, 129th Baluchis.

No. 2292 COLOUR-HAVILDAR SOHBAT KHAN, 127th Bal. L. Infy., attached to 129th Baluchis.

No. 4210 HAVILDAR MUBARAK KHAN, 127th Bal. L. Infy., attached to 129th Baluchis.

No. 290 HAVILDAR RESHMIN KHAN, 127th Bal. L. Infy., attached to 129th Baluchis.

No. 3843 HAVILDAR SULEMAN KHAN, 124th Bal. Infy., attached to 129th Baluchis.

No. 734 COLOUR-HAVILDAR SARFARAZ KHAN, 108th Infy., attached to 129th Baluchis.

No. 290 HAVILDAR SARDAR SHAH, B.M.P., attached to 129th Baluchis.

No. 537 NAIK GUL MUHAMMED, 129th Baluchis.

No. 4781 NAIK HAKIM DIN, 129th Baluchis.

No. 4447 LANCE-NAIK MUBARAK KHAN, 127th Bal. L.I., attached to 129th Baluchis.

No. 35 NAIK ZAR GUL, 127th Bal. L.I., attached to 129th Baluchis.

No. 307 NAIK MIRZA KHAN, 127th Bal. L.I., attached to 129th Baluchis.

No. 4160 NAIK BABRI KHAN, 124th Bal. Infy., attached to 129th Baluchis.

APPENDIX VIII 275

No. 485 NAIK PAHLWAN ULLAH, 124th Bal. Infy., attached to 129th Baluchis.
No. 308 NAIK NIAZ ALI, B.M.P., attached to 129th Baluchis.
No. 600 NAIK FAZAL AHMED, 129th Baluchis.
No. 1311 NAIK SHAMAS DIN, 108th Infy., attached to 129th Baluchis.
No. 521 LANCE-NAIK ATTA KHAN, 129th Baluchis.
No. 778 SEPOY HAZRAT GUL, 129th Baluchis.
No. 636 SEPOY MAIN SHAH, 129th Baluchis.
No. 4453 LANCE-NAIK MUSA KHAN, 129th Baluchis.
No. 193 LANCE-NAIK LAL GUL, 129th Baluchis.
No. 2736 LANCE-NAIK BYRAM KHAN, 127th Bal. L.I., attached to 129th Baluchis.
No. 4450 SEPOY MUHAMMAD ALI, 127th Bal. L.I., attached to 129th Baluchis.
No. 4463 SEPOY DITTA KHAN, 127th Bal. L.I., attached to 129th Baluchis.
No. 38 LANCE-NAIK AWAL MIR, 127th Bal. L.I., attached to 129th Baluchis.
No. 517 LANCE-NAIK FARMAN ALI KHAN, 127th Bal. L.I., attached to 129th Baluchis.
No. 1782 LANCE-NAIK TAJ MUHAMMAD, 108th Infy., attached to 129th Baluchis.
No. 1789 LANCE-NAIK BAHADUR KHAN, 108th Infy., attached to 129th Baluchis.
No. 1977 LANCE-NAIK SARDAR ALI, 108th Infy., attached to 129th Baluchis.
No. 2087 LANCE-NAIK MUHAMMAD ALI, 108th Infy., attached to 129th Baluchis.
No. 2102 LANCE-NAIK KHAN MUHAMMAD, 108th Infy., attached to 129th Baluchis.
No. 1132 LANCE-NAIK SULTAN, 108th Infy., attached to 129th Baluchis.
No. 864 LANCE-NAIK ABDUL REHMAN, B.M.P., attached to 129th Baluchis.
No. 436 LANCE-NAIK MIR JAN, 129th Baluchis.
No. 456 SEPOY ASAL MIR, 129th Baluchis.
No. 716 SEPOY FAZAL KHAN, 127th Bal. L.I., attached to 129th Baluchis.

No. 290 COLOUR-HAVILDAR RESHMIN KHAN, 127th Bal. L.I., attached to 129th Baluchis.
Showed conspicuous gallantry with the rear-guard under

Lieut. (A/Capt.) G. E. Hawkes, at Mwiti Water, on 26 November, 1917. (2nd mention.)
Recommended for I.D.S.M.

No. 3394 HAVILDAR MIR SHER, 127th Bal. L.I., attached to 129th Baluchis.

Showed conspicuous gallantry with the rear-guard under Lieut. (A/Capt.) G. E. Hawkes, at Mwiti Water, on 26 November, 1917.
Recommended for I.D.S.M.

Identical recommendations, for the same occasion, and in the same terms, on behalf of the following:

No. 4225 NAIK JUMA KHAN, 124th Baluchis, attached to 129th Baluchis.
No. 4565 SEPOY ABDULLAH KHAN, I.O.M., 124th Baluchis, attached to 129th Baluchis.
No. 759 SEPOY JEMADAR, 127th Bal. L.I., attached to 129th Baluchis.
No. 416 SEPOY AMAL AMIR, 127th Bal. L.I., attached to 129th Baluchis.

No. 294 LANCE-NAIK SHAH URAM, 129th Baluchis.

Brought up ammunition and water under heavy fire to the firing line—Mwiti Water, 26th November, 1917.
Recommended for I.D.S.M.

The following four N.C.O.s were recommended for the award of the I.D.S.M. for

'Having brought away two machine guns and a Lewis gun when the ammunition had been expended and the rest of the crews hit. All had their shoulders burnt'.

No. 489 LANCE-NAIK HAYAT MOHAMED, 127th Bal. L.I., attached to 129th Baluchis.
No. 1863 LANCE-NAIK WARIS KHAN, 130th Baluchis, attached to 129th Baluchis.
No. 1342 LANCE-NAIK BOOTA KHAN, 129th Baluchis.
No. 4104 LANCE-NAIK MUHAMMED SADIQ, 127th Bal. L.I., attached to 129th Baluchis.

# APPENDIX IX

## DECORATIONS

### V.C.
No. 4050 Jemadar (then Sepoy) Khudadad Khan.

### C.B.
Brigadier-General J. A. Hannyngton.

### C.I.E.
Lieut.-Colonel W. N. Hay.

### C.M.G.
Brigadier-General W. M. Southey.

### D.S.O.
Lieut.-Colonel J. A. Hannyngton.
Lieut.-Colonel W. N. Hay.
Lieut.-Colonel H. Hulseberg (bar).
Major M. A. Hamer (not with the regiment).
Captain R. F. Dill.
Captain H. V. Lewis.

### M.C.
Major M. A. Hamer (not with the regiment).
Brevet-Major F. M. Griffith-Griffin.
Captain H. V. Lewis (bar).
Captain A. N. Dickson, I.M.S.
Captain G. E. Hawkes.
Captain H. J. D. O'Neill.
Captain A. C. Gover.
Lieut. C. W. Palin.
Lieut. V. G. Robert.
Lieut. W. S. Thatcher.
Lieut. R. G. Woodward.
Subedar-Major Zaman Khan.

### O.B.I.
Subedar-Major Zaman Khan.
Subedar Makhmad Azam.

## I.O.M.

Subedar-Major Sarbiland (bar), 127th.
Subedar Makhmad Azam.
Subedar Mir Bad Shah, 127th.
Subedar Muhammad Afzal, 124th.
Subedar Zerghun Shah, 127th.
Jemadar Ayub Khan (bar), 124th.
No. 3836 Jemadar Fateh Haider.
No. 2524 Colour-Havildar Ghulam Mahommed.
No. 4280 Colour-Havildar Sar Mir.
No. 3151 Havildar Mirza Khan.
No. 4333 Havildar Redi Gul.
No. 436 Naik Mir Jan.
No. 118 Naik Nek Amal.
No. 453 Naik Sahib Jan.
No. 653 Naik Shah Nawaz, 21st.
No. 3814 Lance-Naik Habib Gul.
No. 4565 Sepoy Abdullah Khan, 124th.
No. 596 Sepoy Munsibdar.
No. 471 Sepoy Raji Khan.
No. 250 Sepoy Saiday Khan.

## I.D.S.M.

Subedar Durani.
Subedar Ghulam Jilani.
Subedar (then Havildar) Nur Khan I.
Subedar Nur Khan II.
No. 290 Colour-Havildar Reshmin Khan, 127th.
No. 1342 Havildar Boota Khan.
No. 3394 Havildar Mir Sher, 127th.
No. 44 Naik Fateh Khan.
No. 4030 Naik Najib Khan, Somaliland Contingent.
No. 453 Naik Sahib Jan.
No. 4104 Lance-Naik Muhammed Sadiq, 127th.
No. 294 Lance-Naik Shah Uram.
No. 447 Lance-Naik Torsum, 127th.
No. 1863 Lance-Naik Waris Khan, 130th.
No. 3600 Sepoy Afsar Khan.
No. 2012 Sepoy Aulia Khan.
No. 105 Sepoy Kassib.
No. 2813 Sepoy Lal Sher.
No. 4267 Sepoy Mehrab Gul.

## APPENDIX IX

### I.D.S.M. (*contd.*)

No. 4182 SEPOY SAID AHMED.
No. 1894 PENSIONED HAVILDAR TAJ MUHAMMAD, Sistan (Persian).
No. 44 HAVILDAR FATEH KHAN, Waziristan.
No. 1974 LANCE-NAIK ROSHAN ALI, Baluchistan.
No. 1842 SEPOY WARYAM KHAN, Baluchistan.
No. 4321 SEPOY GHULAM HUSSAIN, 124th.

### I.M.S.M.

No. 290 COLOUR-HAVILDAR RESHMIN KHAN, 127th.
No. 290 COLOUR-HAVILDAR SARDAR SHAH, B.M.P.
No. 2792 (2292?) COLOUR-HAVILDAR SOHBAT KHAN, 127th.
No. 1671 COLOUR-HAVILDAR ALI BAHADUR.
No. 3635 COLOUR-HAVILDAR FAZIL ILAHI.
No. 261 HAVILDAR GUL AHMAD.
No. 3151 HAVILDAR MIRZA KHAN, 127th.
No. 4210 HAVILDAR MUBARAK KHAN, 127th.
No. 2968 HAVILDAR NAWAB ALI.
No. 308 HAVILDAR (then Naik) NIAZ ALI, B.M.P.
No. 1311 HAVILDAR (then Naik) SHAMAS DIN, 108th.
No. 4288 HAVILDAR SHARAF DIN.
No. 192 HAVILDAR SHER BAHADUR.
No. 307 HAVILDAR ZAR GUL, 127th.
No. 456 NAIK ASAL MIR.
No. 521 NAIK ATTA KHAN.
No. 1789 NAIK BAHADUR KHAN, 108th.
No. 1342 NAIK BUTA KHAN.
No. 517 NAIK FARMAN ALI KHAN, 127th.
No. 600 NAIK FAZAL AHMED.
No. 537 NAIK GUL MUHAMMED.
No. 578 NAIK HAZRAT GUL.
No. 2102 NAIK KHAN MUHAMMAD, 108th.
No. 193 NAIK LAL GUL.
No. 436 NAIK MIR JAN.
No. 4453 NAIK MUSA KHAN.
No. 1132 NAIK SULTAN, 108th.
No. 1782 NAIK TAJ MUHAMMAD, 108th.
No. 864 LANCE-NAIK ABDUL REHMAN, B.M.P.
No. 38 LANCE-NAIK AWAL MIR, 127th.
No. 4160 LANCE-NAIK BABRI KHAN, 124th.
No. 2736 LANCE-NAIK BYRAM KHAN, 127th.

#### I.M.S.M. (*contd.*)

No. 2087 LANCE-NAIK MUHAMMAD ALI, 108th.
No. 1977 LANCE-NAIK SARDAR ALI, 108th.
No. 4463 SEPOY DITTA KHAN, 127th.
No. 716 SEPOY FAZAL KHAN, 127th.
No. 636 SEPOY MAHIN SHAH.

#### *Croix de Guerre*

SUBEDAR GHULAM JILANI.

#### *Medal of St George*
#### 4th Class (Russian Decoration)

No. 3836 JEMADAR FATEH HAIDER.
No. 118 NAIK NEK AMAL.
No. 4297 SEPOY SULTAN BAKSH.

#### *Medal of St George*
#### 1st Class

No. 4355 HAVILDAR WASIM KHAN.

#### *Italian Silver Medal for Military Valour*

CAPTAIN H. V. LEWIS.

# INDEX

Abdullah Khan, Subedar, 63, 65, 118, 172
Abdullah Kitambi, 135, 140
Acacia, 91
Adair, Captain W. F., 2, 11, 12, 15, 19
Adam Khan, Subedar, 30
Aden, 73, 80
Afsar Khan, Sepoy, 17
Ahmed Din, Subedar, 35
Alexandria, 3, 72, 73
Algerian Division, 45th, 44
Alim Khan, Sepoy, 93
Allenby, General, 11
Ambush Hill, 142, 159
Amettes, 72
Amir Khan, Subedar, 35
*Arcadian*, H.M.T., 72
Army, 2nd, 46
Army Corps, 1st, 13
Arques, 7–9, 72
Arusha, 88
Atal, Major P. P. L., 18, 23, 24
Aubers ridge, 21
Ayub Khan, Naik, 56, 57; Jemadar, 61, 62, 154, 155
Azad Gul, Subedar, 19
Azam Khan, Subedar, 65

Bagamoyo, 117, 118
Bagh Khan, Havildar, 163
Bailleul, 9
Baluch Regiments, (124th), 35, 38, 52, 57, 64, 80; (126th), 43, 62; (127th), 3, 26, 38, 41, 72, 80, 195, 196, 198, 199; (129th), *passim*; (130th), 23, 83, 111, 181, 195
Baluchi Road, 63, 64
*Bandra*, H.M.T., 73
Bangalla River, 209, 211
Bannerman, Lieut. H. D. A., 199, 200, 215
Bareilly Brigade, 38
*Barjola*, H.M.T., 118, 120, 216
Bavarian Corps, 2nd, 13
Beaumetz-les-Aire, 72
Beka, 199
Bendela, 111

Berlin, 75
Bethune, 30
Beves, General, 158, 165
Bhopals, 9th, 22, 23, 48, 60
Bickford, Lieut. M. H., 57
Big Hut Hill, 146
Bissel, 79, 80
Blegier Pierregrosse, Caporal Le Comte Louis de, 4
Bois du Biez, 21, 40
Boma ja Ngombe, 84, 86, 88
Bond Street, 65
Borely Racecourse, 4
Borton, Captain C. E., 73
Boshoff, Lieut., 191
Bostan, 218
Boulton, 2nd Lieut. A. G., 5
Bournemouth, 61
Bout Deville, 55, 56
Brilliant, Lieut. L., 104, 180
British Expeditionary Force, 27, 44
Brock, Captain B. de L., 151–153, 173
Brown, Lieut. A. H., 157
Browning, Captain C. S., 3, 30, 41, 55, 56, 116, 118, 120, 139, 146–148
Buffs, 2nd, 48
Buist, Major A. H., 23, 28
'Bump', the, 153, 155
Bura, 83
Burd, Captain E. P., 63, 65, 71
Burma Infantry, 93rd, 63
Burne, Colonel, 165, 166
Burne's Column, 165, 166
Busnes, 72
Bweho, 198
Bweho Chini, 198

Cairo, 3, 4
Caldicott, Captain A., 146
Campbell, Lieut. F. C. G., 42
Canadians, 44
Cape Corps, 80, 86, 167
Cats Post, 71
Caudescure, 62
Cavalry Brigade, 3rd, 9, 14
Cavalry Corps, 9, 13

Cavalry Division, (1st), 11, 91, 117, 140; (2nd), 9, 11, 14, 19, 117; (3rd), 11; (7th), 11, 117
Central Railway, 107, 117, 121, 122, 183, 184
Cercotte Camp, 5
Champagne, 66
Charriers, Adjudant de la, 4
Château Redoubt, 64
Chemera, 168, 174, 179, 180, 186
Chemera Hill, 136, 137
Chigugu, 207, 208
Chimney Crescent, 64
Chingwea, 206, 207
Chiwata, 208, 209
Christian, Brigadier-General, 218
Christopher, Lieut. W., 182
Chumo, 131, 132, 149, 153, 157, 158
Chumo Road, 157
Church Redoubt, 64
Clive, Major H. W. F., 216
Cocoa Nut Village, 143
Connaught, H.R.H. Prince Arthur of, 6
Connaught Rangers, 23, 24, 47, 48, 50, 66
Contour 30, 11
Copse Keep, 66
Cornet Bourdois, 39, 72
Cox, Lieut. G. A. T., 105, 126, 137, 138, 156
Crawford, Major A. G., 38, 56, 87, 104
Croix Barbée, 56, 71
Croix Marmouse, 64
Culverwell, 2nd Lieut. J. S., 53

Dadin, Jemadar, 26, 53
Dar-es-Salaam, 117–120, 181, 183, 193, 216
Dasin Khan, Jemadar, 104
Davies, Captain R. D., 26, 30, 35
Defu River, 96, 102, 104
Dickson, Captain A. N., 61, 120, 149, 150, 157
Didan Khan, Jemadar, 53
Dill, Captain R. F., 3, 11, 16, 19, 35, 39, 42
Dodoma, 117
Domundo, 205
Dothumi, 158
Doulieu, 53

Dreyer, Major G. V., 190–193, 195, 198
Du Pree, Lieut.-Colonel, 45
Durani, Jemadar, 113, 118

East African Brigade, (1st), 106, 165; (2nd), 79, 80, 84–86, 88–91, 94, 96, 97, 106, 118, 139, 168, 172, 173; (3rd), 168–170
East African Division, 1st, 84, 86, 87, 88
East African Mounted Rifles, 84
East Kware River, 88
*Edavana*, H.M.T., 120, 124
Edelstone, Lieut. E., 178
Edward's Post, 66
Elephant's Skull, 80
*Ellenga*, S.S., 2, 4
Engare Nairobi, 86
Engare Nanjuki Marsh, 86; River, 84
Estaires, 9, 19, 71
Euphorbien, 95
Euphorbien Hill, 90

Factory Post, 71
Fakhar Din, Jemadar, 208
Farfan, Major, 153
Fateh Haider, Jemadar, 64, 146, 147
Ferozepore, 2
Ferozepore Brigade, 2, 9, 19, 20, 28, 40, 41, 47, 49–53, 69
Festubert, 20, 24, 72
Fitzgerald, Lieut.-Colonel T. D., 108, 110
Force Reserve Column, 202, 203
Forrester's Lane, 66
Foster, Lieut., 201
Fox, Lieut. H. V., 195, 199
French, Lord, 8, 9
Frere Hall, 216

Garangua, 89
Gaskell, Captain J. C. T., 172–174, 181, 182, 187–190, 192
Geddes' Detachment, 48
Geragua, 86, 87
Geragua River, 86
Ghafar Khan, Jemadar, 53
Gheluvelt, 44
Ghulam Hussain, Sepoy, 52, 57

## INDEX

Ghulam Jilani, Jemadar and Jemadar-Adjutant, 63; Subedar, 130, 172
Ghulam Kadar, Havildar, 163; Jemadar, 194
Ghulam Mohamed, Subedar, 19
Ghulam Muhamad, Sepoy, 17, 39
Givenchy, 20, 26, 28, 31–33, 37, 72, 147
Gloucesters, 7th, 71
Godewaerswelde, 43, 45
Gold Coast Hill, 152, 157, 159
Gold Coast Regiment, 148, 151, 152, 185, 200, 201
Goldsmith, 2nd Lieut. W. S., 104, 114, 139, 156, 178
Gonya, 110
Gover, Captain A. C., 173, 176, 179, 180, 182, 187, 190, 191, 194; Major, 200–202, 204, 205
Graham, 2nd Lieut. E. M., 126
Grant, Colonel, 185
Great Ruaha River, 122
Greek House, 88
Green's Post, 171
Grey, Lieut.-Colonel, 56
Griffith-Griffin, Major F. M., 9 n.; Lieut., 34, 52, 53, 61, 63, 68; Captain, 116, 119
Guarbecque, 39
Guiton, Lieut. L. W., 206
Gunja Peak, 119
Gurkha Road, 64
Gurkhas, 1/1st, 64
Guy, Lieut. N. G., 178, 195; Captain, 215

Ham, 39
Handeni, 107, 111, 113, 114, 116–118, 121
Hanforce, 203
Hanga, 158
Hanga Valley, 158
Hanna Valley, 218
Hannyngton, Brevet-Colonel (Temporary Brigadier-General), 13, 16, 28, 51, 52, 56, 57, 86, 104, 106, 108, 121, 123, 126, 127, 184, 212, 215, 218
Harman Hill, 157
Hasham Din, Jemadar, 173
Haverskerque, 62

Hawkes, Lieut. G. E., 199, 212, 213
Hay, Lieut.-Colonel W. N., 199–201, 204, 212, 217, 219
Heliopolis, 3
Hen's Post, 66
Hill 620, 112
Hill Top ridge, 48, 50
Hill's Redoubt, 64
Himo, 95, 101
Holbrooke, Major B. F. R., 38, 41, 49, 52, 53, 61
Hollebeke, 9–11, 13, 15
Hollebeke Château, 13, 14, 17
Hong-Kong, 6
Hoskins, Major-General A. R., 106, 165
Hotel Heliopolis, 3
Hull Howitzer Battery, 182, 185, 205
Hulseberg, Lieut.-Colonel, 41, 55, 73, 91, 119, 126, 134, 138, 156, 172, 173, 181, 188, 193, 199
Humphreys, Major G. G. P., 3, 11, 12, 14, 19
Hussars, (4th), 9; (18th), 18

Id Mohamed, Jemadar, 29, 35
Igumi, 207
Imandar, Jemadar, 30
Indajit Singh, Lieut., 24
Indian Cavalry, 25th, 196, 197, 205
*Indomitable*, H.M.S., 4
Ismailia, 218

Jafar Ali, Jemadar, 19
James, Major C. A., 43, 53
Jardine's Farm, 11
Jenkins, 2nd Lieut. J. D., 110, 113, 157
Joffre, General, 27
Johnstone, 2nd Lieut. N. W. W., 136, 138
Jullundur Brigade, 40, 47–52

K.O.S.B. (13th Brigade), 46, 48
Kadir Khan, Jemadar, 26
Kahe, 84, 91, 94, 96, 100, 102, 104, 114
Kahe Hill (Kopje), 94, 96, 97, 102, 103, 105
Kahe Kwa Ruwu, 90, 91

Kajiado, 77–79
Kalamba, 111
Kampfontein Road, 84
Karachi, 2, 3, 104, 215, 216
Karachi Brigade, 216
Karam Bakhsh, Subedar, 211
Karam Dad, Jemadar, 173, 202
Karam Dad, Subedar, 53, 182
Karim Khan, Jemadar, 35
Kashmir Rifles, (2nd), 108; (3rd), 116
Kasigao, 83
Kassib, Sepoy, 17
Keary, Major-General H. D'U., 54
Kedongai, 79, 80
Keili Hill, 110
Kemball, Major A. G., 42, 43
Kemmel, 19
Khudadad Khan, Sepoy, 17, 26, 39
Kibata, 126–128, 130, 133, 134, 136–138, 140–154, 156, 158, 159, 161, 163, 164, 168, 169, 171–174, 176
Kibata Fort, 143
Kibongo, 165
Kilaganeli, 186
Kilimanjaro, 82–84
Kilimatinde, 117
Kilindini, 76
Kilossa, 117
Kilwa, 119–121, 123–126, 134, 138, 140, 147, 166, 167, 169, 172, 174, 180, 181, 183–185, 187, 196, 203, 204, 207, 208
Kilwa Kisiwani, 124, 125, 167
Kilwa Kivinje, 124, 174, 181
Kimamba Hill, 186
Kimbambawe, 158, 165, 166, 184
Kimbarambara, 128, 129, 134
King's African Rifles, 77, 87, 89, 126, 142, 144, 146, 156, 157, 160, 163, 167, 169, 171, 213; (1st), 99; (1/2nd), 126, 128–130, 133–135, 137–139, 142, 146, 147, 151, 156, 157, 159, 164, 169; (1/3rd), 185, 188, 190–194, 201, 203, 205; (2/2nd), 123, 125, 135, 137, 147, 151, 176, 185, 200, 201; (2/3rd), 181, 185, 198; (3rd), 108, 110, 113; (3/3rd), 186

King's African Rifles Mounted Infantry Company, 108
Kirongo(ware), 180–182, 186, 187
Kiruwiru, 173
Kisangire Railway Station, 102, 103, 105
Kisegesse, 165, 166
Kisiwani Harbour, 186
Kissingere, 140
Kitambi, 136–138, 148, 151, 169–171, 173, 176, 179
Kitandi, 198
Kitengari, 208, 209
Kitshi Hills, 168
Kiturika Hills, 183, 184, 186, 187
Kiurubi, 169
Kiwambi, 171
Kiwambo, 210, 211
Kiwatama, 181, 182
Kleine Zillebeke, 13
Koehl, Captain, 196
Koge, 165
Kondoa, 107, 117
Kondoa-Irangi, 105, 107, 114
*Königsberg*, war-ship, 75
Korogwe, 107, 111, 113, 118, 122
Kukday, Major K. V., 61
Kwa Mdoe, 111, 113

L'Épinette, 56, 61, 64
La Bassée, 67
La Bassée Road, 66
La Brique, 45, 48, 52
La Clytte, 19
La Flandrie, 38
La Gorgue, 23, 63, 71
La Quinque Rue, 23, 32
Lacouture, 40
Lahore Division, 2, 20, 23, 31, 37, 39, 40, 44–46, 51, 53, 55, 67, 68
Lahore Divisional Artillery, 46
Lal Sher, Jemadar, 35
Lal Sher, Sepoy, 17
Lancers, (5th), 9, 10 n., 14; (16th), 9, 10 n., 14
Langata, 112
Langemarck, 46–48
Lansdowne Post, 71
Laome Hill, 109
Lasa, 111
Lasa Hill, 111
Latema, 88

## INDEX

Leese, Lieut. C. F. W., 195, 215
Lembeni, 110
Lens, 66
Les Lobes, 40
Lettow-Vorbeck, General von, 75, 92–95, 97, 126, 127, 140, 146, 155, 158, 167, 174, 175, 183, 196, 204, 205, 207, 209, 210, 213
Lewis, Lieut. H. V., 15, 16, 19, 29, 34, 38, 55, 61, 63, 73; Captain, 77, 92, 110, 116, 118, 120, 126, 134–136, 139; Major, 144, 145, 153, 154, 156, 157, 159, 162, 164, 170, 172, 181; Captain, 187
Lewis Gun and Stokes Mortar School, 172
Libangani, 180
Light Infantry, 5th, 116, 118, 119, 138
Ligny-le-Petit, 24
Lillers, 38, 72
Limbanguku, 160
Lindi, 120, 167, 174, 183–185, 187, 196, 204, 207, 208, 213, 215, 216
Liwale, 123, 125, 127, 167, 169, 183, 186, 206
Lock, 11
Lodgement, 141, 144, 146, 147, 151–156, 158
Londons, (1/4th), 48, 66
Longido (West), 77, 79, 80, 82–84, 89, 105
Loos, 19, 66
Loretto Road, 57
Loyal North Lancashires, 118, 123, 125, 154, 161, 162
Luatala, 210, 211
Ludhiana Lodge, 64
Lugonya River, 166, 170, 171
Lukuledi, 203, 204, 207
Lukuledi Mission, 203–205, 207
Lukuledi River, 200
Lulindi, 210
Lungo, 195
Lunguani, 136, 137
Lutshemi, 208, 209
Lys, 9

McCormick, Major G., 215
MacIvor, Lieut. R. S. P., 79, 84, 114, 139, 169, 178, 180
Mackinnon, Captain F. D., 181, 182, 187, 201, 202

Maclean, Captain F. A., 3, 11, 18, 19
MacMahon, Captain G. D. R., 38, 53
Madaba, 127, 186
Magadi, Lake, 78
Magoza, 119
Mahenge, 183, 185, 196, 206
Mahenge Plateau, 122, 123
Mahiwa, 207, 208, 215
Mahomed Bakhsh, Jemadar, 190
Mahonga, 180
Makangaga, 186
Makhmad Azam, Subedar, 42
Makonde Plateau, 193, 208, 210
Maktau, 83, 105, 120
Makuyuni, 113
Mala Khan, Subedar-Major, 35
Malasin, Subedar, 212
Malleson, Brigadier-General, 83
Malta, 72
Mametz, 72
Manacho, 207
Manga, 80
Manyamba's, 210
Mapinga, 119
Maraisse, 62
Marathas, 105th, 38
Marles, 35, 38
Marne, Battle of the, 3
Marseilles, 2–5, 56, 71, 72, 104
Masaod Khan, Jemadar, 35
Massai Kraal, 88, 90, 91
Massai Steppe, 107
Massassani, 119
Massassi, 183, 186, 196, 207, 209
Matandu, 134
Matandu ford, 125
Matandu River, 124, 128, 170, 174
Matola, 181
Maungu, 76, 79
Mauquissart, 20
Mauri, 113
Mauser ridge, 48
Mawarenye, 197, 199
Mawudji River, 182, 187
Mazar Khan, Signalling Naik, 10
Mazinde, 112
Mbemba, 203
Mbemkuru River, 197–200, 203
Mbindia, 160, 169, 173, 197
Mbiriri, 88

## INDEX

Mbuyuni, 83, 105, 108
Mbwara, 169
Meerut Division, 9, 23, 31, 37, 40, 55, 67–70
Mehdi Khan, Subedar, 71
Mehr Jan, Sepoy, 156
Menin, 44
Meru, 84
Merville, 56, 61, 62
Messines, 9
Meterem, 53
Mewa Khan, Jemadar, 200
Mgamba, 114
Mgeta River, 121, 122, 166
Mianbondo, 130, 131
Miesse River, 213
Mihambia, 187, 196, 197
Mihambia-Ndessa, 188
Mikesse, 166
Mikindani, 119, 120, 126
Mikokani, 110
Mikurumo, 148, 157
Mingumbe, 158
Minindi Post, 182
Minjumbe, 158
Mir Bad Shah, Jemadar (127th), 19
Mir Bad Shah, Jemadar (129th), 31, 39; Subedar, 92, 156
Mir Kambir Khan, Subedar-Major, 72, 130, 131, 156
Mirza Khan, Havildar, 156
Mission, the, at Mtumbei Juu, 138, 148, 152, 169, 171, 173
Mission Road, 157
Mitchell, Lieut. F. M., 195, 199
Mitchell, Major W. J., 35, 42, 56
Mitole, 133, 134, 136, 137, 147, 168, 170
Mitoneno, 200
Miwale, 209
Miwale Hill, 208
Mkalinso, 158, 165
Mkindu, 166
Mkumazi, 110, 112
Mkumbala, 112
Mkundu, 165
Mnasi, 182, 186, 187
Mnero, 203
Mnero Mission, 203
Mnindi, 186
Mohamed Sadiq, Jemadar, 152
Mohoro, 140, 144, 158, 168, 173, 184

Mole Hill Keep, 66
Mombasa, 73, 75, 76
Mombo, 112, 113, 116
Money, Major C. A. G., 23, 30, 53, 104, 113, 119, 126, 134, 138, 151, 152
Mons, 4
Mont des Cats, 9
Morogoro, 158, 172, 173, 180, 181
Morris, Major G. M., 64, 80
Moschi, 84, 88–90, 94, 103, 119, 183
Mountain Battery, (22nd) (Derajat), 185, 188, 190, 198; (27th), 86, 89, 96, 108, 147, 153, 158, 159, 161, 162, 185, 201
Mouse Trap Farm, 44
Mpotora, 126, 136, 137, 167, 168, 174
Mssindy, 188, 192–195, 197
Mtaba Hill, 125
Mtama, 216
Mtandawala, 188
Mtavi, 173
Mtimbo, 210
Mtshakama, 182, 186
Mtumba Hill, 195, 197
Mtumbei, 135
Mtumbei Chini, 134, 135, 176
Mtumbei Juu, 135, 137, 138, 148
Mtumbei River, 136
Mtumbi Mountains, 123, 126
Mue, 90, 91, 104
Muhammad Afzal, Subedar, 154–156
Murray, Major L. G., 164
Murtaza, Jemadar, 188
Mushroom Tree Hill, 163
Mwengei, 139, 140, 144, 152, 159, 163, 173, 207
Mwiti, 208, 209
Mwiti Water, 211, 213, 215

Nahende, 186
Nahungu, 197
Nairobi, 81, 104
Namakongwa, 208, 215
Namanga, 78–80
Namatewa, 168, 170, 171, 176, 178, 186
Nambanditi, 186
Nambanji, 137, 178, 179
Namehi, 200
Nangagchi, 188, 195

Nangano, 197
Nangoo, 207, 208
Nangue, 171
Nanguiwe, 179
Nanyati, 187, 188, 194, 195, 202, 209
Narungombe, 182, 187, 197
Narungu, 199
Nasuras Shamba, 188
Naumann, 184, 185
Nawab Khan, Jemadar, 30
Ndanda Mission, 207
Ndarema, 114–116
Ndende, 134
Ndessa, 187, 195–198
Ndessa Chini, 198
Nek Amal, Sepoy, 12, 42, 64
Nek Mahomed, Jemadar, 189, 194
Neuve Chapelle, 20, 37, 39, 40, 53, 63
New Moschi, 90, 100
Newala, 167, 207, 209–211
Newton, Captain E., 173, 192, 193
Ngambo, 114
Ngandi River, 202
Ngarambi, 136, 137, 148, 168, 171, 178
Ngarambi Chini, 170
Ngasseni, 84, 86
Ngasserai, 84, 85
Ngata Hill, 105
Ngaura River, 186
Ngoha River, 112
Ngoya, 109
Ngulu Gap, 108
Ngulu Hills, 117
Nguru Mountains, 121
Nigerian Brigade, 165, 166, 184, 187, 196–198, 208, 209
Nigerians, 2nd, 193, 198
Njimbwi, 171
Njinjo, 125, 126, 134, 136, 140
Nkiu, 199
Nkulu, 173, 178
Noote Boom, 53
Northey, General, 158, 165
Nur Khan I, Jemadar, 113, 172; Subedar, 190
Nur Khan II, Jemadar, 179; Subedar, 207
Nyakisiki, 166
Nyandote, 165

Oblong Farm, 47
Observation Hill, 159
O'Grady, Brigadier-General, 153, 184
Olekenoni, 79
Olorungoti, 87, 88
O'Neill, Lieut. H. J. D., 38, 49, 61; Captain, 79, 92, 97
Orchard Keep, 66
Orchard Redoubt, 41
Orleans, 5
Orr, Colonel, 165, n. 1, 185, 203
Ouderdun, 45, 46, 53

Palin, 2nd Lieut. C. W., 120, 125, 134, 137; Lieut., 139, 145, 158, 163, 169, 173, 180, 181, 189, 190–193, 209, 216
Palm Tree Village, 159
Palm Village, 144
Pangani, 94, 96, 99, 108, 113, 116
Paradis, 42, 55
Paré Mountains, 82, 106, 107
Passchendaele, 19
Pathans, 40th, 56, 72, 108, 118, 119, 120, 123, 125, 128, 134, 148, 170, 176, 186, 216
Persian Gulf, 80, 104
Phillips, Captain G. A., 57, 65, 105, 118, 157, 158, 160, 161, 163, 169
Picquet Hill, 139, 142, 144, 146, 148, 151, 152, 154, 155, 159, 169
Pilckem, 44
Pili Pili, 215
Pilkington, Lieut., 195
Pioneer Keep, 66
Pioneers, (61st), 124; (121st), 173
Piper, Lieut. R. L., 195, 201, 203
Plain Hill, 146, 157
Platform Hill, 159
Ploegsteert Wood, 9
Plum Street, 65, 66
Plumer, General Sir Herbert, 45, 46, 54
Plumer's Force, 54
Poelcappelle, 44
Pont Fixe, 35
Pont Logy, 63
Pont Riqueul, 64
Poperinghe, 9
Port Arthur Redoubt, 57
Port Said, 73
Port Tewfik, 3

## INDEX

Potter, Major H. W. R., 14, 18, 28, 30, 31, 34, 35
Pratt, Lieut. A. R., 195, 199
Price, Brigadier-General C. H. U., 73, 117
*Princess*, liner, 216
Pugnoy, 35
Pungatini, 139
Punjabis, (20th), 23; (21st), 41; (24th), 23; (29th), 80, 85, 89, 93, 94, 98, 99, 101, 103; (31st), 42; (33rd), 185; (46th), 26; (62nd), 104; (67th), 206; (69th), 172; (84th), 38, 64, 104; (89th), 56
Putz, General, 44

Quetta, 218

Radcliffe, Captain A. Delmé, 38, 41, 42
Rahim Ali, Subedar, 53, 104, 172
Rahim Dad, Jemadar, 53
Raji Khan, Sepoy, 51, 57
Rajwali Khan, Jemadar, 179
Rasthaus, 91, 95
Rasthaus Hill, 90
Rau River, 102
Reata, 88
Reserve Valley, 157
Reshmin, Havildar, 195
Richebourg l'Avoué, 20
Richebourg St Vaast, 40, 71
Ridgeway, Colonel, 165, n. 2
Rifles, (55th), 196, 213; (57th), 5, 22–24, 32, 47, 56, 178, 185; (58th), 41; (59th), 20, 22, 42, 57
Robecq, 72
Robert, Lieut. V. G., 72, 120, 126, 130, 137, 138, 157, 159, 161–163, 171, 172, 179, 180, 217
Roberts, Lord, 23
Robinson, Captain D. G., 26
Rome, Captain H. C., 23, 31
Roosebeek, 11
Rose, Colonel, 165
Rouges Bancs, 20
Rovuma River, 123, 206, 207, 209, 211, 213
Royal Engineers, 64
Royal Fusiliers, 25th, 80, 96
Royal West Kents, 1st, 48
Ruangwa Chini, 200

Rue de Bacquerot, 20
Rue des Berceaux, 40
Rue du Bois, 41, 57, 61, 66, 70, 71
Rue du Puits, 42
Rue Tilleloy, 64
Rufiji River, 121, 122–124, 127, 136, 140, 141, 158, 165–167, 170, 184
Rumbo, 174, 186, 187
Ruponda, 200, 202–204, 206
Russia, H.I.M. the Emperor of, 64
Ruwu Pangani River, 101
Ruwu River, 90, 92, 94, 96, 97, 99, 100–102, 108, 109, 118
Ruwu Village, 105

Sahib Dad, Subedar, 179
Sahib Jan, Lance-Naik, 29, 32, 39, 153, 154
Said Ahmed, Sepoy, 17
Saiday Khan, Sepoy, 13, 42
Saif Ali Khan, Subedar, 194
Salaita, 82, 83
Samanga, 158
Same, 110
Sanja, 88
Sar Mir, Naik, 39
Sarbiland, Subedar-Major, 178, 179, 182, 195, 201
Sardinia, 72
Schulz, Major, 126
Secunderabad Cavalry Brigade, 20
Serengeti, 83
Sevrieures, General, 5
Shah Zada, Jemadar, 56
Sheep's Hill, 84
Sheppard, General, 80, 84, 91, 92, 94–97, 106, 108, 158
Sher Baz, Jemadar, 65
Sher Jang, Jemadar, 53
Sherbat Khan, Subedar, 172, 179, 194
Sign Post Lane, 63, 64
Sikandar Khan, Subedar, 104, 162, 163, 172
Sikh Pioneers, 34th, 23, 24
Sikhs, (15th), 28, 30, 64; (47th), 48; (52nd), 199; (54th), 199; (57th), 56, 71, 195
Simba's, 209
Simla, 2, 80, 111
Sind desert, 3
Singa, 118

# INDEX 289

Single Palm Village, 144
Sirdar Shah, Jemadar, 104
Sirhind Brigade, 8, 32, 33, 40, 47, 52, 53
Smith, 2nd Lieut. M. I. L., 72, 120, 139, 145
Smith-Dorrien, General Sir Horace, 46, 54
Smuts, General, 75, 76, 82, 83, 90, 94, 95, 97, 106–108, 117, 119, 121–123, 127, 158, 165
Soko Nassai River, 93, 95, 96, 98, 99
Somme, 19
South African Brigade, (2nd), 90–92, 96; (3rd), 90, 91, 94–97; (7th), 186; (8th), 182, 185
South African Field Battery, 96; (6th), 108; (7th), 108; (8th), 171
Southey, Lieut.-Colonel (later Brigadier-General), 11, 14, 17, 22–25, 33, 34, 38
Ssingino, 181, 182
St Cyr, 41
St Eloi, 9
St Jean, 45, 46
St Omer, 65, 66
Steel, Captain H. P., 181, 188, 189, 192
Steell, Lieut. J. W. G., 173
Steenstraat, 44, 45
Steffans, Ober-leutnant, 131
Stewart, Captain A. E., 64, 65, 80
Stewart, Major, 14
Stewart, Major-General J. M., 79, 83, 84
Stone, Lieut. A. P., 88
Store, 91, 93
Strazeele, 19
Stuemer, von, 184, 185
Sudi, 120, 126
Suez, 73
Suffolks, 4th, 63
Sundar Ali, Jemadar, 66

Tabora, 106, 122, 183
Tafel, 206, 209–212
Tanga, 107, 117, 118, 122, 183
Taveta, 76, 82–84, 89, 104, 105
Tawa, 137, 138
Taylor, Colonel, 186
Tel-el-Kebir, 3
Territorial Division, 87th, 44

Thatcher, 2nd Lieut. W. S., 62, 71, 120; Lieut., 154–156, 158, 159, 162, 163
Thornhill, Lieut. C. M., 23, 35, 57
Tor Khan, Lance-Naik, 163
Toulon, 72
Tschirimba Hill, 210
Tunduru, 167
Turkestan, Subedar, 53, 136

Uberoi, Lieut. T. S., 195
Uganda Railway, 83
Uhlans, 16th, 61
Ulanga River, 122
Uluguru Mountains, 121
Unterer Himo, 90, 92
Usambara Mountains, 106, 107, 117
Usambara Railway, 84, 105
Ussher, Captain S., 3–5, 23, 30
Uteenge Lake, 174
Utete, 136, 140, 158, 166, 168, 173

Van Deventer, Lieut.-General Sir J. L., 90, 94, 96, 107, 108, 117, 158, 165, 184, 196, 213
Vaughan, Brigadier-General, 9, 10
Victoria Nyanza, 82
Vincent, Captain P. C. H., 3, 12, 13, 19, 42, 64
Voi, 76, 77, 79
Vootmezeele, 19
Vuruni River, 113

Wahle, General, 197
Wales, H.R.H. the Prince of, 23
Wali Dad, Jemadar, 64
Walton, Colonel, 217
Wasim Khan, Havildar, 64
Water Picquet, 157
West Indian Regiment, 2nd, 118
West Kware River, 88
Western Usambara, 107
Westoutre, 19
*Weymouth*, H.M.S., 4
Wieltje, 48
Wieltje Farm, 48
Wilhelmstal, 113
Willcocks, General Sir James, 6, 23, 26, 32, 38, 54, 57
Wilson, Lieut. R. B., 64, 88, 139, 157
Wolseley, Lord, 3

Woodhouse, Major C. G., 62, 68, 73, 80
Woodward, Lieut. R. G., 199, 201, 211, 212
Worcesters, 56
Wungwi, 186
Wytschaete, 9

Ypres, 8, 9, 20, 43–48, 55, 57, 72

Zaman Khan, Subedar, 19, 39
Zandvoorde, 9
Zerdad, Havildar, 102
Zerghun Shah, Subedar, 38, 53, 66
Zerim Gul, Lance-Naik, 102
Zindeni, 113, 117
Zonnebeke, 44
Zugimoti, 113

www.ingramcontent.com/pod-product-compliance
Lightning Source LLC
Chambersburg PA
CBHW020639300426
44112CB00007B/170